Teaching is No Picnic

Teaching is No Picnic

WRITTEN BY:
Rudolph Rogers
&
Ruth Foley

EDITED BY:
Jack Foley

Order this book online at www.trafford.com
or email orders@trafford.com

Most Trafford titles are also available at major online book retailers.

Printed in the United States of America.

ISBN: 978-1-4269-5880-9 (sc)

Trafford rev. 03/30/2011

 www.trafford.com

North America & international
toll-free: 1 888 232 4444 (USA & Canada)
phone: 250 383 6864 ♦ fax: 812 355 4082

All school teachers

PREFACE

When this work is published, it is going to come in for a great deal of derogatory criticism, and the author is going to reap a harvest of scorn and derision. this is true for two reasons: it points up the real weakness of the American public school system, and the writer is one of that most despised and least honored group of all the people who are concerned with it--the class-room teachers.

Many authorities have essayed to examine the demerits of the system, and evaluate the merits (if any). They have nibbled at the edges, all around; they have speculated from several standpoints, and no critic, to date, has gone to the heart of the matter.

One reason for this failure is the fact that every explorer has tapped the wrong sources of information. Each has gone to the headquarters of the county school system-- to the comfortable, air-conditioned repository of the records and plans. They have asked their questions of the administrative officers of the system. The questions have been of the kind that elicit favorable answers that indicate that the system is conducted according to the best methods employed in the Army, the hospitals, and business corporations. The organization is that of the Line and Staff -- adopted from the Army. The staff consists of the Superintendent, his directors, supervisors, and all of the multifarious girls-Friday, together with the building principals. The personnel would like very much to wear the titles of General, of the various grades, and from that, down through colonel and major through captain, lieutenant, and sergeant. At that point, however, they shift to the hospitals for inspiration. The title of highest authority is Doctor. The ideal title of everybody who has his name lettered on his office door is Doctor. All these gentry hope that some day they may become a doctor of something or other; but oh! the long, weary, rocky, difficult road that leads to an earned doctorate in any field! Recently the requirements for Doctor of Education have been watered down until surely that exalted title should be within the reach of every educator (because the boys and girls in the county offices are Educators), but alas, few there be that attain to it, for some reason or reasons. One wonders what those reasons could be!

But these folks move in an aura of mystery. Their ways are not ordinary ways, and their methods are past finding out. All their plans are top-secret, and they put them into practice by executive decree. Their function is to command. Such is the Staff.

The Line consists of the classroom teachers.

Their job is to teach Johnny to read, write, and figger. It is up to the Line to impart the tools of learning, pass on the heritage of the race, and condition the pupils for adult citizenship. It is their duty to do this if they have time and energy to do it after they have produced the data and made the records that are kept on every pupil, from the day he enters kindergarten until he leaves school by graduation or drops out for some cause.

At first consideration, the innocent layman would suppose that the first duty of the Educators would be to make it possible for the teachers to do the best possible job of teaching. He would form the mistaken notion that the first duty of the teachers is to teach. But the innocent investigator is in error there. The first responsibility of the Staff member is to command. The chief duty of teacher is to obey. His not to reason why; his but to do and die!

Our school authorities have gone stark raving mad on the subject of Records. To name a few, there are the test records. These begin with the A B C's of the medical check-up. Then comes the attempt to measure the I.Q. of each child at age five and a half. Each subject grade he makes is recorded, during his school career. A running anecdotal record is included, that purports to measure his social growth from year to year. (And good friend, every entry in that record had better be complimentary!) When that record is complete, one has only to read it, to turn inside out, the body and soul of each pupil. A completed record is open to prospective employers, so that when the young man moves into adult citizenship, his new Lord doesn't have to give him a chance -- he looks upon the heart, and channels him in the way he should go.

Besides producing these data, and recording it all, the teacher must see to it that all pupils are fed, watered, and sent to the bath-room at regular intervals. He must collect and account for all monies, conduct a half dozen fund raising campaigns during the year, conduct the thrift club, turn in the money, keep accounts and distribute the stamps. He must keep a sharp eye on the physical welfare of all pupils, and report any indication of illness or physical mal-adjustment to the proper administrative official. If any request for information comes from the school office, the teacher must stop whatever he's doing, and prepare the report. In triplicate. All reports must be prepared in triplicate.

The teacher is the source of all statistical data. Administration must run smoothly, without a hitch, if it requires the major portion of the teacher's day. Teaching is the least important part of the teacher's whole duty. Teaching is done only when, as, and if, all administrative details have been taken care of.

While we are studying in College, we are taught that administration is an auxiliary to teaching. Supervision has, as its first function, the improvement and perfecting of the learning-teaching situation in the classroom. The first duty of a teacher, according to the training he receives in College, is to establish and maintain a learning-teaching situation, and to plan and carry out, learning-teaching processes.

The reality, as we see, is quite different. Instead of administration acting as the handmaiden of Education, it acts as the mistress. Instead of Supervision acting to improve the learning-teaching situation, the supervisors busy themselves with interfering with the teachers' activities, and ferreting out the "incompetent and unworthy." The educational pyramid is resting on its apex instead of its base. Administration and supervision are on top. Teaching is on the bottom -- the least important part of the process.

So the investigators go to the county or state administrative offices, read statistics, and interview administrators, who stoutly and everlastingly maintain that there is nothing the matter with the schools. Our schools are the best of all possible schools, in this best of all possible worlds.

If the top educational and political authorities are going to find out why our high schools are turning out whole classes of graduates who can't pass a college entrance examination to save their collective face in the matter of preparing young people for adult citizenship, they'll have to abandon the administrative offices, and get out into the schools, observe what goes on in the schools, and consult school teachers.

This book contains anecdotal records of this kind, with comments. Some of the experiences recounted here are the experience of the writer, who has served the teaching trade for wages over a third of a century. Most of them are the experiences of his colleagues.

Names of towns and persons have been changed to protect the innocent. But the incidents related here, occurred. The conditions described, exist.

This is not the protest of a single disgruntled teacher. These things have happened and are happening, to untold multitudes of teachers.

If anybody's name has been used, it is purely coincidental.

CHAPTER ONE

Azurville, Florida is a small town in the central part of the state --population about 6,000. There are several small cities in the county, which is of considerable extent and fairly thickly populated. There is a county superintendent of schools. The administrative head of the schools in and around each town is called a supervising principal. Under him are the building principals -- one for each school.

Azurville is the center of the citrus industry of Florida. The great "Second-Maid" processing plants are located there. A large part of Azurville's population is employed by Second-Maid. The rest are chiefly engaged in working in the groves.

Wages in the citrus industry are not so high that the head of a family is able to support it on his earnings. His wife also must bring in a weekly pay check. To do it, it is necessary for her to be absent from home during the day. A large amount of itinerant labor finds employment there during the rush season.

Their children, of course, attend schools -- many of them only when they feel so disposed. During the year I'm speaking of, the attendance fell off to such an alarming extent that it was apparent that something would have to be done about it.

When the school administration reported to the parents that their children were not attending school, the parents betrayed an attitude of angry resignation. They confessed their helplessness in dealing with their lazy off-spring. They left their homes early for work. It was up to the children to go to school. If they persisted in laying out, they could do nothing about it.

There are state laws requiring the attendance in school of school-age children. A stiff fine of three dollars per day is prescribed as the penalty for non-attendance.

Now the administration, one would think, would take proper steps to see that these parents paid their three dollars per day for each day their children were absent from school. It is the general experience that when a child's unauthorized absence from school costs his parents three dollars, those unauthorized absences come to a sudden halt.

Did the school administration take action appropriate to the situation? Did they take any action at all? Remember that the school's average daily attendance was down to the point at which teachers would have to be discharged, only to be desperately needed a few months afterward, when school opened the next Fall, and unavailable, because the number of teachers who can be hired for service next year is determined by this year's A.D.A. Affairs had clearly reached a crisis. That action did the administration take? Gentle reader, I will tell you!

The supervising principal called a meeting of his building principals, and spoke:

"People, you all know what a pass pupil attendance has brought us to. I have given this matter much thought. I have come up with a masterly solution to this very serious problem. I'll send my attendance officers out -- far and wide, and compel the pupils to come in. When they get here, have the teachers pour on all the work the pupils have missed. When this has been made up, erase the record of their absences, and count them present, just the same as if they had really been present. Thus the pupils will have done all their work, accomplished their normal amount of learning, and derived the normal degree of benefit from full attendance; our A.D.A. will rise sufficiently to allow us to retain our full quota of teachers to open school next fall. Call your teachers together and acquaint them with this plan. Get going."

The building principals each called a faculty meeting, and relayed the orders from the high. In our school, I asked leave to speak, and was given the floor.

"Ladies and gentlemen," I began, "we all recognize the seriousness of the situation, but I doubt if this plan proposed by the supervising principal is the right remedy for it. We know that the teacher's daily register is a legal document, and that to falsify it is a serious offense against the law. If we did this, and it became know, I have a feeling that swift and crushing punishment would fall upon us. For this reason, I feel that some other method of dealing with the situation should be sought. There is ample provision in the law for this situation and I urge that we avail ourselves of that provision, rather then embark upon a course of action which is fraught with such peril to us all."

That afternoon, I was summoned to the office of the supervising principal. He received me urbanely.

"Mr. Porter, I've been told that you don't approve the plan I've ordered for solving our attendance problem. How do you stand on that?"

I replied, "Mr. Damron, if this thing got out, we'd have more misery than we could cope with. We'd all be ruined. For the love of Pete, rescind that order, and save our lives, because if you permit in it, we are gone suckers! It seems a fool-hardy thing to do, especially as we don't have to do it. The law makes ample provision for this situation. Let's do it that way."

During my speech, Mr. Damron had settled back in his swivel chair and fitted his finger-tips together. He sat glowering at me, over his spectacles. When I stopped speaking, he said:

"So <u>you</u>, an insignificant classroom teacher, presume to take your employer to task! You dare to question the orders of your superior! You presume to substitute your puny judgment for mine!"

"Now, I brought you into this state, and I'm not going to fire you for insubordination. I've never fired a teacher in my life. But there are more ways of killing a cat than choking him to death with butter. Boy, there's another year coming up. I promise you that I'll fix your bill for snappin'. But good."

Little did I suspect how sincere he was!

As I resumed my seat, another teacher clamored for recognition, and got the nod. He bellowed:

"Madam chairman, this proposed plan entails much extra labor for the teachers, and a great deal of vexation of spirit. However, I feel that we can carry this through with next to no risk of discovery, and with no real harm done to anyone. I think we should show ourselves loyal to our dear good chief, and back him heartily on his proposal. Madam chairman, I so move."

This move was instantly seconded, and immediately put to vote -- and carried.

Much the same experience was gone through in the other faculty meetings in the district; and teachers who had low average daily attendance, swung into action -- not, however, without misgivings.

The classrooms filled. The teachers worked overtime and all the time, to bring up those pupils who had fallen so far behind in their work. The next month's attendance average looked much healthier. Teachers who needed to, altered the reports for previous months, and all seemed serene.

But suddenly calamity came upon us. We had a young man on the faculty of the Junior High School who found himself at odds with his fellow teachers, the school administration, the government of the United States, and indeed, with everything and everybody American. He saw his chance to bring down the house on all our heads. He wrote an expose of what had been done -- two copies. One he sent to the State superintendent of public instruction; the other he sent to the Tampa Daily Tribune. All hell broke loose.

Now it happened that a state election was coming up the next year. The county superintendent of Jackson county was a prominent contender for the state superintendency. The present incumbent read the young man's report, and went into transports of glee. Here was presented, ready-made, the means of crushing opposition and still be doing nothing but what was his clear duty and wholly right.

The hearings on the matter rocked the state. They were headline news for weeks. The supervising principal who cooked up the scheme went on trial before the county education board, and sat throughout the hearings with nothing of his countenance visible but the top of his head. The young betrayer thoroughly enjoyed his notoriety, and read prepared statement galore.

Finally, at long last, the verdict was reached: The supervising principal was fined six hundred dollars and placed on probation for three years. The betrayer was blacklisted as a teacher, forever. County staff members came to Azurville and stood over the sweating teachers who had altered their records, while they realtered the alterations.

The shouting and the tumult died. The captains and the kings departed. All was serene. Everybody was satisfied. The schools settled down to the even tenor of their ways, ready for opening in the Fall.

CHAPTER TWO

*W*hen the county education board found the supervising principal guilty of malfeasance in office, they did not fire him. They only fired the classroom teacher who reported him. The teacher didn't do anything wrong. He acted unwisely and vindictively, but he did nothing wrong. He exposed shady dealing; he caused a great deal of trouble and suffering to his innocent colleagues -- they had only reluctantly obeyed the orders of an autocratic boss -- working as they did, in an organization in which the principal wields the absolute powers of economic, social, and professional life and death over the teachers in his school. He acted ruthlessly and cruelly, and sent the chips flying in all directions. But he did nothing wrong. One might even say that he acted as a good citizen.

Contrast the punishment inflicted on him, with that laid upon the supervising principal -- the offender who really offended: the teacher was blacklisted. Never again would he be allowed to earn his living by the practice of his profession. The supervising principal was fined a couple of weeks pay, and placed on probation for three years -- but not removed from office. No, he was still carrying all the powers, prerogatives, and responsibilities that had been his before. Only he was paralyzed by the fear that he might do something wrong.

During the first day of the pre-planning period preceding the opening of school that Fall, the supervising principal called a meeting of all building principals and teachers. He rose and spoke:

"Ladies and gentlemen, we are treading extremely precarious ground. We don't dare allow anything to happen that would give rise to any complaint that might reach the county office. We must not arouse the hostility of any pupil. Punishments are entirely out. Infractions of school rules and regulations must be ignored. We must proceed as if we were treading on rotten eggs. Good luck to you."

We had a situation in the high school that year, which we experienced teachers knew was going to be a source of trouble -- apart from the fact that the head of the system was on probation. For several years previously, we had held the scholastic standards high. Any pupil who failed in his work received the actual grade he made and was retained. As there had been the usual percentage of drones and dead-beats, they had piled up in the junior high until it was so overcrowded that the junior high could no longer hold them. Our educational Napoleon decided to relieve conditions there by draining off this surplus into the senior high.

I drew my home-room group from this body. The first morning I walked into the room to call my group to order and proceed with the registration, they began to howl and screech. They kept it up for forty-five minutes. I sat at my desk and read, waiting for them to run out of steam. But they proceeded according to plan. Half their number would howl while the other half rested. But a sufficient number kept at it all the time. At the end of the period, they piled out of the room -- flushed with triumph.

When that group met again the next morning, the building principal was there. He read them a stern lecture, ending with the assurance that they were'nt going to drive anybody out of that school. They replied with gusty hisses, catcalls, and howls. The principal retired amid a rain of spit-balls and derisive laughter.

We could get attention, sometimes, by saying things like, "You people will get no credit at all unless we can get organized and going. You have to swing into action some time, or you'll have to go over the material next year that you failed to cover this year."

Such reminders worked some of the time, so we were able to keep a semblance of order, some of the time. We teachers laughed off as much of the disorder as we could, since we could do nothing else. If all the classes had acted like that one, we couldn't have even pretended to run a school. We had six hundred pupils there, of which eighty were juvenile delinquents, and of the eighty there were perhaps a dozen who were out and out criminals, and should have been in the penitentiary.

The teachers would find notes on their desks containing insults concerning the previous year's padding of the records. They called the teachers all the kinds of crooks they could think of -- and reader, they knew all the kinds.

I will not mention the name of every teacher to whom each outrage happened, because there were only four who were treated with much human consideration: the coaches of football, basketball, baseball, and track. These were young, big, physically formidable men. The hoods and thugs were literally afraid of them. The supervising principal noticed that they were given less trouble than the rest of the faculty, and he gleaned a lesson from the circumstance; since that time, he has never hired any man to teach who was not big, formidable, and as rugged-appearing as possible. If they can be ugly, it is a point in their favor. And above all, they have to be young.

Signal bells for changing classes were obeyed by the majority of the pupils. But in each class, there were representatives of the hood element, who went to class when, as, and if they pleased. They strolled in after the class activity had begun, laughing and chatting in full voice -- likely as not, loudly demanding, "Where's my seat? Now, what dirty bastard took the pencil I left here yesterday? I'll be God-damned if it ain't a fine thing -- a fellow can't lay nothing down without some son of a bitch stealing it!" Or, they might simply turn their chairs facing each other, seat themselves, and go on with their conversation without such scabrous behavior as that just described. This last was more the standard procedure. It is next to impossible to set up, and maintain a learning-teaching situation, with such behavior on the part of some.

One young fellow, just beginning his teaching career, had a very pretty, attractive-looking girl in one of his classes. Those were not all of her qualities. She was also low class, profane, uncouth, scatter-brained, and foul-mouthed.

Her favorite gambit was the bathroom routine. Of course there were a half-dozen other pupils in the class, who laughed uproariously at her witty sallies. She'd sit down, and draw her face into a mask of suffering. Then, in a tight voice, she'd gasp,

"Mr. Ferguson, I have to go to the bathroom'"

A titter of laughter.

"Of course, Lana. You are excused. You don't have to ask. Go ahead."

"I don't want to go alone. I want you to go with me."

Uproarious laughter.

"You are so inspiring, Mr. Ferguson. This is going to be a big operation, but I can swing it, if you're there holding my hand!"

The poor young fellow ordered,

"Lana, go to the office and report to the principal! This is outrageous! I won't have it!"

"Aw, Mr. Ferguson, why you want me to report to that little pip-squeak? He ain't nobody. I couldn't do nothing if he was holdin' both my hands! I need you with me, honey, at a time like this."

Uproar.

"Lana, stop it! Go somewhere! But leave the room this instant!"

Lana rose. Three other girls rose with her. Laughing merrily, they strolled out. The teacher finally quieted the class. But the period was pretty well shot.

In the hood group, we had two girls who were well-known to be whores. One of them left a note on the desk of one of her teachers which read,

"Always notice my hair, Mr. Griffith. If I'm wearing a flower in it, that means I haven't any panties on."

Those two especially, and numerous other pupils, rose and strolled out of the room at will, without permission. Generally they went to the washroom, for a chat and a cigarette.

The favorite bathroom routine of the boys, which caused gales of laughter, was a favorite one in the classes of the older teachers -- dignified old ladies who were highly respected in the community; a young man of six feet two, weighing a hundred ninety-five pounds, would screw up his face and bellow,

"Mrs. Cunningham, it looks like I'm going to have to go to the bank. And by God, I have to go right now!

The first such outburst brought a shocked question from the innocent old lady!

"Why James, why must you go to the bank just at this time?"

"By God, I've got to make a deposit, that's why!"

Gales of fiendish, bellowing laughter from the boys, and a prolonged season of screeching from the girls.

When the poor old lady bowed her head in tears, the hilarious group would come to some semblance of order, awed by the possibility of trouble that might come of such brutality in the presence of so highly regarded an old lady

But the period would be pretty well shot.

There is nothing so discouraging to a teacher or destructive of the purpose for which a school exists, as persistent smearing of that teacher's efforts to set up and maintain a learning-teaching situation. Such is his duty and responsibility. That is what the administration and the public expect of him. His training has equipped him with the techniques and learnings he needs, to do it! But constant smearing such as has been described, effectively stops him, and he is a frustrated man. His frustration, however, is only secondary in importance; the fact that ninety percent of the student body is thereby denied the opportunity to learn, is the main consideration. They may as well go fishing or bark up a tree, as attend a class in which rowdyism is so rampant.

The ten or fifteen percent who engage in such behavior are militant. Besides these overt and above-board methods of smearing, they engage in many other activities which depane upon secrecy for success. Any pupil who exposes wrong-doing is subjected to a campaign of visious ridicule, sarcasm, and in extreme instances, bodily harm. Economic reprisal is practiced upon them in the form of destroying their belongings and defacing their papers and books. If they drive to school in their own cars, sabotage on the cars is frequently practiced. Even the failure of law-abiding pupils to appreciate such delicious humor as has been described, can bring down strong condemnation upon such as so fail, so that self preservation prompts the habitually decent pupil to give moral support to the rowdy, though he may secretly and privately disapprove.

The most common expression of smearing, on the part of those who would not be guilty of the rougher forms of misbehavior, is refusal to pay attention to instruction. The never-ending yak-yak-yak that goes on, as effectively smears the serious efforts of all concerned, as any other practice yet devised.

Tearing up the furniture and equipment in the school was widely indulged in, that year. Numbers of boys carried pliers and screw drivers and small wrenches with them, which they used in taking the screws and bolts out of the chairs and desks, during the class period. A teacher finds it extremely difficult to detect such activity. Even if he caught the culprit red-handed, there is generally no method of punishing him. Furniture so weakened makes much unnecessary noise, and sometimes collapses completely

-- sprawling the occupant in the floor -- to the unutterable glee of the class. When such accidents occur, the class period is spoiled, though the teacher may restore some semblance of order, and cripple along to the end of the period, somehow.

One would suppose, that, in a high school, spit-ball shooting would not be indulged in. As a matter of fact, it is a practice almost universal. Because of the two-faced attitude of all the building principals the writer has know, towards school disorder in general, to see a young man of six-feet two, weighing 200 pounds or more, thrust his head up, stretch his neck, raise his hands, showing a rubber band and a ball of tin-foil, and snap it against the ear, eyes, or neck of another such young man, is a heart sinking experience for the teacher; the man who serves as target, when hit, emits a heartrending howl of pain, whereupon a half dozen special cronies of the two, burst out with a prolonged fit of howling, screeching laughter. The period is pretty effectively shot.

The principal hauls the teacher into his office, by bellowing into the inter-com.

"Mr. Jones, report to me at once, in my office!"

As the luckless young fellow walks out of the room, amid the jeers and catcalls of the fifteen percent, he'd rather be a hundred miles away. He reaches the office. The "secretary," regarding him through narrowed eyes -- nose wrinkled slightly as if she were assailed by an unpleasant odor, lips pursed, says coldly,

"Have a seat."

The young teacher cools his heels in the outer office for ten minutes or longer. Finally the secretary obeys the summons of the buzzer, and disappears into the sanctum sanctorum. In a minute, she's back out front, and announces, in a sugary, mincing tone,

"Mr. Cantor will see you now."

The other people in the outer office titter softly as Jones enters the sanctum sanctorum.

"Close the door!" barks the principal -- plenty loudly enough to be heard out front. He leans forward in his swivel chair, his elbow

16

resting on the desk. He removes his glasses, holds them by the head-pieces, and slowly twirls them round and round. His facial expression is like a thunder cloud.

"Jones," he says, "when I hired you to teach in this school, I thought I was hiring a young man of at least ordinary intelligence. Instead, it appears that I hired a weak nincompoop who can't keep order in his class. I can hear that racket plum down here in the office! Now, I expect the classes in this school to be orderly. I expect those who engage in fun and games to be sent to me immediately!"

"Mr. Cantor, I'll be most happy to do so, because I believe that when those young men are informed that their teacher is a member of the faculty, and has the support of the principal, their conduct will change for the better."

"Alright! Go back in there and assert some authority. For God's sake, let's have a little law and order around here! On second thought, don't send them -- bring them!"

Jones walks back to his classroom, miserable and ashamed, but thinking, "Maybe I'm not alone, playing a game with me on one team and several other players -- those devoted to fun and games -- on the other. Maybe conditions will improve."

The next meeting of the class was marked by a hush of expectancy. As the teacher began the lesson presentation, the whole sorry performance of the preceding day began again. But this time, the teacher snapped,

"Come with me, gentlemen."

They walked down to the principal's office. This time there was no delay, because one of the boys snapped his fingers under the secretary's nose and snarled, "I want to see Cantor, and I want to see him NOW!"

The secretary smiled brightly and said, with a slight tremor in her voice,

"Go right in, gentlemen!"

The boy led the way. Opening the door, and leaving it open, he advanced to the great man's desk, and snarled,

"What the hell's going on around here?"

"Yeah!" growled the other boy. "It's one hell of a note to be ordered out of the class and hauled down here! What's the world comin' to, anyway?"

"Now, now, gentlemen," purred the principal. "Let's get to the bottom of this." Turning to the teacher, with an expression of exasperation on his silly face, he said,

"Jones, what's the meaning of this?"

"Spit-balls again. Following instructions, I brought them to you," said the teacher.

"Were you boys shooting spit-balls?" gently inquired the great man.

"Hell fire and damnation!" howled the first boy. "Suppose we were! Whose business is it, anyway! We were just having a little fun. We're sick and tired of being ordered around like little kids! If you can't stop it, Cantor, by God WE will! You'll hear from the school board about this!"

"Please, gentlemen, don't report this sorry exhibition of weakness and incompetence to the Board. I assure you that I can handle it, myself," whined the great man.

Turning to Jones, he rasped,

"Jones, how could you bear to expose such weakness and incapacity on your part? If you're not able to maintain order in your classes, I certainly can't do it for you! Now, all of you get back to class, and let's show some STUFF!"

"Untenable situation," sighed Jones. "Damned if I do, and damned if I don't. When my contract expires, he can have this hell hole to himself."

No piece of equipment could be kept intact for long. The big, stationary pieces, like stoves or sewing machines, were frequently out of commission. The small equipment could be, and was, carried away -- all to the serious detriment of the program. Even the trash receptacles, placed through the corridors at intervals, had their swinging lids so twisted that they could not be used.

When one considers the Physical Education program, one would suppose that he had hit upon <u>one</u> activity which "would be suffered gladly." But no. It became just too too much trouble for the girls to get into their gym clothes. They insisted upon strolling three abreast -- arms around each other, around the field, talking about whatever interested them at the moment.

At one end of the field was a spreading oak tree that afforded grateful shade on a hot day. Some of the girls of each P.E. class strolled down to the oak for a cigarette, and a little much-needed rest. Some took bottles of cold drinks with them, available at dispensers in the main corridor -- and left the bottles where they emptied them.

The main attraction of the oak, however, was not its shade. Stimulating and inspiring companionship was furnished by "young-men-about-town," who parked their cars nearby - just off the school property. Numbers of girls enjoyed a lively spin around the lake while they were supposed to be engaged in physical excercises and games, under trained adult leadership. Their teacher tried to keep them on the field and at work, but they paid no attention to her. She could only report their absences from class, but nothing could be done about it. She had to do the best she could with a skeleton crew.

Not even the building itself escaped the wrecking activities of these free spirits. One day everybody's attention was drawn to the ceiling of one of the long corridors. Somebody had toted a long sharp pole from one end to the other, and had jabbed a hole in the ceiling with every step.

Anytime a pupil desired to enter a locked room, he took a crowbar and pried one of the windows open. Of course the window was no good from then on, until it had been repaired or replaced, at considerable expense. There was scarcely a door or cabinet lock in or around the school that had not been forced until it was useless.

No doubt such activity accounts for a large percentage of the financial outlay referred to in the school budget as "maintenance."

The writer remembers having read a statement in his home town paper, to the effect that the education board of the school system he came up through as a boy, had spent twenty thousand dollars to replace windows of schools, broken the day before school was scheduled to reopen for the Fall term.

But to return to Azurville: the girls were not alone in rising and strolling out of class without permission. Our hood and thug element among the boys enjoyed much of freedom in that area. Numbers of them would leave class, stroll out to the parking area, enter a car belonging to one of the group, and drive down town for a few beers and a few games of pool -- arranging to return in time for lunch.

These gentry never took their turns in the chow line -- they swaggered to the head of the line, so they'd have time after lunch for a cigarette in the boys' room, or down under the oak. It was no use for the displaced pupils to object -- that only brought them a dig in the ribs or a crushing blow in the stomach that would last for a couple of days. Nothing could be done about it. If any teacher besides the coaches attempted to put them in line, all they got for their effort was a sneering wisecrack, and an invitation to put them in their place by force, if the teacher thought he or she was big enough.

Naturally, in the complete absence of support from the front office, the teachers soon learned to overlook such behavior as was none of our damned business, and spare ourselves embarrassment and possible injury. We knew that those hoods would not hesitate to hold us, by two of their number, while a third worked us over. Indeed it was only the presence of the coaches, before mentioned, that prevented the actual mauling of the other teachers. I don't know of an instance of actual physical attack upon any teacher, but I remember one instance in which I myself narrowly escaped a beating, by the nimble exercise of my wits.

I am a small man, only a little over five and a half feet tall. I am generally overweight, though not obese -- just fat enough to be in no physical shape for athletic exercises such as wrestling and boxing. At that time I was already past fifty.

It happened that a new boy enrolled in school within two months of the end of the semester. It is an unusual time of year to enroll, but this boy's case was special. And let me hasten to admit that this was an unusual boy. If we had a large number of boys like him, among the pupils, we would not be able to cripple along with a school program at all."

Well, this boy had been attending Seaside high when he and one of his teachers ran afoul of each other. The result of their fracas was, that the boy produced a set of brass knucks and pounded his teacher's face to a bloody pulp. The newspapers in the central part of the state made much of the incident and the trial of the boy in juvenile court. The outcome of the trial of this sweet, innocent, defenseless child of six feet, two and one half inches, and one hundred ninety six pounds was, that he was released to the custody of his mama, with the provision that he would not be allowed to attend Seaside high for the remainder of that year, but would have to attend another school. The teacher was discharged.

He elected to honor Azurville high. Of course his great fame preceded him, and he was received with a hero's welcome. The principal assured him that he would not be molested in any manner -- that his record would not be held against him -- that he could start again with a clean slate. He was invited to simply report to the principal, any teacher who gave him any trouble.

This ill-used child was enrolled in two of my classes. When he entered the room, surrounded by a bevy of beautiful, foul-mouthed molls, and took a look at the teacher, he must have judged that fortune had favored him again. Surely that little old man would not be able to give him serious trouble!

The group moved to the back of the room, and seated themselves. The class was unusually attentive that day. Everybody was agog to discover how this expert would work up his situation.

Two girls moved their chairs close to his -- one on each side. We teachers took no notice of little things like that -- never remonstrated as long as no more noise was made then we could go against, so I said nothing. I went ahead with the program.

Since this was written, this kind of boy is present in considerable numbers.

Toward the end of the period, my new boy abandoned the bass runble he had been using, under his breath, and began talking in full voice -- his girl in each arm -- his rich bass voice filling the room.

I said,

"Gentlemen" (he wasn't the only one talking) -- "let's have a little closer attention to business."

My new boy rose and stood -- feet wide apart in his #12 cowboy boots -- his hair slicked down with grease -- his side-burns reaching elegantly toward the point of his jaws -- pelvis thrust far forward -- his hand feeling in his pocket for his brass knucks -- his teeth showing in a wide, menacing grin, in the best movie dead-end manner -- his eyes narrowed to slits -- calculated to strike terror to the teacher's heart -- and spoke, in a gentle, deadly tone:

"Mister, are you talkin' to me?"

Ignoring him, I went on with my lesson point. He cleared his throat, and raised his voice to a snarl:

"Mister, I asked you a question."

I gave him a wide grin like his own, and replied,

"Did you, now? It must have escaped me. Would you mind repeating it?"

"I'll repeat it. I said 'were you talking to me'?"

I replied, in a deprecating tone,

"Naw! Now why should I be talking to you?"

Tension loosened in the room. Some of my friends were apprehensive, lest I stride back and attempt to handle him, as his Seaside teacher had.

He was taken aback. The wind was gone from his sails. Uncertainty sat upon him. He shifted his stance, and said, lamely,

"I'll bet my muscles are better than yours,"

I replied,

"Mister, I know a hundred horses in this county, each one having muscles that are better than yours, and not one of them will ever be a man."

Gargantuan laughter rocked the room. The uproar was at its height when the bell rang, signaling the end of the hour. I was immensely relieved, yet wondering what would happen when he returned that afternoon to history class.

In the meantime, however, Providence was operating in my behalf. A little girl approached the track coach, whose room was just across the hall.

a word concerning the track coach might be in order at this point. He was built like Joe Palooka -- twenty-nine years old at that time. His favorite exercise, just to keep in shape, was picking up three-hundred-pound barbells, and pushing the weight above his head, at arms length, a half dozen times.

The little girl, knowing what close friends the coach and I were, said to him,

"Mr. Smith, that new boy from Seaside tried to provoke a fight with Mr. Porter, just now."

Smith glanced around over the milling throng, and asked,

"Is that the lad, that tall one with the side-burns?"

"That's the one," the girl replied.

23

As the boy swaggered abreast of Smith, the coach's hand shot out, and gathering a handful of leather jacket, literally lifted the boy clear of the floor. He shook him so violently that the boy must have felt like every vertabra in his spine was shaken loose from all the others. He was dazed and bewildered.

The coach pulled him close and glaring into his eyes, grated,

"Boy, did you know I'm at least two kinds of a fool? I'm fool enough to believe I can thrash you to within an inch of your life; and I'm fool enough to do it, at any moment! On your way!"

That boy didn't even stay for lunch. He made tracks down over the hill, and did not come back.

That evening, the supervising principal sent for Mr. Smith. When the teacher reported to the office and said,

"You sent for me, Mr. Damron," the principal replied,

"Come in and sit down, Mr. Smith" and leaned back in his swivel chair. Looking out benevolently over his spectacles, he placed his elbows on the arms of his chair, fitted his fingertips together, and spoke, in that hesitating, gentle manner of his:

"Mr. Smith, word has come to me that you roughed up one of our boys."

Smith dipped his chin, grinned engagingly, and replied,

"Aw, shucks, Mr. Damron, I reckon I didn't hurt him any."

"Mr. Smith, we frown upon such rough treatment of the pupils. We believe that gentleness and understanding will accomplish more than violence. I want to warn you against a repetition of such disgraceful conduct. I shan't ask for your resignation this time. But he assured that another such exhibition of brutality will be dealt with most harshly."

Smith replied,

"I appreciate your forbearance very deeply, Mr. Damron, and I assure you that such an incident shall not occur again."

In spite of the rebuke to Smith and the implied guarantee of safety to our hoods, they were not able to dispel entirely the healthy respect they had always felt for the young teacher. The thugs had a doubt struggling around in their minds: could they be absolutely certain of their immunity from punishment if one or more of them actually manhandled a teacher? They knew they could depend upon the loyal backing of the administration. But the coaches? They were unpredictable. To the hoods and thugs, the coaches had all the appearance of manhood, not only physically, but spiritually and morally as well. Anyhow, no one made any physical attack upon a teacher that year.

Now, I agree with the supervising principal to a great extent, when he expressed his confidence in gentleness and understanding, in dealing with hoods -- under certain circumstances. When lawful authority breaks down, and a teacher is left to cope with pupil disorder with no support whatever, of any kind; when the recalcitrant is a man in size and strength, feeling no loyalty to his school, his society, his country, or his God, not many teachers feel physically strong enough to deal with him in a test of strength. Teachers are very seldom fighting men; and in the case of women, they never are.

Now, many readers will recall their experiences in the Little Red School House on the Hill. They will remember, with a little effort, the fact that teachers of that era were mostly men; that the most important attribute of a teacher was the ability to thrash the biggest and most war-like of the young men who happened to be members of the pupil group. The teachers were hired on that most important consideration.

In that far-off time, the preacher, when he arrived in a community, first sought out the bully of the neighborhood, and thrashed him, before attempting to hold worship service.

But, as the Roman post horses remarked so aptly, two thousand years ago, times are changed. Coaches are generally muscle men as well as intellectuals; but most teachers, though in reasonable health and fairly good shape, as civilians, cannot qualify as fighters, especially knife fighters.

No, the average teacher, where there is no administrative authority, finds it expedient to use gentleness and understanding -- escaping the missiles, as Cicero put it, by genuflections of the body, and ignoring misbehavior, laughing it off, and crippling through with the teaching program as best he can.

Our school was fairly crowded, so that it was necessary to make classrooms do double duty. Each room in the school was in use every period of the day.

The shorthand room was furnished with writing tables which were somewhat larger than ordinary school desks. The legs of these tables were not even, so that they did not set solidly on the floor. The pupils of my English class that met in that room, amused themselves by wiggling those tables in such a way as to cause each of them to give out a noise like that of an air drill. Naturally the teacher was at considerable disadvantage in presenting the lesson and carrying on the work of the day.

The proper way to handle such a situation is to dismiss the class, with orders to come back in the evening for work. But we couldn't do that. Those pupils had to ride home on the buses, as the school was located out at the edge of town -- and the teachers were under strict orders to cause no one to miss his bus.

Conditions became so bad that the administration finally allowed the teachers to keep pupils after school for as long as half an hour -- provided we delivered them at their homes in our own cars.

Even with this service furnished, the pupils hated to miss that trip home on the bus -- miss the fun of baiting the bus driver, punishing some other pupil by heaping sarcasm or ridicule or bodily harm or humiliation, and calling out witty sallies or insults to passing motorists or folks walking along the street.

One of the most hilarious and enjoyable exercises of the afternoon consisted of shifting their weight back and forth, in unison, so as to rock the bus so violently that the driver couldn't hold it in the road, thus rendering it a danger and a menace to themselves and the general public. Pupils who did not approve this exercise were required to participate in it, nevertheless, on pain of profane and obscene ridicule, or bodily harm.

So it was real punishment to be kept in, and miss all that fun. What to do to break the teachers of keeping the pupils in, became the burning problem of the moment. The solution was not long in coming; it took the form of bearing false witness.

The writer had been familiar with the Commandment "Thou shalt not bear false witness" throughout his life. But this is the first society he had ever seen in which violations of that commandment was a favorite device for getting along.

Reports began to sift into the front office: Miss Strudelheimer had detained young Conrad Kretzelbaum because she desired the pleasure of taking him home in her car. Mr. Mannheim detained little Lorene Thomaskevesky, and on the way home, the poor little thing had to fight him off, and finally get out and walk, so insistent were his improper advances, and so scandalous his proposals.

These reports were brought in by the dams of the delinquents. I don't refer to them as mothers, for they were more like dams. And the fathers were not fathers, but sires.

They trickled into the principal's office in high dudgeon. If the principal didn't make it impossible for these low-lifed scum that called themselves teachers, to continue such scandalous behavior, they'd take the matter up with the county office. They knew full well that the principal could not afford to bring down criticism or inquiry from the county office -- he was on probation!

So the teachers were called in, those who had delivered pupils after school.

Leaning back in his swivel chair, resting his elbows on the chair arms, carefully fitting his finger-tips together, and regarding the teacher steadily over the top of his spectacles, the principal would speak:

"Miss Strudelheimer, young Kretzelbaum's mother came in yesterday, and acquainted me with a situation which I cannot and will not tolerate. Miss Strudelheimer, shame on you! I say again, shame on you for detaining young Kretzelbaum after school simply for the pleasure you get out of the drive home with him!"

The poor young woman would attempt an indignant denial of the brutal charge against her character, at this point.

"Ah-ah-ah-ah-<u>Ah</u>!" the principal would exclaim, with uplifted hand -- palm out. "Let us face the facts! Now, Miss Strudelheimer, we can't have this sort of thing. We have the fair name of our school to consider! We must keep the reputation of Azurville High unblemished! Go, and sin no more!"

Next, Mr. Mannheim would be summoned. On the way, he would see Miss Strudelheimer emerge from the executive suite, in tears, sobbing wildly. He would enter the awesome presence in great trepidation.

He would find the Great man slowly pacing the room. On his entrance, the Great Man whirled and confronted the frightened young fellow:

"Mr. Mannheim!" the principal would thunder. "To what level can a man possibly sink? How dare you so cruelly use an innocent young girl, as to keep her in after school, just to get her in your power on the way home and make indecent proposals to her? Ah-ah-ah-ah-ah! Don't attempt any denial or justification! You should be so ashamed of yourself that you'd want to die! Let me tell you, sir, that I won't tolerate that sort of thing! Let me hear of it just one more time, and you will be out of the teaching profession from here on out! So, and sin no more!"

Poor Mannheim! He has a wife and two babies. He has eight thousand dollars paid on his home, and a seven thousand dollar mortgage. He pays one hundred sixteen-dollars per month toward its liquidation, twenty-five dollars of which applies to the principle -- the rest is interest monthly on the unpaid balance. His wife needs expensive surgery. His job is all that stands between his little family and stark penury. The last thing he can do is antagonize the Great Man. He swallows the indignity and the outrage for the sake of his dear ones; and stalks from the office, angry, humiliated, exhausted, and heart-sick.

Young Robertson is next on the list. Having observed the exit of the other two, he has the wind up to some extent. He doesn't know what's coming, but he figures it's going to be something unpleasant.

He enters. The Great Man takes a fatherly tone:

"Robertson, I am deeply grieved at reports that have reached me, concerning your unprincipled conduct with the young ladies of this school, who are under your authority and protection -- and while you're taking them home after class detention -- at your mercy!"

"Why, Mr. Damron, what are you talking about? What is the matter? What occasions this outburst?"

"I had great hopes for you, Robertson. I thought you had the makings of a fine school man. And now you make indecent proposals to little Debby Blake! If I hear any more reports like poor Mrs. Blake made this morning, I shall have to ask you for your resignation!"

Now Robertson is somewhat differently situated from Mannhaim. He is just out of college, teaching his first term of school. His father heads a great corporation. A teacher's salary means nothing to him. He chose teaching as a labor of love. His experiences so far, however, have not been of the sort to reassure him as to the wisdom of his choice. The more he sees of the teaching profession, the more discouraged he feels. And now this kind of talk from his principal to a man who is a gentleman by birth, training, and education!

Anger uncontrollable and resentment immeasurable boils up from the depths of his soul.

"Anybody who accuses me of improper conduct toward anybody at any time is a damned liar. And you are an unprincipled scoundrel to entertain such charges for a split second. You don't have to ask for my resignation. You already have it. And I invite you to ram it into any orifice of your anatomy that your ingenuity may suggest."

He also stalks out -- light, buoyant, happy, justified, and smiling, leaving the Great Man limp, flabbergasted, speechless.

The schools have lost a really good teacher.

This incident actually occurred, to the writer's certain knowledge. At this point, one wonders how many fine young men and women are driven from the profession each year, over the length and breadth of the nation -- young people who felt dedicated to the work, who toiled through the years of arduous study and training -- spent thousands in money and the best years of their lives in preparation -- for reasons similar to those that prompted Robertson to give up in outrage and disgust.

The principal, on the whole, was victorious. Or was he? He had kept those flap-lipped harpies from going to the county office. He had saved his own precious skin at the expense of driving away a young man just embarking upon a career that held every promise of brilliancy and success. He had embittered the lives and undermined the confidence, and impaired the effectiveness, of two other fine young teachers.

Reader, this sort of occurance is tragically common in America. No wonder there is a shortage of teachers!

Detention had begun to work, even wearing the hand-cuffs and leg-irons imposed upon the teachers in requiring them to furnish transportation home, to those detained. The pupils were resentful, and chafed under so mild and brief an interruption of their freedom.

Some of them went to their dams and said,

"Look here, ol' woman. I'm sick and tired of being kept after school. God damn ya, you've got to do something to get this stopped. Go to the ol' man out in the front office. You know he's under probation. Surely you can come up with some angle that will jerk a knot in the ol' bastard's tail. Now, do it. Like I said, I'm sick of this. If I don't get relieved pretty soon, no tellin' <u>what</u> I might do."

"All right, honey, mama will think of something."

The foregoing was the plan mama thought of. It worked brilliantly. News of what had happened to Mannheim, Miss Strudelheimer, and Robertson, spread through the faculty like wild fire. Form that time on, no one would assign detention on any provocation whatever, naturally.

We struggled along.

The element that seized complete independence for themselves not only felt free to live exactly as they pleased around school, but were independent of, and above the law, around town, as well.

At school, it was their purpose to see to it that no teaching was done, nor any learning accomplished by anyone. The body of rules and regulations necessary to any society, of whatever size, that is necessary to the smooth functioning and purposeful existence of that society, was not only flouted -- its very existence was denied. Contrary to the belief of many citizens that teachers and school administrators are authoritarian in their relations with pupils, those folks are there, not to impose their will on the pupils, but to furnish leadership. Of course, once the fundamental purpose of the school's existence is questioned -- and not only questioned, but boldly denied, there is no common purpose to weld that society into any cohesive whole -- and hence no ideal to really around. So they supplied a new purpose! to exercise perfect license, and impose the hood will on everybody around. Right there in their own little society, they established a brave new world.

If any of those pupils thought of anything he wanted to say to another who was sitting in another room, he rose and walked out of his own class, likely preceding his departure with an announcement in a loud voice, interrupting a mathematical demonstration:

"Oh hell! I forgot to tell Bill to be sure to double the beer order for the party tonight!"

Out he would stalk, over to the other room, where the other teacher was doing the best she could to teach; open the door, stand in it, bellow to that teacher:

"Miss Davis, Doll, I've got one hell of an important message for ol' Bill, back, there. Hold everything a few minutes, will ya, there's a sweet doll, while I cue him in."

Stalking back to Bill, he would have a few minutes consultation -- stalking out when he had finished. The period was pretty well shot. Teachers were interrupted constantly. It did no good at all to appeal to control authority: there wasn't any.

If a teacher whose program was constantly being interrupted and broken up, appealed to either of the principals, he was told off without hesitation:

"Now, Miss Davis, we believe that any teacher worth her salt, can run her own class. If she can't, it's time for her to admit candidly that she is in the wrong kind of job, and hand in her resignation. If you feel insecure as a teacher, you should become a stenographer or a store clerk. It is extremely poor procedure to annoy the principal with difficulties you should be able to handle yourself. The administration takes a dim view of weak, ineffective, incompetent teachers who depend upon the principal to do their work for them."

Miss Davis was a fat, dumpy, little old maid, who had earned two degrees, and had served the trade for wages for fifteen years. She was as good a teacher as ever took charge of a class. But that year, she had to try to teach above the uproar the hoods kept up, from the beginning of the period to its heaven-sent close. Her voice could be heard throughout that part of the building. She was exhausted by lunch time, and hoarse. For her afternoon classes, her voice was a frog-like croak.

On the occasion just mentioned she had been drilling an English grammer class for the forthcoming six weeks test. When that hood stalked to the door, one his way out, she burst into tears, grabbed his arm, and screeched, poor little outraged woman.

"You come with me to the principal, you sorry specimen. I'm calling for a showdown,: and began hauling the handsome, amused young man along the hall.

"Now, doll, there ain't no use to act this way. The principal knows better than to ram his nose into affairs that don't concern him. He knows he might get it flattened."

The little woman had reached the breaking point, and had broken. She refused to release the pupil. She dragged and hauled and sobbed, and they moved the short distance to the office. As they entered the principal's office, she was sobbing and shedding tears. The boy was grinning broadly.

"Hey," exclaimed the principal. "What's going on here?"

"This chick has gone off her rocker, Doc," replied the young athlete. "She suddenly grabs me, and starts carrying on like crazy. I ain't done nothing."

Miss Davis sobbed out the sorry story, ending with the threat:

"You've got to stop this sort of thing, or I'm through with this school, beginning right now. There isn't money enough in Florida to hire me to try to work under these conditions."

The principal was very much on his dignity.

"Miss Davis, your working here, after this disgraceful outburst, is highly inadvisable. I'm sure the thought has occurred to you that you may be in the wrong kind of job. I shall, therefore, not be able to recommend you for reemployment for the coming year. I'm sure you will admit the justice of my action in pronouncing you incompetent and insubordinate. Good morning, Miss Davis. You may leave by the same door through which you entered."

During this masterly discourse, the thug stood smiling indolently. When the teacher had rushed from the room, he softly clapped his hands, and said,

"Bravo! That's telling 'em, Doc. By God, that disposes of one nosy dame, anyhow. Now, I'm getting sick of being pushed around, and -"

By that time the principal had absorbed more than even <u>his</u> stomach could stand.

"Button your lip, you lousy, lazy, impudent, ill mannered, insufferable, lantern-jawed limb and branch of hell! I'm sick of you! Just get your personal belongings together, and let me enjoy the welcome sight of your ass disappearing down over the hill and around the curve. Go!."

"Why doc! Boy, you ain't acting right. Simmer down. Apologize, now, so we can part friends, and let's now hear any more of this crap!"

"No, Fuzzy. I'm mad plum through, and mean everything I say. You're through. Get going."

The boy was mad now.

"You'll regret this before night, you little pip-squeak. You just wait!"

He swung angrily out the door, and high-tailed it to his locker, off the school property, down over the hill, and around the curve.

The principal heard that boy when he snarled that he would regret his action before long. And he believed it. The rest of the afternoon was a time fraught with anxiety for him. The longest days finally wear away, though, and finally the buses pulled in, the final bell rang, and the bellowing, screeching, mob piled in, and peace reigned. Blessed peace! The principal mopped his sweating, aching head with a sodden handkerchief.

His phone rang.

"Hello."

"Mr. Birdsong" This is Capt. Easy," (the county superintendent). "What's the matter over there, boy? I've had a dozen phone calls this afternoon about you. Have you gone stark raving mad?"

"No-o-o. I don't think so. Everything's under control, as far as I know."

"I'm not so sure of that. Suppose you stay put until we get there. I've got to get to the bottom of this. Where there's smoke, there's fire. These fellows are raising general and particular hell. You just hold the fort. We'll be along directly."

Poor Birdsong. No man ever occupied a more unenviable position than his. The supervising principal had not relieved him of any of his responsibilities. He had merely robbed him of the authority to deal with them. He was forever treating him the same way he dealt with him one morning when he noticed a boy sitting on the front steps of the gym, smoking a cigarette. Saying nothing to the boy (he knew better), he sought out the building principal, and beckoned him to approach. His face wore an expression of one who has seen something, but can't credit the evidence of his own senses. He said, and his voice dripped with gentle incredulity,

"Mr. Birdsong, I saw a boy, sitting on the gym steps, smoking a cigarette!"

"Maybe it isn't too late to catch him! choked Birdsong, and he tore out of the building and over to the gym as if the devil pursued him. Sure enough, the boy was still here.

Rushing breathlessly up to the boy, the principal demanded,

"Where are you supposed to be this period?"

"Who want's to know?" asked the boy, grinning neastily.

"Don't give me that stuff. I asked you a question!"

"All right, if it's any of your business, which it ain't. I'M supposed to be in typing this period. But I ain't there, as you can see."

"Well, get there, on the double!"

"Simmer down, Doc. So much of the period is gone, that it's hardly worth while to go there now. Ol' Potter won't miss little ol' me, among the forty-eight members of the class. I'll see you this afternoon. Right now, I've got important business."

And he rose, to his full six feet of height, stretched, yawned, recovered, and strolled into the gym.

The principal went to his office, opened the intercom, and spoke:

"Mr. Potter, will you report to me in the office, immediately?"

The order was heard by every member of Mr. Potter's class. An intake of breath, and a titter swept gently over the room. There were comments.

"Ol' Potter is on the carpet!"

"I wonder what it is, this time?"

"Maybe it's nothing -- just Birdsong wanting some information, the little squirt."

Mr. Potter obediently entered the office. Both principals were there.

"Can I be of assistance?" asked the teacher.

"Tell him, Mr. Damron,:" snapped birdsong.

Damron slumped down in his chair -- his elbows resting on the chair-arms--fitted his fingertips together carefully-- dipped his chin, looked out over his spectacles, and spoke in his gentle voice and hesitating manner:

"Mr. Potter, just now I saw one of your boys sitting on the gym steps, smoking a cigarette. How did he get out of your class?"

"Why, I remember having given some boy a pass to go to the gym, some time ago, replied Potter.

"Why, I never heard of such a thing," said Damron. "Why did you do that, in the name of all that's holy?"

"The boy said he had left his wallet and watch in the gym, and begged leave to return for them," said the teacher. "What would you have done?"

"Tch, tch, tch," slicked Damron, wonderingly. "I never heard of such a thing in my life! Now, Mr. potter, we really must ask you to be more careful and attentive in the future. Such incidents point to incompetence. We really can't have that sort of thing!"

As the little man sat there, waiting for the arrival of his executioner, his mind darted around among the experiences of that year. He thought of the morning his phone had jangled, and the voice of an old nosy informer in the area had announced breathlessly and triumphantly -- thrilled to the marrow of her bones:

"Mr. Birdsong, I just saw two girls and two men crawling into the bushes in the vacant field next to my house. Oh, Mr. Birdsong, I'm morally certain that they are high school girls!"

He had torn out to the parking area at his usual gait, poor little devil -- as if pursued by fiends. He had arrived at the fatal spot. The girls were there, apparently fully dressed, though he did notice that they were wearing flowers in their hair. The two young men-about-town, both high school graduates but under twenty-one, were just pulling up their trousers.

He remembered how gentle and sweet and considerate the judge had been to all four, later in juvenile court. He remembered with what scathing contempt the judge had addressed him -- what searing sarcasm he himself had listened to, for "allowing these sweet innocent children to leave school, and thus furnishing temptation to these fine, handsome boys."

"Yes," he reflected, "The judge dished out to me the same bowl of stew I served to Miss Davis today. Only when I blacklist Miss Davis for incompetence and insubordination her means of livelihood will be gone. How will she support herself and her invalid old mother on a store clerk's wages? And God knows she struggled during those years when she was studying -- figuratively lifted herself by her own bootstraps. How she managed and made ends meet, only He knows. What a kettle of rotten fish! What will become of my wife and children? For I too have struggled. I've devoted my life, my talents, my effort, to the school business. But this looks like the end. I hear cars stopping in the lot."

The men -- a full dozen of them -- trooped grimly toward the office. Birdsong recognized them all. Three were members of the county board of public instruction. One was the county superintendent of schools. The others were members of that mighty body known as "The Downtown Coaches."

He met them at the door and invited them in. His face wore the green pallor of fear. They rudely ignored his jovial welcome. The men ranged themselves around the office. For a few moments, there was an uneasy silence. Presently the superintendent spoke!

"Mr. Birdsong, complaint has been lodged with me by these gentlemen, concerning the perfectly scabrous treatment you meted out today to Fuzzy Jones, our star "forward." From the sound of that disgraceful episode, I should imagine you would find it very difficult to justify your high-handed conduct. You have persecuted this fine, upstanding, innocent boy, simply to placate a hysterical woman on the faculty, who had already subjected the young gentleman to great embarrassment, humiliation, and anguish of spirit. Shame on you, sir!"

"And just on the eye of the Sebring game, too,: grated one of the Downtown Coaches. "Of all the fat-headed, scatter-brained, exhibitions of brutality I've ever heard of in my life, this wins the crocheted slop-jar!"

"What in the hell were you thinking of?" bellowed another downtown Coach. "Or do you even pretend to think? What th' hell you think your head's for -- to keep your spine from unraveling?"

An elderly board member cleared his throat, and spoke in measured tones:

"Mr. Birdsong, experiences in school, during the tender years, can warp a boy's personality permanently. We consider your fault in this matter is very grave. You have acted in a manner totally unworthy the head of a high school in this county. Unless you can mend your ways, we shall have to ask you to tender your resignation."

A second board member hunched forward in his chair and spoke:

"Mr. birdsong, we feel a hesitancy, in spite of the open-and-shut nature of this case, to move to the ultimate solution. It seems to us, despite the bald-faced, inexcusable course you have pursued, a mite extreme, to discharge the principal of a school, without hearing his defense -- if one can imagine the possibility of a defense."

"Have you anything to say for yourself, before the formal request for your resignation," asked the superintendent.

Here it is. At last. How its me, oh Lord. How often have I ground up a ragged school teacher! I didn't think it could happen to a principal. But it is happening.

The sweat poured down the face of the little man. He was at bay -- literally fighting for his life. The only difference between his situation and that of a teacher is, that the teacher is not allowed to put on a defense. The principal had been tried, as teachers are, in secret and in his absence. The teacher is called in only to hear sentence pronounced. The little man was allowed to speak in his own defense.

He had made a lightning decision: he would make no defense -- he would throw himself upon the mercy of the court. He spoke:

"Gentlemen, you see before you a man covered with sin and shame! My soul is filled with anguish! My heart is broken and contrite. My conduct is inexcusable. I have no merit. I can only throw my worthless self upon your mercy."

He lowered his face into his hands and sobbed unrestrainedly.

Except for the sound of the principal's weeping and sobbing, there was silence in the room.

Gradually his grief spent itself, and its noise subsided. The superintendent spoke:

"Mr. Birdsong, I cannot guarantee the clemency of the board. You will be notified of its decision in due time. Meanwhile, I feel it only right and proper that you should make proper amends to the boy you have so cruelly wronged. Someone ask fuzzy to step in."

Fuzzy had been sitting in the next room all the time. When called, he swaggered in, an expression of sullen outrage on his ugly face.

The principal sprang to his feet and approached him with outstretched hands. He smiled up at him through his tears.

"Fuzzy boy, I'm sure sorry for the way I treated you this morning. Ol' Birdsong just lost his head. If you can find it in that big , generous heart to forgive me, let's forget it, and let by-gones be by-gones. I was wrong, dead wrong. And I'm asking forgiveness from my heart."

Fuzzy reluctantly allowed his hand to be shaken. He replied,

"All right, Birdsong, I'm being a brainless sap. I'm doing something my better judgment tells me I hadn't oughta do. Just watch yourself, and don't let it happen again, either to me, or to any of the boys. Just because some screwey dame raises hell about somebody, don't mean you have to go off your rocker. Just remember that teachers are a dime a dozen. Now remember -- behave yourself!"

"Oh, Fuzzy! I <u>will.</u> I'll remember. Bless your big, generous heart -- to forgive a scabrous injury just like that" and he snapped his fingers -- "and take back into favor an undeserving sinner like me!"

Turning to the men, the principal intoned, in a subdued voice, and looking at them with pleading eyes.

"Gentlemen, the remorse I feel, I am sure, will shield me from offending again. If you can possibly take this awful chance, and leave me in office, I think I can assure you, without a doubt, that you will not be troubled again."

"We-el," growled another DownTown coach, let's let it lay awhile, boys. Let's sleep on it. Birdsong, we'll let you know. Come on, I've got an engagement!"

They filed out. Silence reigned once more in the all-but deserted office. A beaten, shamed, broken man sat behind a big desk, with self-hatred in his heart that the passage of time would never assuage -- or did it?

He kept his job. Four years later, he retired. He won the victory. He finished his career.

What price victory?

Reader, you'll never be able to calculate the price that was paid for Fuzzy's victory.

Up to that time, the building principal had not been without at least some vestige of the respect and authority inherent in his title and position. When an affair stank too foully -- when a condition got so patently out of hand that he couldn't help but speak out, he could still do so with some small effect, at least. By using a positive, angry snarl, he could over-awe a few of the smaller boys, and some of the girls who were not completely abandoned.

Of course, eighty-five percent of the student body were just run-of-the-mine citizens in school, just as their parents were run-of-the-mine citizens in the community -- not doing anything wrong if they could help it; participated in wrong-doing only to protect themselves from punishment inflicted by the leather-lunger, brass-throated, swaggering gangsters they feared, and their molls; and whom the teachers dreaded and loathed.

But after Fuzzy's victory, even that little bit of authority no longer existed. Joy was unconfined.

DownTown there were three student "hangouts" -- big drug stores with booths, and soda-fountains. The next afternoon, one of those drug stores was wrecked. The leather upholstering in the booths was ripped with switch knives. The perfume area was overturned, losing hundreds of dollars worth of merchandise. More plate glass was destroyed when the hoods could have paid for, with their combined earnings over a twelve month period.

That was the worst depredation. The other drug stores came in for their share of vandalism. The upholstering was slashed. The tables were whittled until they were no longer fit for use in a public place. They had either to be replaced, or the service abandoned.

The service was abandoned. At this writing, four years later, there isn't a drug store in town where a thirsty traveler can get a soda or a shake.

There are plenty of saloons. But thugs behave themselves in saloons.

The particular cronies of Fuzzy planned an evening outing, in the country, to celebrate the complete and final subjugation of school authority.

They planned a picnic and general jamboree.

According to plan, being tired of hot dogs and hamburgers, they caught a farmer's yearling calf. One of the girls cut its throat with a switch-blade, they skinned it, and barbecued it. A good rousing time was enjoyed by all in the party.

Of course the farmer felt resentful. He appealed to the civil authorities. Several of the thugs were arrested, and tried in juvenile court.

Bt you might as well whistle, as try a thug in juvenile court, because juvenile courts <u>favor</u> juvenile thugs.

The pupils' conduct in school went from bad to worse -- if possible. When the bell rang for change of classes, the observer could glance in any direction, along any corridor, and see couples ambling along -- the boys' hands massaging and kneading the girls's buttocks. Some of the girls liked it. Others endured it out of fear of possibly more serious punishment if they objected. Couples and small groups would drift out to the parking area, sit in the cars, and have a cigarette between classes. These, of course, arrived at their next classes, late. Their tramping in, talking and laughing in full voice, broke up any order that had been established before their arrival.

Sometimes the building principal would take notice of these pupils in the cars. He would trot out there and get the names of their next period teachers. Presently, over the inter-com, would sound the principal's voice, in an angry snarl:

"Miss Davis, Mr. Ferguson, Mr. Porter, Mr. Potter, will you folks report to me in my office immediately, please?

The tittering would sweep the classes of those teachers, and the comments would be made:

"I'd hate to be in their shoes. Boy,. Birdsong is sure on his high horse."

"They'll catch hell, all right."

"Well, they've got it coming, the Bastards!"

"Pour it to 'em, Big Daddy!"

When the teachers arrived at the office, having left our classes in pandemonium, the principal would be angry enough to explode.

"I went out to the parking area and found a dozen pupils sitting in cars, necking and smoking. this is scandalous! Why you let 'em do it is a problem too big for me to solve."

One of the teachers would attempt to answer:

"Why, Mr. Birdsong, we hardly have time or opportunity --"

"Don't give me that crap! If you people were worth a pinch of snuff, you'd plan a program so interesting that the kids would hasten eagerly to their next classes! They wouldn't be thinking of things they shouldn't think of! Oh, what have I done to deserve such a crowd of incompetent dead-beats on my faculty? Don't let any pupil be absent from class! Don't even dismiss one to the wash-room during class. Assert a little authority around here! If one comes in late, slap a half hour's detention on him! We can't have this sort of thing! Now get back in there and show some stuff!"

The administration decided to take action on the matter of butt-kneeding. only they called it "fanny-patting." They stationed teachers at corridor intersections, and at points between, to take the names of the fanny patters. We were to call them in, and assign detention.

We did it. The boys bellowed and swore vengeance on the teachers who called them. The girls wept.

The "Fanny-patting" fell off for a brief time.

One morning, the voice of the supervising principal summoned me to his office. One of the boys yelled:

"Want to borrow my big geography to slip into your pants, Mr. Porter, haw, haw, heah, heah, heah.

The class responded with a gale of hoots, catcalls, and laughter.

I went in. Two big men were closeted with the supervising principal. Their faces were like thunderclouds.

One of them didn't wait for an introduction. He thundered:

"My daughter came home yesterday in tears, because you punished her on a charge that only a sadistic blackguard could stoop to. I'll have you know that my little gal has a father to protect her! You're going to apologize for this outrage, or I'll pummel your hide 'til the devil ain't bigger than a small tadpole!"

I answered:

"Mister, I only work here. I obey the orders that are issued to me, if possible. Personally, I don't care who feels whom, or if he does. But if I see any fanny patting going on, I have orders from Mr. Damron here, to assign detention to the boys and girls concerned."

During this exchange, Mr. Damron had assumed his "great executive" attitude, in his swivel chair. At my mention of his name, he leaned forward, and spoke, incredulously:

"Why, Mr. Porter! Do you mean to sit there and assert that such exercises as, er, ah, 'fanny patting' occur in this school?"

I reckon a really loyal teacher should have begun blubbering, and admitted that the whole game was only a figment of his dirty imagination, and advised that he himself be sent to the psychopathic ward at Chattahoochee for observation. But I wasn't loyal, that way. I'll admit that the big protecting father had me worried. That lad could have tied me in a bow knot. I didn't intend for that to happen if I could weasel out of it. If any hide pounding was forth-coming, I didn't intend for the hide to be mine, if I could get another hide substituted for it. And somehow I had the quaint notion that Mr. Damron should stick to his guns, and not try to pass the buck to his subordinate. The order had been his. Now he was washing his hands of the whole matter, and dumping the whole affair in my lap.

The shameful attempt stirred me to white-hot anger. I believe, from there on out, that I could have given fair entertainment to the protective father -- big and dangerous as he looked. My mind was made up. By thunder, I was ready to fight a buzz saw!

"You're damned right I assert that fanny patting not only occurs here -- but that it is a common and wide-spread practice. It never bothered me, but it excercised you 'ti you couldn't stand it. You told the teachers what to do about it. You're the lad who 'took the bull by the horns', and if anybody raises hell about it, you're the fellow who is going to answer the question."

I turned to the protective father:

"As for your daughter getting her fanny patted, hell yes, she gets it patted! That's why I assigned detention to her -- on <u>his</u> express orders. Now, if you crave to begin hide-pounding, let 'er flicker. I'm your huckleberry. I'll do my damedest to entertain you! I don't reckon I can last long, or put up much of a fight, but I'll stand up to you."

The father's head was bowed. While I puffed and blew, he meditated. Presently he looked up with worry and shame on his face.

"Fellows," he said, "I'm not as innocent as I'd at first have you believe. I know what kind of a girl I've got. I probably hoped for better behavior from her. hell, she's my kid -- a chip off the old block; but I'm ashamed. Do the best you can, will you, fellows?" And forgive me for barging in like this. Well, I'll go now."

He and his companion trailed out.

Mr. Damron said, in his gentle, hesitating way:

"Now, Mr. Porter! I'm sure you must have misunderstood me on this. Your conduct has been most reprehensible. Let us have no more of it."

"Phooey!" I replied. "I've been scared out of a year's growth, and my life saved by a miracle, and you talk to me about reprehensible conduct. Now, look here. Don't you ever give me orders like that again, for I won't obey them. I don't care if every girl in the student body gets her ass twisted plumb off. You may call it insubordination if you want to, and I suspect you do."

He did.

When I got back to class, I was greeted with wild, enthusiastic cheering. The supervising principal had absent-mindedly left the intercom open. They had heard every word that had been spoken.

There were gleeful comments:

"Pretty tight corner, there, for a minute, eh Porter?"

"Our ol' teacher is a fightin' man, by God!"

"He sure used the ol' beach You'll have to give 'im <u>that</u>!"

"I especially liked that one about letting all the girls get their asses twisted off!"

"Heah, man. And I'm just the lad to do the twistin'. Hyah, hyah, hyah, hyah, hyah! He, he, he!"

I said:

"Well, don't do it in my class. Make love on your own time. When you're with me, I've got more important duties for you to attend to."

"Now, Mr. Porter, don't be a square! You know that love makes the world do 'round!"

"yea, man! All the world loves a lover!"

the class period ended in wild disorder.

A condition took shape in one of my classes, which no doubt appeared also in others:

The boys got mighty free with heir hands. a teacher who was attending strictly to business found it extremely difficult to catch them at it, but they formed the habit of feeling the girls' breasts, running their hands under the girls' skirts, and biting the girls' necks. The writer saw one of the teachers get her neck nipped, one one occasion. She yelled:

"Eee-ee-yow! You naughty boy! Ha, Ha, ha, ha, hah! Take your seat, you rascal, and pay attention!"

Some of the girls liked it. Others suffered it. All screamed like a catamount when it happened. Such a scream just about ruined a class period.

Our of this circumstance arose my final decision to leave that school.

I had, in this class I mentioned, a tall, lanky thug who fancied himself a great deal more than somewhat. Preacher's son he was, too. He and his brother both were delinquents -- had been in juvenile court several times. The size of the hero was measured, that year, by the number of appearances he had made in juvenile court.

This dead-end kid liked to handle one particular little girl more than any of the others. One day I happened to look at him just as the little girl tore off an ear-splitting screech. I had him dead to rights. I said:

"Johnson, move yourself into the third seat in the row by the windows. Retain that place for the rest of the year."

He moved.

I had less trouble for two days. The third morning, as my attention was on the class roll, my head was nearly split by that shriek. I looked up, and there was Johnson, back in his old place. I said:

"Johnson, I thought I moved you over on the last row!"

I reckon saying silly things like that is an occupational hazard of teaching.

"Yeah," replied Johnson. "But I moved back here."

I said:

"Johnson, take the place I assigned to you. Quick! On the double!"

Johnson settled back comfortably, and said:

"Now look here, Porter. I'm tired of being pushed around. Suppose you just 'tend to your business, and I'll 'tend to mine. Okay?"

I said:

"Definitely not Okay. When I'm no longer even nominally in charge of this class, I think it's time the case was decided -- one way or the other."

I gathered up my books and papers, and strode from the room.

I knew there was no use to appeal to either of the principals. But this case, if decided at all, was to be decided by one of them. I knew who the principal would support, but I intended to make him do it. I knew he would support the boy.

Knowing that I could find the building principal at the cafeteria, taking his coffee break at that time of the morning, I walked down there, and found both principals. I hated to put a situation up to him after his authority had been so nearly destroyed, but I reasoned that it had not been I who destroyed it -- and it shouldn't be I who should suffer because of its destruction. After all, the administration had the authority to enroll pupils, and place them as they pleased.

I walked over to the table at which sat Mr. Birdsong with the Great Man. They looked up at me impatiently, as they would have looked at a tumbleweed that had blown in.

Uninvited, I pulled out a chair and sat down.

"Mr. Birdsong", I said, "there is a situation."

And I gave him the back-ground, leading up through the final defiance.

"That thug has to get out of that class before I return to it. Naturally, I can't have a boy in class whom I can't even move to another seat."

Birdsong was in good humor. Damron sat and listened to the recital of the facts. They both agreed that the boy couldn't remain in my classes.

"I'll take care of him," promised Birdsong. "Yeah, yeah, yeah, I'll transfer him."

That happened on Wednesday morning. The boy was due at my history class in the afternoon, if he didn't get moved in the meantime.

When the time came for the history class to meet, I looked in on the class, and there sat Johnson -- big as life and twice as natural. I walked down to the library and graded papers that period.

The next day, Thursday, he reported to both classes, and I worked in the library. The closing days of the year were upon us. But I couldn't let that thug defy me and get away with it.

The Great Man waylaid me after school Friday evening. He was trying to repair a twisted waste can.

"May I see you in my office, a few minutes," he asked.

"Yes sir," I replied. "I'm on my way there right now."

When he reached his office, he entered first. I followed, and Birdsong brought up the rear, so that when we got inside, I was surrounded by administrators, grouped in such fashion as made it impossible for me to look at both at the same time. I recognized the maneuver, and understood its purpose. They intended to give me the old whipsaw treatment.

But they never got to first base with it, because I took charge of that meeting, and dominated it form beginning to end. Not once did I answer a question. I peppered the questions at them, and one at a time. When I addressed a question to Birdsong and Damron attempted to answer, or to parry with another question, I said:

"Quiet. Let him answer. I'll attend to you later."

The reason teachers can be brow-beaten and fully-ragged and treated like half-witted children is not because they haven't mind and knowledge enough to take care of themselves in a verbal rough and tumble, but because they are reluctant to antagonize the administrators.

Perhaps if I had know to that extent the administrators were organized in Florida; if I had know how relentlessly they pursue a teacher, even to his grave, I wouldn't have handled them as they deserved. I'm no hero. Possibly I acted from blissful ignorance.

Anyway, we sat down. The Great Man leaned back in his swivel chair, elbows on chair-arms, fingers carefully fitted together, pulled in his chin, and spoke -- in that gentle, hesitating, deadly menacing manner:

"Mister Porter, do you, er, intend to be with us, ah, next year?"

That was my cue to begin blubbering and pleading.

My answer floored them both.

"Why, Mr. Damron", I replied, "there isn't money enough in Florida to hire me back here next year. This isn't a school. It's a retrace."

"Oh no, Mr. Porter. Not a retrace!" interposed birdsong.

"It all depends upon your definition of retrace," I replied. "It fits my definition to a T. To use an illustration, it has fallen apart, and the nuts and bolts have rolled all over the place, and some of them have fallen through the cracks."

I turned to Damron:

"It all began with your masterly plan to raise the A.D.A. I told you at the time we were running our necks into a noose, but no. You went ahead with it -- laid us out, anked, to the tender mercies of the hoods and thugs, after we had been hauled through the wringer by the press, and disgraced throughout the state. Then you walked into your office and shut the door, and here you've stayed. You've pushed Birdsong and the teachers out to be torn and gobbled up as dog-meat, while you busied yourself with planning for the new school over at Bonaventure. This institution has deteriorated into a blackboard jungle. I'd stay and help you fight, if there were any possibility of bettering conditions, but I see no such possibility, because you have two more years of probation, with your authority in question continually, and with you afraid to assert it in support of either birdsong or the teachers. Last year about this time, <u>without</u> this condition, you had driven Birdsong until he suffered a light stroke of paralysis. Right now, more than half your teachers are under constant medical care.

"Last Wednesday birdsong promised to remove a hood from my classes. He hasn't done it. You heard him promise he would. Now I suspect you'd like to skin me alive for refusing to meet those classes while the thug is in them. Birdsong, you promised to move him, didn't you!"

"Yeah, yeah, yeah, yeah! I did. I remember now. I <u>did</u> promise to move him. By George, I've been so busy I just haven't gotten around to it."

"You have him out of my classes the first thing Monday morning, and I'll meet the classes as usual. If you don't, I won't. As for returning to this job for next year, no. I won't be with you. Good afternoon, Gentlemen."

I walked out, leaving them flabbergasted at the temerity of a ragged classroom teacher.

I wasn't the only teacher who walked out of that situation. Altogether, there were five men and three women. The three women and four of the men were suffered to depart in peace. The case of the fifth man deserves special mention:

The basketball coach was, during that year and the preceding one, the top basketball coach of the state. He produced the state champions during those two years. His fame as a coach was, therefore, statewide.

One would think that, being a coach, and one of the rugged young men who stood between the facultly and actual bodily harm, he'd be spared the ordinary trouble that the rest of us were heir to. But he had his own special trouble cooked up for him in the form of administrative interference.

That year, Azurville's basketball score reached over a thousand points, while the combined score of all the opponents amounted to less than a hundred.

As this tremendous lead piled up, the supervising principal began to heckle the coach on the subject. It was "poor sportsmanship" to lead the opponents by so wide a margin. Why couldn't the coach refrain from such efficient drilling? Why did he have to teach such formations and maneuvers?

Was the supervising principal proud of his high school basketball team after a sweeping victory? Gentle reader, he was ashamed! Did the coach come in for any praise, because he was successful? He was rather subjected to carping criticism, and shame was headed upon him!

At the end of that year, the coach had had enough.

He went to Tampa and got himself another job. He sold his house in Azurville, loaded his furniture and household effects on a truck, and set out for Tampa.

In the meantime, the supervising principal was busily making use of his connections in the state-wide organization of administrators. For a coach or teacher to leave the manor without being harassed out by his liege-lord, was an act of lese majeste. Of course, the coach had suffered harassment, but the management wanted him to stay.

So when he reached Tampa, he was told that he couldn't be accepted there after all. They wer sorry, but his present boss didn't want to give him up. There was nothing left for him but a return to Azurville, and a complete knuckling under to his persecutors.

Mention of the state organization of administrators will be made later in this narrative. It's workings are insidious, secret, untrammeled by little considerations such as truth, fairness, justice, or honor. It operates to keep teachers in the position and condition of peons, or of negro slaves of an earlier era.

CHAPTER THREE

It does seem to me that people would recognize the fact that schools are just another social institution; developed, like all the others, for the purpose of serving our needs. We have always recognized a three-fold responsibility resting upon the schools: first, so see to it that children are given the tools of learning; second, to pass on the heritage of the race; and third, to train youth for the responsibilities of adult citizenship.

This is a very large order, but some of our best brains have been enlisted, through the generations, to determine ways and means to develop methods and techniques.

In putting all these ways and means, methods and techniques into practice, pretty nearly everybody concerned has forgotten a few simple truths. If the classrooms are in a state of confusion and bedlam, no teaching can be done, and no learning can be accomplished. If the teachers and officers of a school have no authority to command attention to instruction, all our magnificent buildings, fine equipment, and know-how is like a train of cars without an engine to move them.

I believe that school administrators recognize these truths as clearly as the teachers do. What is the influence that paralyzes our efforts -- that sets administrators against teachers, divide the eschelons in administration against each other, creates distrust and suspicion in the mind of every school man against every other? Why does a schoolman live perpetually in fear of losing his job? Every principal is afraid to have a complaint go into the superintendent's office against him. Every superintendent has an intense -- even painful -- awareness of the coming of the next election.

The members of the board of public instruction are anxious to appear as the "pu-pull's" friend. I believe they want to hold their positions on the board because of the business opportunities it affords them. At one time, every board member of both Dade and Broward counties was a contractor, or was married to a contractor. The school system handles more money, in most of the counties in the United States, than all other businesses in the county, combined.

So everybody wants to hold his job, regardless of what he has to do to hold it.

Now, why is it so easy to dislodge a school man? I think there are several reasons why this is so. In the first place, there is a condition broad enough to furnish the base for all the other reasons; it is nation-wide, and in every way national in scope.

In 1932, Franklin Roosevelt began his hammering on Democracy. He wanted to make the most of the similarity between the words Democracy and Democrat.

Democracy is a term that is not very clearly understood, in its true meaning. Spurious notions concerning Democracy are rife. Mostly it is thought to mean that everybody is equal in intelligence, virtue, talent, and ability, to everybody else. The true meaning of the word is fairly widely known -- government by direct clamor of the people. For a generation, there has been a rash of petitions, agitations, and individual interventions in the affairs of social institutions, particularly in the schools.

It is widely believed, at the present time, that people have the right to call a principal and demand the discharge of a teacher -- as if the teacher were a stable-boy in their own employ, or an odd-jobs man. They feel like they can pick up the phone and demand the dismissal of a principal by the superintendent.

All this comes from the notion that our government is a Democracy -- which means government by direct clamor of the people, whereas our government is not a Democracy at all, but a Republic, which means government by duly elected representatives of the people, in a constitutional framework.

Elected and appointed officials are, in a sense, "servants" of the people, but only in a sense.

We serve the public, but in a strictly professional capacity. Teachers are people who have qualified as practioners of a learned profession through years of arduous study, and at the expense of thousands of dollars. High standards of scholarship, and wide professional training is required.

Besides all this, we are carefully screened for financial probity and for moral character. So thorough has this screening been employed, that the extremely unusual instance of a dishonest or delinquent teacher is as startling and shocking news as that of a defecting preacher.

Government in a republic includes bureaus of professional people who are part of the government, whose responsibility it is, to screen incoming members of their particular profession, to ascertain if they have education, training, admoral character that fits them for performing the duties of that profession, in a safe and satisfactory manner. The laity are not qualified to state that a doctor of medicine is not qualified to practice medicine. They haven't the knowledge necessary to determine whether a lawyer is qualified for admission to the bar. For their protection, therefore, they have set up state authority on whom they can depend with confidence, whether the profession under consideration be medicine, law, dentistry, teaching, or engineering.

Practioners of learned professions are licensed by the state. Teachers' licenses are called "certificates." When a man or woman holds a teaching certificate in any area, it means that he has satisfied the proper authorities of state government as to professional ability and character.

It ill becomes any citizen either in, or outside, the profession, to state that any teacher "can't teach." Such a blurb is ridiculous; and anybody who mouths it should be subject to the laws of slander and libel.

Originally, the law clearly states the causes for which a teacher may be dismissed from his post. They are five in number: Drunkenness, cruelty, gross insubordination, incompetence, or conviction of a crime involving moral turpitude.

There is no "majesty" title in a republic; therefore there can be no crime of "lese majeste," or offense against heavenly anointed rulers. Yet most teachers are "not invited back" for crimes of lese majeste. He is unafraid. He does not tremble at the official frown. He presents the other side of the case. He assumes manhood, and walks upright, instead of cringing. All these are offenses against majesty.

Perhaps our administrators could justly claim unquestioning obedience, if they possessed education and knowledge not available to teachers. If the teachers were handling duties and situation beyond their understanding and ability, they should depend completely upon the superior knowledge and ability of the administrators. But the administrators are possessed of no such superiority. The training they have received is open to all who are engaged in either branch of the profession. It often happens that the teacher has been trained by the same authority who trained the supervisor, yet the supervisor requires the teacher to make a long journey at the end of an exhausting day, then sit and drink in knowledge that was, perhaps, a part of his equipment before the supervisor was born.

There used to be, in an earlier era, genuine need of supervision. At a time when most teachers began their careers at age sixteen, their education being such as they could accomplish in the "little red school house on the hill," during a half dozen three to six-months terms, teachers desperately needed close supervision -- and seldom got it. Now, we seldom get the kind of supervision we need -- leadership in the over-all program. We get the kind of supervision teachers used to need. They call us in for the purpose of teaching us how to teach. Now we need that sort of help no more urgently then we need a hole in the head. We learned how to teach long ago, before we received our certificates.

We are not "hired hands." We are professional colleagues. There should be free discussion as to how to implement the general policies of schools. During these sessions, the talking of a teacher -- his utterances -- should not be recorded, labled "insubordination," and used against him later on. Of course, after an official solution to any problem has been agreed upon, every teacher owes to leadership, obedience and cooperation. But until then, he has not only the right, but the obligation, to participate in discussion! And that applies to any and all teachers -- not just to a few selected old mossbacks who have been selected as those who shall be recognized as human, and treated as such.

There seems to be a heresy rife among administrators that when a man becomes a teacher, he automatically resigns all the privileges, honors, responsibilities and immunities of American citizenship. He is understood by them to have no standing in court. He is outside the protection of the law. From then on, he is conceived to be entirely at the mercy of his masters, who regard themselves as omniscient, amnipresent, and omnipotent. There is an ambition on the part of school administrators to be recognized as being independent of, and above the law of the land, and subject only to the laws they have made, themselves.

This is true not only of school administrators, but also of members of government bureaus and administrative cliques in business corporations. Such people lose sight entirely of the purpose for which their institution exists. They are intent only upon preserving their authority and perpetuating their position in it.

As for Christian morality, in their dealings even among themselves, they have decided to ignore it. They substitute for it, such procedure as seems to them most likely to serve their own interest and happiness. They have reduced school administration to a game of "every man for himself and the devil take the hindmost."

This attitude has a deleterious effect upon the school system. Everybody is afraid to assume responsibility, lest a record of less than brilliant success is likely to be used against him. Try to find out who is responsible for any directive, and you will fail. Ask the present whereabouts of any county office official, and you'll get the fishy stare, and be curtly informed that "we don't divulge that information."

"In short, my man, you couldn't understand the answer if you heard it. Our ways are not your ways. Our thoughts are not your thoughts. We are as far above you as the dogstar is above the barking animal."

It has been said of the law, that "the law is what the courts say it is."

In the case of school laws, the school administrators are determined that it shall be what they say it is.

The law states the causes for which a teacher may be dismissed. When a teacher is "not invited back," it is assumed by all administrators that he is guilty of one or more of the offenses stated in the law. If he doesn't choose to return to the position he occupied throughout any year, they assume that he "was not invited back," because he was guilty of some offense spelled out in the law.

* Since this was written, the administrators have drawn together. Once a person signs an administrative contract, he is guaranteed against a reduction in salary, or transfer to any

58

position of less authority or title less prestigious than the one he now holds.

Administrators are increasingly absorbing the prerogative of deciding what constitutes insubordination, incompetence, cruelty, drunkenness; and they have even substituted words for those used in the law, for example, in "conviction of a crime involving moral turpitude." For "conviction" they have substituted "being accused by innuendo." Each supplies his own definition of "crime," and each depends upon his private understanding of the meaning of "moral turpitude." They maintain that that which would be moral turpitude in one citizen is Christian rectitude in another.

The writer known of instances in which drunkards, wife-beaters, dope pushers and homosexuals, rate as these gentry are, have been retained in the schools while they were "away taking the cure," while people of honor and rectitude were "not invited back" because of having been accused of wrong doing by innuendo. The offenders favored are generally those who have been granted emergency certificates by the administrators.

Besides the broad social and political belief that the individual citizen has the right to interfere directly in the management of social institutions -- which interference is almost bound to be hurtful to the institution meddled with -- is the burning desire for personal prestige and power among school administrators.

Bacon said that power corrupts. Back in the beginning of our national history, at a time when the whole concept of representative government was something new in the world, Jefferson recognized that even an elected official tended to become headstrong and arbitrary -- to believe himself possessed of greater ability, wider and deeper knowledge, and clearer understanding, than his fellow citizens.

Louis XIV., king of France, exclaimed, on one historic occasion, "I am the state." Philip II, king of Spain, bellowed, "I am Spain." Those fellows were strictly big-time operators, born to their positions; believed that they were divinely appointed, and responsible only to God.

But a man or woman doesn't have to be a chief of state, to savor deeply, the intoxicating taste of power. If they can build themselves up to a position of biggest frog in a very small puddle, it is sufficient to inflate their ego to gargantuan proportions.

The most harmful development we have experienced in the public schools, is the inordinate growth of the authority of building principals over teachers. In Florida, no teacher can obtain employment except by recommendation by a building principal. Elsewhere, teachers are engaged by a director of personnel, on the basis of work done, courses completed, degrees held, and testimonials submitted. In Florida, teachers are engaged on the basis of whether the applicant is a man or woman. If the applicant is a man, the questions in the principal's mind are: Is he young? If not, how young is he? Is he big? Is he physically formidable? If not, how big is he? How tough looking is he? If he has all those qualities, and is ugly to boot -- he's in!

If the applicant is a woman, the main question is, is she pretty? How pretty is she? Is she young? Considering the fact that she has to be a college graduate, there is no danger of her being too young. After that, the younger she can be, the easier it is for her to obtain employment in the most desirable positions.

If a man applies for a position, and happens to remind the examining principal of somebody who did him wrong in his youth, or reminds him of someone he dislikes, he's sunk. It is an instance of "no Irish need apply."

Koas and Kefauver, outstanding authorities on personnel management, sum up the qualities principals look for in teachers: they want girls from twenty-one to twenty-three years of age, with one or two years of teaching experience. If possible, they should be pretty and personable. They want them to stay two years, then move on.

That's the ideal. Of course, it is seldom attained. There just aren't enough sweet girl graduates to "man" the schools. There just aren't enough rugged young men of sufficient scholastic attainment, who choose teaching s a career, to man the schools. The principals can rarely find what they're looking for; they have to settle for approximations, but they approximate the ideal as closely as they can.

There are many men in school administration who thirst for authority, power, and social prominence. If, collectively, they can gather the reins of power into their own hands so securely that they can wield it irresponsibly and permanently, that thirst is assuaged. They resemble the centurion who said to Jesus:

"For I also am a man of authority -- having others under me; and I say unto one, "Go," and he goeth; and to another, "do this," and he doeth it."

So they go out on Saturday and play golf with other fellows who head the businesses of the community. They are associating with tycoons and captains of industry. Maybe they are invited into the homes of these gentry, and those who happen to like them, treat them as equals, and their teen-age daughters meet boys of wealthy families, and their boys make social contact with girls of wealth and position. Their wives sip tea in the company of women prominent in social activities. When they enter a swank restaurant, the sneering head-waiter addresses them by name. When they walk into a saloon, the barkeep smiles on them, and says:

"Good evening, Mr. Whosis! What'll you have -- the same?"

And lesser breeds look up admiringly and whosper:

"That's Whosis, principal of Wingding School, big-shot educationist."

"Ah!" to quote Omar, "'Tis paradist enow!"

On the job, they have the powers of life and death over the teachers, professionally, and of course, economically and socially. Now, in government and in the courts, a man can't be deprived of his life, liberty, or property without due process of law. But a principal, dealing with a teacher, can destroy him utterly by simply "not recommending for further employment." He doesn't have to prove anything. The fact that the teacher isn't recommended, is accepted by all other principals as sufficient proof that the teacher is guilty of drunkenness, gross insubordination, cruelty, incompetence, or has been convicted of a crime involving moral turpitude.

The first question a man is asked, when he applies for a teaching position is not, "how did your pupils score on their achievement test," but, "where did you teach last year? Who is the principal there? What is his phone number?"

The inference is, "if he didn't want you for this year, I don't want you either. If you offended majesty there, chances are you'll offend majesty here. I must confer with your former owner, ol' hoss."

Such procedure titillates the principal's thirst for omnipotence. Few who hold in their hands unlimited and wholly irresponsible power can refrain from wielding it. Those subjected to arbitrary injustice while carrying the great weight of responsibility all teachers carry, have been permanently crippled. Like the lark with the mended wind in the poem, he will never fly on high again.

Young people who choose teaching as a life career don't know it, but they can, and probably will, stamped with the label of sheep-killing dog during their first year in the business. Multitudes of them are undeservedly and arbitrarily and secretly ruined before they are fairly started. Ruined, just to satisfy some phys-ed instructor's thirst for the thrill he gets out of pronouncing the death penalty. I say phys-ed instructor because that is what most principals are -- ex coaches.

"ONE HUNDRED SEVENTY-FIVE THOUSAND TEACHERS SHORT THIS YEAR" scream the headlines.

"We need men in the schools of the nation!" the Educators exclaim.

When they <u>have</u> men in the schools, they won't let them stay. They must use them for their own private purposes. It does something for a man, to be able to kill another man who is at least his equal, in every way, shape, manner and form, and be independent of responsibility. There are too many principals who are too deeply thrilled by leaning back in a swivel chair, looking coldly into the eyes of another man, and asking:

"Has it ever occurred to you, Mr. Hutsinpillar, that you might be in the wrong business?" and watching the color drain from that man's face; to see the look of sickness come into his eyes.

Hutsinpillar and all the other men take that sort of bully-ragging and brow-beating because they are reluctant to antagonize the administrator. There is not much percentage inopposing a power-drunk pip-squeak who is completely devoid of honor, integrity, feeling of responsibility, or sense of justice, when that power-drunk pip-squeak wields the power of life and death over you.

Of course there are a few who have a living independent of their jobs. Once in a blue moon a principal jumps the wrong man, and gets told to "Go and kiss your ass, you bastard!"

CHAPTER FOUR

Most teaching positions are obtained by knowing a fellow who knows a fellow.

While I taught at Azurville, a young man was engaged as librarian, who, furing the months he was with us, became a close friend of mine. He stayed long enough to organize the library and start it functioning properly, but soon he received the offer of the position of supervisor of audio-visual materials and programs, in another county. We will meet this man later in the narrative.

When I answered the supervising principal's query as to whether I was "going to be with them next year" in the negative, I began to cast around for another job. It had never occurred to me that this supervising principal and the building principal, would try to see to it that I was never employed again, as a teacher. I don't know, now, why I failed to recognize them as permanent and mortal enemies. I suppose the training and conditioning of a lifetime was stronger than mere knowledge recently gained. Through the years that have passed since Azurville, it has become painfully apparent that those two men have used their influence against me every time they have had an opportunity to do so.

This is not a series of whines and cries from a single teacher who has experienced the seamy side of the workings of the system. Thousands of teachers in Florida, and other scored of thousands throughout the nation, have been and are being, victimized by a conspiracy of false witness being used against us secretly. When a teacher makes some effort to maintain a learning-teaching situation in his class, or to enforce some rule or regulation else-where in school -- which it is his duty to do -- he is in grave danger of incurring the displeasure of some pupil. Of course, it is one characteristic of youth that it resents authority, and tries every means at its disposal to defeat any grown person who represents it. They begin as soon as they can talk, and many begin before they can talk, to line up papa against mama, and mama against papa. They do it quite successfully. Then they get to school age, they seek divisive measures which can be applied among the grown folks of the school.

The conditions in a school constitute fertile ground in which to plant the seeds of discord. First, there is a principal who is afraid of discord in any form, or to any degree. Adverse criticism is what he avoids, and he is continually ingulging in Cicero's "genuflections of the body" as he dodges criticism or its results.

Next comes the assistant principal and the deans of boys and girls. These folks can be, and are, blamed whenever effective opposition is organized by a group of pupils or their parents, or both.

There are the faculty members, who, I am sorry to report, show the attitude of chickens packed in a coop, and the coop set in a stinking alley, back of the butcher-shop. Every day, the hairy arm of the butcher reaches into the coop, and the hand seizes the leg of a chicken, which is hauled out, and its head chopped off on a stinking, bloody block. Do his fellow chickens feel a sense of outrage or anger, or sympathy? As the days go, and their number dwindles, do they begin to dread the sight of the hairy arm reaching and fishing among them? They circulate casually, unhurriedly, each trying to get behind all the others. One wonders whether they notice the diminution of their numbers, and look forward to the final outcome of this imprisonment -- brutal murder of the last one of them. One hopes they haven't that much intelligence.

When a teacher has worked three years in one school it is the practice to give him a continueing contract." But he must work three years "successfully." That generally means that he has been able to pussy foot behind the other chickens successfully; has been able to push other teachers forward in the performance of the common duty, so that efforts at retaliation have been directed against others, and they themselves have so far escaped serious criticism.

But even then, they may be denied this slight measure of security, and placed, instead, "on probation" for a year. This means that some small effort at retaliation has been made, but fortunately by people who still retained some sense of decency and fair-play. Most often, when a parent or group of parents organize to punish a teacher for having made a pupil behave as a human -- or tried to -- they are the sort of people who will go any length they need to, to gain their point. They will distort the truth, circulate lies, bear false witness -- even under oath -- to win the game.

But some teachers, against whom there has been no opposition by sufficiently influential agitators, are awarded the continuing contract.

That means that they can't be summarily liquidated. There has to be a hearing before the school board, to determine whether they are guilty of any crime, before they can be hauled form the coop. Even after exhonoration by the school board, the teacher is generally so brutally punished by the administration -- pressures deliberately built up around him such as to render his position so untenable, that he has to go anyhow. More about that presently.

In a situation in which the individual is under attack, and there is no organized, collective security, individuals tend to seek security for themselves by hiding behind other. Teacher, poor devils, resort to those tactics as often as any other segment of society.

Let one teacher allow the feeling off outrage and resentment to overflow, and exclaim, as he drops wearily into a chair in the teacher's lounge.

"That Willy Jones had a brand new program today. I am so tired of being frustrated and checkmated each day by that boy, that I am half out of my mind."

Some other teacher (climbing behind the other chickens and seeking to come to terms with the butcher) will speak out, in a gentle, wondering tone:

"Well sir, you know, Willy never gave me the slightest bit of trouble in his life. I've always found him sweet, cooperative, and obedient."

She might just as well say:

"How do you have the heart to speak against this sweet, innocent child? My experience with him is that he responds satisfactorily, when he has a worthy efficient teacher to deal with. Of course, when he has to endure a mere jack-leg masquerading as a teacher, the poor lamb can't be held responsible."

Surely such a teacher has been wide-enough awake to notice that one pupil seldom seeks to break up more than one class in any one semester. No, he works on one teacher at a time. It is one of his divisive devices. Work up a good reputation in your classes -- tear loose and have fun in another. Harass one ol' hen and refrain from bothering the others. Of course it is the professional duty of the teacher to act in opposition to disruptive tactics, and the game is on. The hens who are not being harassed, get a feeling of special professional competence amounting to a thrill of blamelessness and virtue.

"These jack-leg teachers -- these lesser breeds without the law -- lead difficult lives and they deserve to. Some are already hauled out of the coop, and killed. Serves them right. We are glad to have the incompetent and the weak weeded out of our ranks. And that they are weak and incompetent, goes without further need of proof, because aren't they having their lives filed down by sweet little Willy, who responds to my masterly leadership in a perfectly satisfactory manner? Boy, the butcher will never catch <u>my</u> leg. <u>I</u> am an established professional person -- safe from all possible harm."

The fact is, that, like the other hens in the coop, she will eventually be hauled forth, unless she reaches retirement age before the butcher gets around to her. Next semester there will be another Willy, to work on <u>her</u>., but right now, here's a chance to make a little time with Willy's mother -- a flap-lipped gossip -- whom it is good politics to have on one's own side.

So, at the next P.T.A. meeting, at the season given over to sipping bitter punch and gossiping, she'll put it over that "a certain teacher" -- not mentioning any names -- was throwing it into Willy a few days ago, "but I just had to testify to the truth! I just had to compliment Willy on his manliness, decorum, and eagerness to learn!"

Of course, the flap-lip will effuse with thankfulness, and spread the work of how fine Willy is getting along at school. Maybe that will counteract, in some measure, the effect of Willy's hair-raising curses the other morning when she tried to wake him in time to catch the bus, and heard by all the neighbors.

The writer remembers a pair of boys he had in class one semester. it was a ninth grade class in Civics, but the text was written on the seventh grade reading level. These two read lamely and haltingly on the seventh grade level.

They had each perfected a disruptive technique that could hardly fail: one would swath his face in his handkerchief, and make snorting, nose-blowing noises through his mouth. If he had tried snorting that loudly through his nose, he would have broken his own ear-drums and salivated himself -- perhaps blown the top of his head off.

As soon as the teacher would begin to make the assignment for the next meeting of the class, he would go into his act. Snort, snort, snort! At first, the other kids though it was perfectly marvelous, and funny, too.

The teacher would stop until the snorting ceased, then seek to go on with the assignment.

Snort, snort, snort, snort, snort.

Every time the teacher attempted to teach, he would be snorted down.

There were only a couple of counter-measures which the teacher could take: he could assign detention, or send the snorter to the principal's office, in the hope that the snorter might heed the admonitions of the senior officer of the system.

The attempt at detention failed. The boy presented to the principal a note from his dam, averring that she needed him to act as chauffer for her, right after school -- every afternoon. The teacher was therefore ordered to assign no more detention.

The snorter didn't go into his act every day -- only every other day. His side-kick had perfected as disruptive a technique as the snorter had. He had a method of making a noise: he inflated his lungs, held his breath, and pounded his chest with his fist. It sounded as if he were kicking a bass drum.

Both these boys were given F in deportment.

Forthwith, their dams descended upon the principal's office. The principal called the teacher in, to explain the presence of the F's on the cards.

When the teacher first told the simple story, the snorter's mother was aghast.

"Well, for the ord-de-oh!" she exclaimed. "He does the same thing ot me when I try to talk to any one. Often when we are out driving together, I have to make him leave the car. And at the dinner table, when anyone else attempts to speak, he snorts him down. But I never thought he'd be guilty -- I didn't think he'd <u>dare</u> to do that at school!"

The other woman deplored her boy's bass drum tactic:

"I don't send him to school to act a monkey. But I can't help wondering why he doesn't act that way in his <u>other</u> classes."

"Ye-es," agreed the principal. "There's more to this than meets the eye. I can't help but feel that the boys are victims of teacher incompetence and irritability."

The principal had, by an owlish, judicious pronouncement, satisfied the woman, at no cost to himself, but with the same pronouncement, he had crippled not just one teacher, but every teacher on the faculty!

The writer looked at the Principal, and caught the signal:

"For God's sake, change those deportment grades from F to A. Don't walk out of here and leave me undefended."

Genuinely liking and respecting that principal, before that "incompetence and irritability" blurb, and willing to believe, on the basis of past experience with him, that he was saying that only because he was in a bind, and that the blurb was not to be taken seriously, the writer made a terrible mistake: he changed the grades on the cards. He can only plead youth and lack of experience, for this incident occurred nearly a third of a century ago. But that principal was an experienced and seasoned school man at the time. Right there he showed himself to be one who will weasel out of an embarrassing situation at no matter what the cost to a young man who, all his life, had trusted him, respected him, and liked him.

When the teacher changed those grades, he threw down the most formidable weapon he possessed. He felt he should change whatever other poor deportment grades he had assigned, to be absolutely fair; and he felt, further, that if those two boys, who were among the worst behaved boys in the school, were to have A's in deportment, no one else deserved a B.

The precedent had been set. Every teacher in the school was hamstrung. All a pupil had to do was send his dam over to the principal's office, and have her demand alteration of the record, to get it. The principal had brow-beaten one teacher into compliance -- he must be consistent and require the same service of all.

He ruined himself, too, in a way. Until then, his teachers had respected and liked him. After that, they knew their respect had been mis-applied. Their liking had been bestowed upon one unworthy. Suspician and distrust succeeded respect and affection.

The old security was shattered. No longer was it possible to plunge in and do our best -- and strive always to make that best, better. From then on, every teacher considered everything he proposed to do, in the light of the possible consequences to himself, his professional reputation and his financial security.

The worst effect was visited upon the young teacher, just beginning our careers. We saw that the man we had trusted was a weak reed to lean on. We saw that he would throw us to the wolves merely to save himself embarrassment. We had to admit that he didn't have principle number one.

CHAPTER FIVE

Mention has already been made of the librarian whose acquaintance and friendship I had won, and of his joining the Putnam County school staff as supervisor of audio-visual materials and programs.

Knowing that I had severed connections with my former job, and was in need of a new job, my friend exerted his influence in his new place, to obtain employment for me and my wife, who is a first-grade specialist and whose services are always, therefore, in brisk demand. First grade teachers are hard to get, for there is such great need of them, and they are so few in number. Teachers are very reluctant to take on thirty-five or forty or more beginners. It is a situation which is almost beyond human endurance.

In California it is strictly against the law to place more than twenty beginners in one class. In Florida, there is no limit to the number that can be dumped upon one teacher. I've known my wife to have as many as forty-five in one beginning class.

The law of Florida does unequivocally state that children must be six years old before they can start to school. The administrators, yielding to popular clamor, modified the application of the law, for the sake of garnering a little precious popularity for themselves.

72

They interpreted it to mean that children must be six by the following January after the September school begins. That let the bars down. Now first grade teachers are inundated by swarms of five-year olds. Many of these little tots are still unable to take care of themselves in the bathroom. They don't even know the difference in value between a nickel and a quarter. They will lay down a quarter for their 10 o'clock daily milk for the week, and as soon as the teacher enters the transaction in the record, pick up the quarter again and pocket it.

About the only thing a few are sure of is, that nobody is going to get them to do anything they don't want to do. Conversely, everybody else, including the teacher, is going to obey them unquestioningly and instantly. The worst of the crop know only one law -- their own whim.

One little boy beginning first grade was seen approaching the room, hand in his mother's, weight thrown backward, heels desperately trying to dig into the sidewalk, and knees stiff. His head was thrown back. His eyes were closed. From his leather lungs, and up through his brass throat, heart-rending cries issued. He was caterwauling.

"No no no no no! Oh, Nao, nao, nao, nao. Oh nao! Wah! Wah-ah-ah-ah! Ooh wah wah wah!"

But his mother hauled him along. They reached the room, and were met by the teacher. Introductions over (registration had been completed the previous Fall), the mother put on a killing smile, and spoke in dulcet tones:

"Now, lovey, you must go in with the other little children, and begin school. This is where little boys and girls learn to read and write, and do many other things. It's going to be lots of fund, and you will be very happy here. Be a nice little boy, and go in with the teacher."

"I don't <u>want</u> to learn to read and write or anything else!! I wa a a nt to g-g-go home!"

The woman's voice deepened, and the rest of her utterance came out in a guttural snarl:

"You little devil, you. You've nearly run me nuts for five years, and the first time I get a chance for a little rest, you try to crab it! You're going to school all right, and you're going to start right now! Thank God I can get a little rest for awhile!"

"Don't be afraid. There's no danger. you're going to have a lottof fun, and you'll be glad you're going to school. Mama will come and get you at noon. It won't be very long."

The child yelled "No!", dug his heels in, and surged backwards. The way he jerked the teacher off balance showed that he had practiced the maneuver a great deal. When the teacher was off balance, he swung a vicious kick at her shin. She either had to let go of him or absorb the punishment. The turned him loose. His kick missed, but his ass struck the floor with a dull thump.

His mother glared at the teacher. Her face livid with rage, she grated:

"How dare you teat a little child so shamelessly and brutally?" and turning to the child, she tenderly helped him to his feet.

No sooner had the little boy gained his feet than he caught a double handful of his mother's hair, (she was stopped over him) swung himself clear of the floor (she had straightened up when her hair was grabbed) and landed a solid kick in her stomach. The breath left her body in a hissing "whoosh," but she recovered instantly.

"You ornery little whelp," she screeched. Flopping him over her knees she poured blows to his rear that must have blistered him, and started every joint in his skeleton.

The little boy was so astonished that he actually stopped bawling. The teacher said to the mother:

"You'd best go now. We always get along smoother without the parents."

The woman stalked off to the school office. She said to the principal:

"That teacher over there hasn't much patience with little children. She let go his hand and let the poor little fellow sit down heavily and violently on the floor."

"Oh, no!" replied the principal. "Mrs. Porter is as patient a teacher as we have in the whole school, and she is one of the best. Any child who is lucky enough to begin his schooling with her is fortunate indeed!"

Generally, principals don't stand up for a teacher under the parental frown. But in this instance, this one did. A little word of confidence and appreciation, at the right time, would prevent worlds of trouble. But alas, the common response to parental criticism is agreement and sympathy. Two objectives are thus reached -- the desire of the principal to save himself embarrassment or annoyance, no matter at what cost to the teachers and the school -- and the desire to appear as the only truly professional person in the institution. They like to appear as the kindly, broad-minded, all-knowing, benevolent, brave, long-suffering, but marvelously efficient big wheels that function smoothly despite the "ignorant," "vicious," "inefficient," and "lazy" teachers they have to work with.

The fact that is most prominent is, that in spite of the way she had raised her child, all his life up to then, that woman trotted to higher authority and tried to throw the teacher for avoiding a vicious kick.

Fortunately, pretty nearly all the children are just the opposite of that little boy. They come to school eagerly -- anxious to do what they're told -- liking their teacher from the first. If it were not so, we couldn't have school at all.

People have the notion that at school, incorrigible pupils will be cured of the mental and emotional maladjustments which they themselves have fashioned from their babyhood.

One teacher of my acquaintance had two little boys in first grade, who were incorrigibles, and one little girl.

There is generally good and sufficient reason for childrens' misbehavior at that age. In the case of this little girl, she had been to kindergarten for a year in New York, and retained for a second year. At the end of the second year, she was still regarded as unready for first grade work. The therefore was taken into first grade here in Florida because we have no kindergarten system."

If, by some chance, she did prepare a paper, her little hand trembled so, when she handed it to her teacher, that it appeared to be blown by a fitful wind.

While being instructed, she gazed out the window, or somewhere else. Other times, she could play with some simple toy for half a day. But take instruction? Impossible. Her I.Q. was below seventy. What she needed was placement in a special school in which the program and procedure are fashioned to meet the needs of pupils like her, in very small classes. But once a child has been enrolled in a school, it takes the better part of a year to get him transferred to another, so slow and cumbersome is the procedure that must be followed.

A little boy had a structureal defect -- he had no palate in his mouth. He couldn't speak understandably to save his life. As there was nothing wrong with his intelligence, he wanted to participate very prominently in all class activities. But he couldn't do so efficiently because of his speech defect.

His teacher, however, gave him his part of the time devoted each morning to "show and tell." His attempts at communication were, of course, in vain. Yet his efforts were made with great gusto. Less disturbance occurred than

* since this was written, a kindergarten system has been set up.

one would expect, for little children are tolerant and helpful with each other. But through the day, his whole interest was centered in fruitless efforts to communicate and participate. When he spoke to another child and the other couldn't understand him, his patience would wear thin, and presently he would be striking them with his hands or kicking them, or otherwise hurting or bothering, or by snatching their tools and materials. The patience of the others would wear thin, and they would fight back, and call on the teacher constantly for regulation.

The third child turned out to have a disastrous background. He was the unexpected and belated baby brother of a family of grown people; and sired late in life by a neurotic father who resented him, and punished him often and mercilessly. With his inderitance, and unfavorable home environment, he had as poor a chance of normal development as anybody you could find.

But this information was slow in coming.

At first, this child's father would visit the room, then tell the teacher:

"You're just too easy on Johnnie. Get you a strap and wear him out for disobedience. He knows he has to step around at home, or get half killed."

The teacher thought the "half-killed" bit was rough humor. But subsequently she found that it was literally true. His father beat the child until his bruises were deep and extensive, and sometimes had to be treated by a doctor.

Their neighbors had a swimming pool, surrounded by a high fence. The child frequently climbed the fence to view the bathers. His perch was precarious, and at times when he dropped inside and entered the pool, he was in grave danger of getting drowned. The neighbors were apprehensive for his safety all the time.

At school he would not stay in his seat. He roamed around at will, entertaining himself as interest dictated. In a first grade, teaching aids are placed on the walls of the room, on tack boards, and on easels. This child would move a chair, table, or desk to the wall, climb up the wall, and pull down valuable pictures and other teaching aids, and tear them to pieces. When groups of little children were working from models placed on tack boards or easels, he would pull them off, and cut them up with his scissors.

If the teacher's back was turned on him for one moment, he was destroying something of value.

It is the principal's responsibility to take note of such pupils, and start procedure to place them in schools provided for such children, where they can be dealt with individually, or in small classes. But teachers are reluctant to report such conditions, because the principal's attitude is, "don't bother me. I'M swamped with problems of administration. A good teacher overcomes her own difficulties. Only the weak and incompetent call on administration for help" -- another instance of the refusal of administration and supervision to serve as the hand-maiden of education. There was a teacher, with forty-two beginners, including three that had no more business in there than an alligator. Yet such is the attitude of administration that the teacher didn't dare to make the situation know, until her nervous system was shattered and her soul broken.

Children's acts of destructiveness were not the only symptoms of that child's abnormality. Young as he was, he couldn't keep his hands off women. He would come to his teacher and stroke her arm, with the tips of his fingers. His hands would close tenderly around her neck -- stroking and feeling -- the pressure gradually increasing, until she would have to remove his hands forcibly when the pressure had increased to a squeeze, and his face had developed an expression of slavering demoniacal intensity.

Clearly this child will be a sex maniac when he reaches puberty, unless the direction of his development can be changed.

The teacher happened to know the county school psychologist personally. She went down to see him, and said:

"Bill, I've got three problems who, I'm sure, are in your department. I don't dare refer them to the principal, and I don't want her to know I've appealed to you. Is there any way you can get on them without anybody knowing that I initiated action? You know the parents of these children are adamant in their stand that their children are 'just as good as anybody.' and that they are no no different from the average. The principal would never dream of taking the risk of incurring their displeasure. She has her precious 'public relations' to keep intact. So my initiating this investigation must not be made known. My doing this is clearly an act of lese majeste.

So she gave the psychologist a complete report on the three pupils.

Bill replied that he certainly could horn in, and without incriminating the teacher. He did.

After his first visit to the school, and on the completion of his preliminary investigation, there followed tests, physical examinations, hearing of the parents before the psychologist -- a long process of weaning the parents from "Democracy," and winning their approval and cooperation in getting their children into the schools in which they belonged. The process dragged on for eight months.

In the meantime, the teacher had to carry on as best she could. If the principal's attitude had been unfriendly toward the teacher, the procedure could have ended in the teacher's "not being invited back" for the ensuing year, on the charges of incompetence and insubordination.

If a society of flap-lipped gossips had been organized, and had swung into action in the neighborhood, that is exactly what would have happened. One determined campaign by one parent of one of those troubled children, could have resulted in the dishonorable dismissal of the teacher. Similar cases do end that way -- all over the nation. So the teachers are disposed to suffer, while it is possible to stand it and cripple on, than initiate action to help the children, the school, and the teacher. It is an illustrative incident in showing the way fear pervades the school system, and shows one way in the schools are falling down in the matter of discovering abnormality early in a child's life, and taking corrective measures in time.

Soon that little boy would have been drenching the family cat with kerosene and setting it afire -- just for fun.* A little later, he'd be staking some little child in the sun, in a secluded place, all day, just for fun. When he reaches puberty, he would wring the neck of some little girl, just for fun. Later, he'd be on trial for his life, for multiple murder.

Not long ago a young man went to the electric chair, bitterly protesting that the authorities had known he was sick, from his boy-hood.

That young man had the misfortune of having a teacher who didn't have the connections needed for by-passing authority, and for acting outside of channels. His teachers were afraid.

This little boy's teacher was afraid, too. But because of her tact, connections, and carefulness; because of her prestige in the system, and the fact that the principal happened to like her, she was not punished for acting "outside of channels."

The average teacher would have felt the full rigor of official wrath, by being banished form the profession. No doubt we would be astonished if we knew how many qualified and experienced teachers are banished from the profession every year, in this nation for similar offenses.

Question: How many, of the one hundred seventy thousand shortage, can be accounted for in this way?

The reader may exclaim: "Oh, Porter, come a squirrel or two! Surely

* The year after this was written, exactly this incident occurred. principals are not as quick to refuse to "invite teachers back" as you would have us believe!"

Following is the true account of an incident that occurred in that same school, under that same principal:

A young man teaches sixth grade there. He had, in his class, a big boy, I.Q. around seventy, who amused himself by playing painful and humiliating practical jokes on his classmates. One day during lunch in the cafeteria, he saw a little girl shuffling cautiously along, balancing in her hands a bowl. It was a golden opportunity in no wise to be missed or wasted. When she drew abreast of him, he thrust out one of his #10 shoes and sent her sprawling -- her face in a bowl of hot clam chowder.

The teacher witnessed the whole shameful episode. His patience was at an end. The boy saw him striding over to him. He rose, and in a crackling baritone, he warned:

"Don't you hit me, Mr. Cameron. You know you're not allowed to punish the kids!"

The element knows all about the duties, responsibilities, and limitations of authority of the teachers; but they recognize none of their own. Indeed, there aren't any.

The teacher grabbed that boy and gave him a good shaking -- slamming him against the wall a few times.

The cook dodged out and rushed madly to the principal's office. You may depend upon the cook to hold the teacher in line, every time, for she outranks any teacher on the faculty.

Rushing breathlessly into the principal's office, she gushed:

"Mr. Cameron is punishing one of the boys! Do something! Quick!

Instantly, the voice of the principal rang out authoritatively and incisively -- heard throughout the whole cafeteria:

"Mr. Cameron! Report to me at once!"

Cameron obediently trudged over to the executive suite.

"What were you doing, Mr. Cameron," asked the principal? "And why? It is reported to me that you were roughing up one of the pupils! You know that is strictly against the policy of this school!"

Alas, poor Cameron knew this only too well. That was the reason the big brutal moron effectively checkmated every instructional effort he made, every day.

He related that latest incident of the big moron's cruelty and brutality, and told the principal exactly what he had done.

The principal said, shaking her head mournfully and reproachfully:

"Tch, tch, tch, tch, tch. You'd better give me your resignation right now, Mr. Cameron. Let's do it quietly -- no fuss. When that boy's mother calls me this afternoon, I want to be able to tell her that the problem is solved and the whole incident liquidated -- permanently."

She thus sought to save herself blame in the neighborhood, and possible embarrassment.

"I'm not resigning," replied Cameron. "I have a continuing contract, and you can't break it except by taking it to court." He walked out.

If he hadn't been protected by tenure, he would have been banished from the profession.

Shortage of one hundred seventy thousand teachers.

CHAPTER SIX

*W*ell, my friend got his superintendent to call me long-distance, and offer positions to both me and my wife. Having consulted with her, I had the answer ready: we would be very happy to accept the position offered.

While my wife was sweating it out in summer school at Gainsville that summer, I had been busy finding new jobs for us. Having made connections in Putnam County, I went to Fort Digby and attempted to find a house to live in. There were only two vacant houses for rent in Ft. Digby. One was unacceptable; the other rented for ninety-five dollars per month. It was a gem of a little house, in a fine residential section.

More details had to be attended to. I engaged the services of a van-line there, and presently the van appeared in Azurville. The truck driver was a specialist in packing furniture and household goods. We worked like beavers until everything was ready to load. He went to niggertown and engaged a couple of sleepy, lazy, satchel-footed darkies to help us load. Finally the lading was completed. I locked the house, and we set out for Ft. Digby.

When we reached Ft. Digby, we had the help of other professional movers in unloading, placing the furniture, and getting settled. I had to engage telephone service, gas, water, and electric services -- plunking down "deposits" at every office.

The bill for moving was three hundred and fifty dollars.

I had traveled extensively over the state, in my search for a job. Every time I interviewed a principal, he asked,

"Where did you teach last year?"

When I told him, he'd reach for his telephone, put through a call to Birdsong or Damron, and get told that I was a jack-leg teacher, insubordinate, incompetent, and a trouble maker. Watching his face, I could tell just about what the speaker at the other end was saying. At the conclusion of the conversation, he'd say:

"Well, I can't be sure we'll be allowed to hire another teacher -- the enrollment being somewhat uncertain. Tell you what: I'll let you know. Don't call me. I'll call you."

And that would be the end of that.

My mighty executives in Azurville were proving to me that there are more ways of killing a cat than by choking him to death with butter.

Qualified and experienced and dedicated teachers are being branded that way, all the time. The shortage of teachers could be cut down immensely, if we were not being forced out of the profession by administrators who have no reason to do so, beyond their determination to indulge personal pique, show their authority, and punish somebody else for their own fears and weaknesses.

In counties where the staff is bellowing "teacher shortage crisis" the loudest, their filing cabinets are bulging with the applications of qualified and experienced teachers who have incurred personal displeasure of some principal, and are, therefore, outside the paoe.

The Clear Springs school is located twenty-three miles north of Ft. Digby. It is part of a village of perhaps one thousand population, with two hundred pupils in grades one through nine, with a faculty of six. The first, second, and third grade classes were very large, and consequently, unwildly. The junior high classes were not too large.

The village boasted a nice hotel with handsome grounds, including the Springs. There were some fairly nice dwellings, but most of the houses were small, set in limited grounds -- presenting no suggestion of Florida luxury or opulence.

There was a native Floridian element in the population, which supported itself by fishing and shrimping. Several of the Jr. High boys got away with coming to school armed with switch-blade knives, on the plea that they were part-time fishermen, and the knives were regular and necessary tools of their trade. I'll have to admit that I never saw anyone threatened with a switch-blade while I worked there. Certainly I never had one drawn on me. However, there were some boys who felt a solid sense of security because they had them handy.

There was a population element consisting of winter visitors from the North -- principally New Jersey. My experiences with those gentry cause me to look upon New Jersey and its people with dislike. Too bad, too, because these folks were too few to be taken as truly representative of that great state -- especially as New Jersey-ites, most of them, live in New Jersey. The state ought not to be judged by the behavior of a few winter visitors to Florida.

The building was a rambling brick structure, mostly one-story; two-story partly. Out front was a lovely little auditorium running all the way across the building -- the seats rising gradually in tiers toward the back of the room. Down front was a small stage, with curtain and scenery.

Towards the back of the building, one of the classrooms had been converted into a kitchen and dining room. We needed to serve meals in that school like we needed a hole in the head, because the area served by the school was quite small, and the children could very handily have gone home to dinner. But no.

Every school has to serve "hot lunch" -- principally to relieve the dams from having to cook at home in the middle of the day.

Lunch at home used to provide the mid-day break as necessary to the self-satisfaction and well-being of the pupils. The little folks got to see Mama at noon instead of waiting until the day's end. The big kids got to be free, for an hour, of school authority and routine and discipline. There was freedom and relaxation just when it was needed most. There was the opportunity for comradeship and socializing so natural to children. When such an opportunity and body of experience and change of scene is denied, and replaced by the most rigid regimentation, there's something precious lost from the school day, and replaced by a body of experience that's unnatural, repressive, and irksome to children of all ages.

Mealtime is a time of natural relaxation and indulging in fellowship. Friends like to eat together, and chat on the subjects most interesting to them. They resent having to march to the cafeteria, go through the chow line, take assigned seats, eat with those who happen to be in classes with them, and keep quiet.

Especially they resent having to keep quiet. Of course, if noise were permitted in the cafeteria, there would be bedlam. Some few would want to act like apes and hooligans -- wrestle, fight, throw food, pour soup down each other's collars, and otherwise misbehave. With all our careful supervision, there is a certain amount of horseplay. The children don't act that way at home, but some of them do it at school just because they are held down so tight by authority, at a time of day which should be given over to fellowship and conversation.

Some of the worst trouble we have in school lunch rooms, grows out of pupils' efforts to seat themselves in congenial groups, and being forbidden to do so by the necessity of having numerical regularity so that large numbers may be fed in the allotted time.

Then there is the loss of benefit derived form the physical exercise of walking home and back. The pupils used to come from dinner, play some in the school yard, and associate together along the way and back at school, before classes resumed for the afternoon session. The whole arrangement was conducive to regularity and normal human behavior.

When the pupils had gone home to dinner, the teachers had an hour's break in the middle of the day, for eating, resting, enjoying each other's company, and the blessed quiet and dignity that ensued on the departure of the children.

All these blessings have been replaced by the most rigid regimentation. "Step up there, child! Close the ranks. Move along. And keep quiet! Sit in your assigned seat. keep your place in line! Say nothing!"

The teachers get no relaxation either. They must exercise supervision every second. As soon as lunch has been bolted, they must line up the kids and march them back to class, and the grind continues.

The writer remembers a principal whose policy it was, to prevent all communication between teachers. If he spied two teachers talking, he'd trot up to them and dismiss one of them. That was especially hard to take because some of those teachers had had him in school as a boy. They'd tell him to trot along and attend to his own business. So help me, he'd report them to the board of public instruction for insubordination! He actually tried to banish some of his teachers from the profession because they wouldn't let him rob them of human dignity. That was several years ago, in a smaller school system than those in the sizable cities of Florida. In this state, at this time, the administrators have organized so solidly that they are able to drive the teachers like cattle, and rob them of the last shred of human dignity. They have the power to secretly put the mark of Cain on a teacher's record -- making it impossible for him to obtain employment elsewhere.

That young fellow would be happy in a Florida principalship, where his power would be unlimited, and completely irresponsible. I suppose it's a trait of human nature to want authority, and at the same time want to avoid having to answer to anyone for the way it is exercised. It is certainly the nature of government to expand. It is the nature of school government to function "on the administrative level" -- to achieve complete irresponsibility. If a certain kind of personality can worm his way into a county school office, he has achieved a position such as he conceives God as occupying. But God is a responsible being, whereas these boys and girls are not responsible to anybody, nor to anything -- not even to the laws of their own nature. They don't make decisions with their brains; they think with their guts. If it gives them a visceral thrill to ruin a colleague, and they have it in their power to do it, it's done. Considerations of ethics, morality, or common decency don't weigh with them at all.

A few years ago we had an elderly lady teaching in an elementary school here in Ft. Riverdale, Fla. She had served the trade for a third of a century -- brilliantly. She was popular in the community. She was within three years of retirement.

It happened that year that her pupils were from financially poor homes, and out of that circumstance arose the trouble that resulted in her dishonorable discharge from the school system of Bunk County.

Mention has been made of the several fund-raising campaigns that the teachers are required to conduct. This teacher's pupils were not financially able to contribute to the funds, or participate in conducting them. She frankly told the principal the facts of the case. When he remonstrated with her, she argued.

Now, no classroom teacher can argue or reason with a principal. His function, as we have mentioned before, is not to reason why -- but to do and die. But this old lady had been a human too long to be suddenly transformed into a beast.

Her stand in this matter, and the positive way she asserted it, deeply angered the principal. He wanted a "one hundred percent" record in the campaign, and she was keeping him form achieving it.

At the end of the year, he refused to renew her contract.

At the very time that she was being nationally honored as an outstanding teacher, she was fired from her job! She was humiliated, grieved, outraged, ill-used, insulted, and degraded.

A national patriotic society had issued her a citation and struck a gold medal for her, and the county office gang refused to confer it upon her -- even sent it back to the donors. Their excuse -- "they had not been consulted!"

The community was up in arms. The newspapers made it a "cause celebre." Independent citizens flooded the principal and county dignitaries with letters of protest. The state superintendent of schools and the president of the University of Florida interceded in her behalf. All to no avail. The little tin gods had spoken. They closed ranks and stood like the rock of Gibralter.

At the end of her career, that old lady would have faced the loss of her retirement benefits, had she not enjoyed high standing in her home community up-state. In that city, a principal took his life in his hands -- braved the displeasure of his fellow principals, and gave her a position.

No doubt he has been made to feel the crushing weight of their animosity, for he is a member of the principals' organization, whose chief aim is to consolidate the authority of principals over teachers. One of their number who hires a teacher who has had the misfortune to offend another, has committed the unpardonable sin.

I don't know why these gentry thirst so, for the power of professional life and death over classroom teachers. The writer remembers a time when no such power resided in their hands, and the schools functioned more smoothly than they function now. They achieved the purposes for which they had been established. They imparted the tools of learning. Now, they are doing a notoriously poor job of it. They passed on to each school generation the heritage of the nation. Now, they are doing it poorly, if at all. In the matter of conditioning youth for adult citizenship, they are not doing it at all.

I suspect that one of the reasons the schools are crippling along so painfully and ineffectually, is precisely this passion on the part of school administrators to make themselves a master group, and at the same time, to reduce the teachers to the status of beasts.

We are here to train and educate the sons and daughters of free men. To do so, we must have the respect and cooperation of those children. We are the schools, as far as they're concerned. We meet them daily, in position of leadership. It is difficult to see how children can respect teachers who are robbed of security and human dignity by administrators seeking to consolidate their positions at any cost.

Free men cannot be educated by a gang of scared hired girls and hired men.

To get back to the building at Clear Springs: it was well equipped. It had a nice little library -- books well chosen. There was ample equipment for teaching general science. The state provided text-books for all pupils. We had playground equipment in plenty, and extensive play-space. To look at the physical plant made a teacher's heart glad, for the chance of doing a good job appeared to be above average.

Extensive repairs had been in progress on the building throughout the summer, and the place was in the wildest disorder when the pre-planning period began. New floors had been built, necessitating the removal of everything in the place.

The writer was given the task of getting the library straightened. It was a task requiring several days of hard labor, but it was a labor of love.

Our principal was a true Georgia gentlemen who had headed the institution for seven years. He was familiar with every nook and cranny of the building he could put his hand on every article of equipment in the school, and he knew all the pupils of permanent residence, the parents, step-parents, grand-parents, and half-siblings. He knew who had served jail sentences, and what the charge had been in each instance.

The solid majority of the village population respected and admired the old principal. The whole student body respected him one hundred percent. As the year wore on, and as those whose purpose it was to destroy the school got better organized, and their influence was increasingly felt, with the accompanying increase in deliberate pupil disorder, there was never a time when his mere appearance on a scene of disorder was not sufficient to induce instant quiet and perfect order.

We new teachers went in there, that year, liking and respecting the elderly principal (he was sixty-five years of age), liking each other, and liking the pupils -- all of us looking forward to a great year.

None of us knew of the condition of social and political unrest that existed in the neighborhood.

Our school was located out on the edge of Putnam County, so that the towns over in neighboring Susanne County were nearer to us, and their affairs of greater interest to the old residents than those of Putnam County.

At Frondisi -- a town nearby -- a brand new school was under construction. The people of Clear Springs wanted two things: a new school building and a new principal. Their old building was adequate and their old principal was better than most, but they wanted new ones.

More than a hundred residents of the village met and organized what they called the school improvement association. They elected president, vice president, secretary, and treasurer, and they hired a mouth-piece. I can't call him a lawyer, because his subsequent activities showed him to be, not an attorney at law, but a mouth-piece, in the best gangster tradition.

Their plan was to start raising hell, to interfere constantly in school teaching and administration, and to take every opportunity to wreck the school which presented itself, or which they could stir up.

One of their plans, indeed their grand plan, was to exert their influence on members of the student body to the end that they should reject the leadership of their principal and teachers, and defy their authority. As subsequent events proved, these tactics, supported and abetted as they were by the county superintendent, proved to be highly successful.

We straightened the building and its contents, organized the classes, and swung into action. The committee, too, began to operate, under cover to a great extent -- openly when they had to. Openly at P.T.A. meetings, in which they followed a policy of obstructionism from a prayer that ran.

"Oh Lord, open the eyes of this principal and these teachers, to the end that they may realize the extent of their ignorance, unworthiness, and incapacity. Help them, Lord, to realize that, far from possessing understanding, they really know nothing. May we all depend heavily upon thy divine wisdom,"

to refusal to wait for recognition from the chair before speaking, and shouting down the principal or any teacher who attempted to speak.

In the words of one big, brash, ill-mannered and unprincipled young father,

"By God, we want a new school building, and we want to select our own teachers, and we figger that if we raise enough hell, and keep at it long enough we'll get what we want. The folks down at Frondisi are getting a new building, and they're not a damned bit better than us. (Democracy at work). We want it and we're going to have it."

The county superintendent journeyed out there for one of those meetings. He carefully explained that specific conditions had to be present in a community before a new building could be constructed -- that Frondisi was located in another county -- that it was a new and rapidly growing community -- that a new school building was needed there -- that the financing of a school building was a major undertaking, involving exhaustive surveys of all kinds, and the cooperation of state and local governments, and the floating of bond issues.

He reminded them that a great deal of money had been set aside and spent on the Clear Springs school -- that the building, though not new, was in first flass condition. He reminded them that their present facilities were better than adequate. He saw no hope in the near future, for a new building.

The superintendent was an army colonel. He could recognize danger when he saw it. The meeting broke up in the wildest disorder. He and a couple of his supervisors lost no time in getting into their cars, and shaking the village dust from their whells.

From that moment on, he began to get the principal and any teacher he could conveniently use, ready for the dog-meat sacrifice. He certainly had the ravening dogs at the rear of the sled. He was desperately in need of meat to throw to them. Elections were coming up the next ear, and he intended to succeed himself in office, if humanly possible. He couldn't give them a new building, but he could save his hide at the polls by throwing them a principal and maybe a teacher or two.

Now the principal had done a fine job there for the past seven years. He owned his home there in the village. He was active in the Baptist Church, and he had a circle of good friends -- that is, there were people who wished him well. But the opposition believed he was too old. They accused him of many derelictions of duty of which he was not guilty, and they were determined to replace him, by fair means or foul. They had tried the fair means to no avail. Now they would try the foul.

The easiest and most obvious method of wrecking a school is to encourage rebellion and disorder among the pupils, and then give them adult support in the community, and official support from either the school office and/or the county office.

It happened that recalcitrant pupils were given support from all three sources. The committee members had resolved to "raise hell" until they should get a new building. It was up to them to stir up insurrection among the pupils until it would be impossible to have an educational program functioning there at all.

The superintendent had no recourse in smoothing his way through the next election but in throwing those fine upstanding citizens somebody to chew on -- to take their minds off the badly-wanted new building. They wanted to select their own teachers (which is not the manner of placing teachers prescribed by law) so the superintendent would and did, support any wrong perpetrated by a pupil, so as to hamstring the principal in the performance of his duty, and thus make him a fair candidate for the dog-meat honor.

The principal had been well-aware of the determination to retire him from service, and he didn't intend to be shelved. He was determined to remain in his position until he reached the legal retirement age of seventy.

The best method of saving himself was to select a teacher to whom he could divert cricicism and animosity. His personal strength prevented the immediate break-down which the committee expected. No matter how great the turmoil, in or around school, his appearance on the scene instantly quelled it. If he could have been everywhere at once, the school would have functioned smoothly. Yet that very influence of his militated against the successful wrecking of the teacher whom he had selected to take his place on the chopping block.

He had, of course, seen the teaching certificates of all the teachers in his school. The writer had the misfortune to be issued what he has come to regard as a "kiss of death" certificate; that is, it includes supervision and administration. The minute our principal saw those items on the writer's certificate, he concluded that this was a man selected to succeed him. According to his thinking, the writer had been sent out for one year, to learn the ropes -- after which, the second year, he himself would be dismissed, and the new man appointed to succeed him.

So it seemed advantageous to him to discredit the new man. More ardently than ever before, he labored to prove that his teachers, and especially the one with supervision and administration on his ticket, was weak and ineffectual, and that he himself was the indispensable man.

This he did by postponing the release of supplies for the teachers to use; by retaining all authority in his own hands; by refusing to instruct his teachers in the use of the audio-visual aids which we had there.

Anybody who has ever dealt with office equipment knows that it rapidly becomes obsolete, and that many machines develop pecularities in their functioning that require instruction in their use, and practice at it. He insisted upon operating the duplicator himself, or having his secretary do it. If a teacher needed copies run off, he had to wait for his material until the principal or the secretary would find time to do it.

If one of the teachers needed supplies, he didn't even know if any were available, for the principal kept the supplies under lock, with the key in his pocket. When the teachers had constantly to tag along at his heels, asking questions, it made them appear inept and ignorant.

When the teachers wanted to plug in so simple a machine as a phonograph, the fuss would blow. (Not his fault, unless not ordering the wiring strengthened would be a fault. The wiring <u>was</u> strengthened, toward the end of the first semester, but a great many programs and teaching plans had been scrapped during the time the wiring was at fault.)

If a teacher wanted to move a class into the auditorium and run a film at just that point in the course, he had to wait until the principal could get around to running the film for him. He would not teach anybody else to do it. It was an old, complicated machine, and his baby. It wouldn't work for anybody but him.

On one occasion, the writer was working at trying to thread the projector, before school took up in the morning. One of the more intelligent boys was at least lending moral support. The principal bustled up to us and panted,

"Almost time for the bell. Get to your class, Winston. And you, Mr. Porter -- hurry to your room. Hurry up. Trot -- run -- you'r late!"

There were loafing onlookers there, and he was treating me like a half-witted child in their presence. They laughed appreciatively, and ambled toward their rooms.

Early in the year, the teachers were innocently planning and sincerely trying to carry on learning-teaching processes. We didn't know that the disintegration of the school had been carefully planned in detail, by the committee of improvement. We were all new on the job, except the principal and his wife, and we were on the ball, sincerely trying to run a school.

One morning before classes began, the writer was seated at his desk when a boy came running down the hall, dribbling a basket ball. As the floor was wood, the sound he made was as if he were pounding the building to pieces. The writer called to the boy.

"Play basket ball outside, Robert. Keep it quiet inside the building."

The principal was sitting at his desk, in the room across the hall, reading the morning paper. At the sound of the teacher's voice, he glanced up over his paper at the pupils loafing in his room, and raised his eye-brows -- at the same time turning his mouth down and pulling in his chin. The gesture said, as plainly as if he had pronounced the words.

"Now, who des he think he is?"

The kids laughed derisively, and the teacher was put out of countenance. The boy continued to play there with the ball, and the principal said nothing.

The writer concluded that it must be standard procedure to race along the hall, dribbling a basket-ball, so he resolved to take no notice of such things in the future.

The worst condition all of us had to contend with was the refusal of the pupils to come to order, when it was time to call the class to order. Right in the middle of a mathematics demonstration, one boy would call across the room to another.

"Hey, Charlie, you coming straight to the shack this afternoon?"

"Sure," Charlie would answer, "But you were late yesterday, yourself!"

"I was not, you big liar!"

"Hey, you can't call me a liar," and he leaped across to the other boy, who had risen, and they were locked in a wrestling embrace -- rolling and kicking -- grunting, panting, exclaiming and laughing.

A half dozen girls would, by that time, be shrieking like factory whistles. They shrieked at everything. If one girl had on a new blouse, the others gathered around it and shrieked. If somebody told a funny story, or any story, they shrieked. If one of them dropped her pencil, she shrieked. if there was nothing to shriek about, some girl would carefully mark her place in her book, tilt her chin up, close her eyes tightly, and shriek until she was exhausted, while the others laughed and kept up a general uproar.

We had comedians with us -- the best in the business. We had Laurel and Hardy, The Three Stooges, and Jerry Lewis. Especially Jerry Lewis. One big boy from New Jersey must have spent practically all his leisure before a mirror, practicing Jerry's facial expressions, and going through jerry's motions and routines.

He was six feet two, and had feet to match. He could sit down, turn sideways, with his feet in the aisle, and do a clog dance, sitting down, with appropriate facial expressions, that sent the girls into fits of the screaming meemies. This entertainment would be provided for us during literature class. When the dance was concluded, and the class would be at last restored to some semblance of order, the period would be just about shot.

Of course, in his innocence -- not knowing that this performance was part of the over-all plan to wreck the school, the teacher would try to deal with it in regular, orthodox ways. He talked to the pupils -- reasoned with them -- admonished them -- appealed to common sense. Of course he, nor any teacher, ever accomplished anything in that direction. But we tried to keep up the effort, and did.

When testing time came, we gave them their tests, in good faith. Tests were just as carefully and conscientiously built as if the pupils were trying, and the directions were as carefully given.

A fifty-minute test, they raced through in ten, and shambling forward, dropped them on the teacher's desk. When they had finished, they formed in groups and indulged in a bull session.

Of course, the teachers were trying, all the time, to set up and maintain, order. None of us had any success.

At the end of each day, the men were in a towering rage and the women teachers were in tears.

Sometimes, when the uproar was greater than usual, the principal would appear in the door-way. Instantly, there was silence. Those who were out of their seats would quickly and silently take their seats.

As soon as the principal's back was turned, they resumed their bull sessions.

Surprisingly enough, there were a few, even there, who did not join in these festivities. I remember one family especially, two girls and one boy, who behaved themselves perfectly during the whole time. They worked faithfully, and treated the teachers with respect. Of course, brutal retaliation was taken on them. They were "chicken."

Nothing violent occurred until one evening when the pupils were on their way home from school. One of the wreckers actually laid hands on one girl in that family, whereupon her brother whipped him until he couldn't stand up. That boy was able to whip any other boy in the 8th or 9th grade class. After that, the wreckers confined their punishments to talking, and not much of that. The few others, besides that family, who refused to join the hoods and thugs, made it possible to keep up the routine of school, in spite of the uproar.

The writer had long looked with appreciation upon the strong influence that the principal exercised over the thugs. it occurred to him that the principal possibly could help the situation permanently, if he were to deal with an individual on a specific issue.

The next time the young man from New Jersey did his sitting clog dance, he took him to the principal, and told what he'd brought the young man in for, describing the dance and its effect upon the class.

The teacher said,

"Just look at those shoes!"

They looked like flat-boats.

"Now, now, now, now, Mr. Porter. Let's not make any personal remarks. Go back to your class, Mr. Porter. Don't' try to answer back. Just go!"

Turning to the boy, he said,

"Son, I'm sure Mr. Porter didn't mean to be unpleasant when he called attention to your shoes. I sure hope you won't hold it against us. We try to do as fine a job of educating young people as we know how. Try to forgive him, because sometimes he feels bad or tired, and he's liable to let temper get the best of him. Now, you just go back to class, and don't you worry about a thing!"

His attitude in any situation involving a clash between a pupil and a teacher was,

"Now, now, now, now, Boys! Tch-tch-tch-tch-tch-tch! Surely you fellows can do better than that. We have to live in harmony, you know. Mr. Teacher, you are the grown, mature person in this trouble. Surely you should be able to handle this situation in a smooth, dignified manner. I have to admit I'm disappointed in you. Go now, and sin no more."

The pupils couldn't all be fed at the same time in our little dining room, so it was necessary to stagger the lunch periods. As soon as the first lunch period began, we might as well have dismissed school. The other classes acted like the hogs in the other pens, when the hogs in the first pen began to be fed. It was with the utmost difficulty that the teachers were able to keep them in their seats, who were not already eating. At first we succeeded in doing that. But later on, we would have had to lock the back door and stand at the other one -- club in hand -- and use it, too, to knock some of the pupils unconscious, if we hoped to keep the class from leaving the room. By and by, they dismissed themselves at the first lunch bell, and filled the corridor leading to the lunch room. They milled and screeched and howled, as the first group finished eating and left the dining room, to be succeeded by the second group, and so on, until all had been fed.

Lunch time at that school was a nightmare. It more closely resembled feeding time at the zoo. There was shouting and shoving and overturning of benches.

But the most revolting thing that occurred in that dining room, was the stomach-turning sink talk that some of the boys indulged in. As little prestige and authority as the teachers had, the boys didn't let them hear this. They leaned over and whispered it to the girls. Some days there would be a literal procession of girls going to the refuse cans, and scraping their plated empty.

But the girls never reported this to the grown folks around school. They reported it to their dams, and the dams tramped into school, and cussed out the teachers for letting it happen.

One dam tramped up to me, and putting her fists on her hips, exclaimed:

"Look here, Mr. Teacher. I want to know why in hell you stand there and allow them nasty boys to talk so dirty that my little girl has to scrape her dinner out in the slop-bucket. If you wuz hald a man, you wouldn't allow it!"

She had probably drilled her own boy carefully in the technique, and rehearsed him, so that he'd be letter perfect at getting it done without the teacher's hearing it.

I said, "If you'll give me the names of the boys, I will personally see to it that they wait until the others have finished, and eat by themselves."

"What?" she yelled. "You want me to name the boys, and have them and their parents mad at me? No siree boddy-tater-o. Don't you try to unload your burdens on me! Why, some of them people would burn my house down some night. Hell no, I'm not gonna name 'em! I never heard of such nonsense in my life! Now you get on the ball, and make 'em behave theirselves, or I'll ask the county superintendent if he can send a teacher in here who at least calls hisself a man!"

Whirling, she tramped off, down the hall, sniffing and switching her tail as she went.

I want to emphasize the fact that we teachers, at first, didn't know of the existence of the school improvement league. We were honest and innocent. We tried, in good faith. It took until almost Christmas for the improvement society to build its so called case to a degree of completion that they thought would stand up in court.

In the meantime, the pupils, under the inspiration and careful coaching of the members of the improvement society, were having fun.

These gentry, by the way, were well qualified to coach.

Later on we learned that when one prime over in the association was a boy of high school age, he had stolen the ignition key out of the school-bus one afternoon, and kept them in his pocket until dusk -- marooning a bus load of school pupils until the sheriff arrived and threatened to arrest the whole crowd less the keys were produced while he counted ten. The prime-mover gave up the keys then, and the pupils, at long last, were delivered to their homes.

A woman who provided yeoman leadership to the other members of the improvement association had recently flown home from California, to re-establish residence in her old home village, preparatory to divorcing her husband and the father of her little boy.

We learned later, that when she was younger, she herself had been expelled from that same school for habitual truancy and other charges, which must have been fairly scabrous, to bring punishment on a girl. She was a delinquent, all right. But the ex-juvenile delinquent was considered worthy of helping to head up the school improvement association.

We had, in the ninth grade class, two boys, both of whom had spent time in the psychopathic ward of a hospital in New Jersey.

One of them couldn't keep his hands off girls and women. He was adept at meeting a woman suddenly at a corner, and smashing into her as if he was playing football. He was expert at catching her in his arms before she fell. Then he would shower her with excuses and endearments, while his expert hands explored every inch of the surface of her body.

The other hated to feel rejected. If he seized a girl to kiss her and she resisted, he wanted to throttle her.

Now we teachers weren't vouchsafed this information at all, until we worked it out for ourselves, by observation and experience. As I though back over my experiences with those two fellows, I was amused to remember that the two girls whose brother was so powerful a fighter, never seemed to run into the one, or attract the other -- though both were very attractive girls.

These psychos were finally the reasons why we left that school, though our leaving was still some distance in the future.

An illustration of disruptive tactics: In a history class for seventh graders, one little boy had picked up a quotation from John Paul Jones, which he made yeoman use of, in class. He worked up a routine with another boy whose place was at the other side of the room. He would stand up, hold his cupped hands to his mouth like a megaphone, and bawl across the room:

"Have you struck your colors?"

And the other boy would bawl back,

"I have not yet begun to fight!"

Well, the first time they did that, it raised an appreciative laugh. They were fairly cute kids. But to have it endlessly repeated, at short intervals, along with other ugh provoking sallies, gets old, finally.

It was the working of that particular plan that finally moved the writer to action. One morning I tried to stop those comedians, unsuccessfully. I stepped down the hall to the principal's office, picked up the official paddle, and said to him:

"Come on, and witness a few paddlings. I have five boys that have it coming. They deserve it so richly that this time, they're going to get it. These months I've had experiences that convince me that this campaign of disorder is organized -- probably rehearsed and directed from outside."

The principal assented, and we walked back to the door of the class-room. I called the first boy out, stooped him over, and gave him the six regulation whacks over the rear.

I sent him back in, and called the next one -- and the others, one by one, until I had paddled the five chief offenders.

When I re-entered the room, there was such a difference in the atmosphere that would have astonished any observer. Gone was the expectant smirks. Present instead, was a sane attitude of respect and decency that had not been seen in there since semester had begun. The pupils acted, as the scripture expresses it, "clothed, and in their right minds."

It is impossible to express, adequately, the change that had come over that class. The very boys I had paddled looked at me with respect, and even with affection. They knew they hadn't been acting right; they felt, for the first time, clean, straight, and right.

Although the laws of Florida confer the paddling authority on school teachers, we use it reluctantly and seldom. So many people have lost confidence in, and respect for, classroom teachers, because of the way they are bull-dosed and brow beaten and discredited by the principals, and everybody else connected with administration, that they actually regard teachers as people against whom they have to protect their children.

Too many children are sent to school with the assurance:

"Now, honey, if any teacher bothers you, or arouses your displeasure in any manner, you just report him to mama, and mama will attend to him in the proper way."

Like we said earlier in the book, it is the nature of children to assert and maintain their independence. They begin to explore in that direction at a very early age. The method is, try and probe; divide and conquer. Some children probe continuously at parental authority and at school regulations relentlessly and unceasingly. No barbarian horde ever probed more industriously at the northern borders of the Roman empire than some children explore the possibilities of getting away with infractions of home and school discipline.

Parents who oppose each other, or oppose school teachers, in the matter of holding children to strict observance of home and school and social regulations, are making an awful mistage. A moment's consideration of facts would convince any thinking parent of the truth of that statement. All human endeavor has to be governed by rules and regulations. Even a game of marbles has to be played according to rules which are equally binding on all players alike, or else the game breaks up in disorder. And so it is, in the whole human experience of living together. Any pupil in school who challenges the regulations, or acts in an unsocial manner, is as a burr under the saddle, or a disease in the body.

Children don't need protection against their teachers. Fifty years of school experience, as pupil, teacher, and principal, convinces me that teachers are, in the aggregate, high class citizens in every way, shape, manner, and form. I have yet to meet a teacher who looked for trouble. Common sense indicates that absence of strife is the condition most conducise to success in learning and teaching. Tension of any kind hinders the efforts of pupil and teacher alike. Teachers know that a pupil learns more rapidly and easily under the leadership of a teacher he likes and admires, than he does under a teacher he fears or resents.

Teachers are in school with a definite purpose. The things they do are designed to help hem accomplish that purpose. Conversely, they try to leave undone every thing that would militate against the accomplishment of that purpose, which is to accomplish the three-fold duty of the public school system.

Now, in spite of the penchant of children to assert their independence, they expect the grown folks to lay down the rules of the game, and see that they are obeyed. If we don't do that, we're criminally negligent in the training of our youth. One of our prime obligations is to prepare children for adult citizenship. If we allow children to grow up, believing that they can play the game by their own rules, and that they will be protected from the consequences by higher authority, they are certainly not being prepared to play the multifarious games of adult life, where we do everything by rigidly prescribed rules, and are punished for breaking them.

If a youth attains physical and chronological maturity, believing that traffic ordinances are like pie crusts, he will soon find that when the policeman issues him a ticket, it takes money to square that ticket. Mama can't make the policeman take it back, nor can she order the punishment of the policeman.

So when mama storms into a school, demanding the punishment of a teacher for having incurred the displeasure of a child, she's doing that child a positive disservice, because as schools are set up in Florida, and doubtless in states all over the union, she can get the teacher punished. Maybe he isn't discharged forthwith, but the fact that she complains, makes the teacher, in the eyes of his principal, a trouble maker, and a person to be viewed with suspicion. If several complaints are lodged in the course of a year, no matter how unfounded they may be, and no matter how intemperate and irresponsible the source, the teacher is not likely to be "invited back" for the coming year.

That is because the principal is afraid the parent might go to the county office with her complaint. His superior officers have the same attitude toward him that he entertains toward the teacher. His success in holding his job depends upon holding down the number of complaints that are lodged against him. His dictum in regard to teachers is, to paraphrase a famous scriptural passage:

"It must needs be that a teacher, in the performance of his duty, will stir up opposition; but woe unto the teacher against whom opposition is stirred up."

Fear pervades the school system of America. It is present in all eschelons of administration. It has grown to colossal proportions -- to a strength that has already well nigh wrecked the system. Fear that causes men to stoop to lying, tyranny, and injustice -- to the bearing of false witness -- all to the destruction of integrity in one of our most important institutions. "Democracy" in action! Direct interference in the functioning of institutions!

But let us consider the true, spelled-out meaning of "Democracy": Quoting from U.S. Army training manual No. 2000-25, democracy is defined as "government by the masses. Authority derived through mass meeting or any other form of direct expression. Results in mobocracy. Attitude toward property is communistic -- negating property rights. Attitude toward law is that the will of the majority shall regulate, whether it be based upon deliberation, or governed by passion, prejudice, or impulse, without restraint or regard to consequences. Results in demagogism, license, agitation, discontent, anarchy."

Several times during the course of this book, instances of "democracy" in action are related, showing the deleterious effect they have had upon the school system of the nation.

Our government is a Republic, not a Democracy.

Let us consult training manual #2000-25 again for a definition of Republic:

"Republic": Authority is derived through the election by the people of public officials best suited to represent them. Attitude toward property is respect for law and individual rights, and a sensible economic procedure. Attitude toward law is the administration of justice in accord with fixed principles and established rules of evidence, with a strict regard to consequences."

A greater number of citizens and a larger extent of territory may be brought within its compass.

Avoid the dangerous expreme of either tyranny or mobocracy.

Results in statesmanship, liberty, reason, justice, contentment, and progress.

It is the standard form of government throughout the world."

We have been public, not a democracy. Our institutions, including the school system, are based upon republican ideals -- not democratic.

But we have been suffering a drift toward socialism since 1932. Being a school man, the writer has had borne upon him the results of socialism and democracy on the school system.

We have a superintendent of each system, elected by the people. He is supposed to be a man well suited to represent the people in the running of their schools. We have a board of public instruction whose duty it is to formulate policy. They in turn engage other people, professionally fitted to implement policy and direct the proper functioning of the schools. They hire teachers, who are professionally qualified to teach.

* Editorial in "Ft. Lauderdale News" September 20, 1961.

Then we yield to individual brashness and mobocracy in the process of applying the republican principles on which our public system is based.

Our school principals give sympathetic ear to the most ridiculous palaverings of women who don't know beans with the bag open, against teachers who are professionally qualified end long experienced as leaders of youth. Superintendents will give tender and reverent treatment to the same women, if some principal has failed to assuage their thirst for vengeance.

We must stop this sort of thing. The public must stop this demogogery and mobocracy that cripples our schools. The death penalty must be wrested from the hands of school officials who use it against those placed on a lower exchelon of authority. The school prople of all positions must be held responsible for their actions, but the checks and balances msut be restored, so that school people may go ahead and work without fear.

Right now, school people are scared hired men and hired girls. The American public school system is too vital a part of our society to allow to fall apart. It has tried valiantly to take up the slack left by the home and the church in the training of youth, caused by changes in our methods of making a living.

But the schools cannot function in the grip of fear. What a pity that we should allow our schools to disintegrate, when they are the last bright hope we have.

The quiet and order established by firm paddlings was of short duration. The teacher had broken at long last, and had applied common sense, under law, and according to regulations laid down by the law of the state, to meet a situation which had become intolerable.

The principal knew what consequences to expect, and was delighted. Now the teacher would come into a storm of persecution, the brutality of which could scarecely be surpassed, short of actual murder. But hallelujah! The heat would be off him!

And it was -- until the end of that school year, at which time the committee turned their big guns on him -- with disastrous results.

The next morning, that school presented the appearance of a sane school, such as it and all others should be at all times. It was the calm before the storm. Toward the end of the first period, all hell broke loose.

The dams of the paddled boys arrived singly, one at a time. The first one appeared at the writer's door, and asked, vivilly enough, if she could have her boy. She wanted to take him to the hospital.

Of course, the teacher and principal excused the boy to his dam.

Presently another dam arrived, and collected her offspring -- to take him off. He needed hospitalization!

And so on, until all five had been taken to a hospital for a check-up.

A few munited later, the writer was asked to report to the principal's office. As he entered the room, his visitor was hidden by the opening door. The door was closed, revealing the irate, protective father.

"What kind of man are you," he yelped. "My boy came home, beaten black and blue! You sadistic brute! You wolf in sheep's clothing! You cruel tyrant! I'll have you know that another such performance and you'll answer to me!"

The writer at first, being taken by surprise, was speechless. During a tirade of abuse that was much longer than the one quoted, he held his peace.

By the time his traducer had gotten out the words, "You'll answer to me" he had gotten his bearings.

He picked up the gauntlet.

"You son of a bitch. I'll answer to you right now. Just come outside!"

At that point, the principal jumped at the teacher, grabbed him around the neck with one arm, and picked up the phone receiver with the other hand.

"Operator, give me the sheriff's office, quickly!" he panted.

The irate father went out of there like a bat out of the Carlsbad caverns, kicked up sand as he crossed the school yard, jumped into his delivery truck, and roared away from there. If the engine had stalled, he would have keeled over, dead.

The ninth grade class, ten feet away, was vastly diverted. Oh, boy! What delicious excitement! Of course, if they could have witnessed a knifing or a fist fight between the teacher and the irate father, they would have been better satisfied. But the instant readiness of the teacher to satisfy his traducer, cheated the class of the fun of seeing two grown folks having at each other, hammer and gongs; and also, perhaps it saved their teacher from a thrashing! Anyhow, the teacher intended to entertain his attacker as well as he could.

Gradually the kettle stopped bubbling, but it continued to seethe. One would think we had had enough for one day. But no.

When the ninth grade class filed into the writer's room for an English class, one big girl said to him:

"Mister, you're sure going to catch it! My mama is going to fix your clock. Make no mistake about it. Your name's mud!"

Just then, the principal's secretary called the teacher to the telephone. The teacher left the room amid a chorus of jeers and derisive laughter.

When he picked up the receiver, there came to his ears a storm of vituperation and filth such as he had not believed any American woman capable of.

The teacher was lost. The woman had not even given her name. The teacher asked.

"Who are you? What's your name? What are you talking about? I can't make head or tail of this palaver!"

For answer, there came fresh floods of abuse.

The teacher handed the phone to the secretary.

"See if you can find out who that is, and what she's palavering about. She sounds crazy."

The secretary took the phone, soothed the virago, and presently hung up.

"It's Mrs. So & So," she reported. "She owns that saloon and beer joint at the edge of the village. I don't know what she was talking about."

The evening papers in Ft. Dibgy reported, in screaming head-lines:

"Committed of parents seeks morals warrant against teacher," followed by the sorry story of a carload of improvement committee members charging into Ft. Digby at midnight the night before, demanding the immediate arrest of the teacher on a morals charge. The rousted the circuit judge out of a sound slumber.

"Why do you want to apply for a morals warrant against this teacher?" asked the judge.

"Never you mind why we want it!" yelped one virago. "Just give us the warrant, and we'll go ahead with the action!"

"Easy!" admonished the judge. "You answer a few questions. Now what has this teacher done?"

"He paddled five boys!" spat another beer/parlor loafer.

"Well," mused the judge. "that's hardly cause for issuing a morals warrant. You'll have to give better reason that that if you expect to get it. The request is denied."

The committee representatives had returned to the village, balked in their design, tired, disappointed; sullen and very ugly.

the next day came the irate father and the phone call from the beer-joing owner.

The teacher was a fairly long time finding out what that call was about. But finally the shocking truth was revealed:

The girl had told her dam that her teacher had knocked her down with his fist; that when she scrambled to her feet, the teacher

111

had slapped her several times and knocked her down again; that when she tried to rise, the teacher had kicked her so brutally that she couldn't rise.

If that girl had gotten what she so richly deserved, she would have gotten all that and more. As a matter of fact, the teacher had not only never laid finger or paddle on her; he had never even so much as given her a cross word.

When the girl went home and told that story of assault and battery, the old saloon keeper had apparently not even inspected the girl for marks and bruises, but had taken all night to wind herself up, and deliver her cursings and ravings over the phone the next morning:

Thinking the matter over afterwards, the writer was amused by the memory of what Mark Twain wrote once, concerning his anger at a man. He said he put on his hat and tramped out as far as the gate, on his way to the man's house, to give him a good cursing. When Mark reached his own gate, a brilliant inspiration struck him: he could do it just as well over the phone!

That afternoon, the superintendent arrived at the school, surrounded by a body-guard of three men. He had his plan pretty well worked out. Here was opportunity to throw a teacher to the mob, and divert the mob's attention from himself. He needed all the support he could muster in the election coming up, and here was a heaven-sent opportunity for him to appear as the great executive, the stern disciplinarian -- the friend of the pee-pull, and the stalwart guardian of each little helpless chee-ild.

He arrived just after school. He and his body-guard filed into the writer's room. After amenities, he addressed the teacher:

"Mr. Porter, what in the world have you been doing out here? I've never known a community to get into such an uproar. Boy, I never though you were that rugged. Slappings, kickings, beatings, threats of bodily harm to a father represented in your class --"

"Colonel Lipton," the writer replied, "I paddled five pupils, strictly according to regulations, in the presence of the principal.

All the rest is lies -- not even based on fact. I paddled the boys. That's the whole story. That's all I've don."

"Well, now, we've got to do something to quiet this end of the county. I have a suggestion to make. If we take the bull by the horns, and you request a hearing before the school board, they'll have to accept the verdict of the board, shut up, and simmer down. Finally we can have peace."

Well, the teacher didn't know that the newspapers would feature the case in scare heads, publish a blow-by-blow account of the public hearing, and open its agony columns to the slanderous and irresponsible writings of the improvement committee members and their sympathizers. He knew he had nothing to hide. He knew he had done nothing wrong. Of course, he was still under the mistaken notion that truth would triumph -- that virtue would be victorious. He didn't know to what extent Democracy had taken over the state.

"All right, Colonel," said the teacher, out of his consciousness of moral rectitude. "I'd welcome an opportunity to put these gentry on the stand, under oath. They'll sing a different tune. And I'd like to have peace around here myself.

Silly boy! Peace was not the objective of the school improvement committed. They were going to wreck that school, and wreck it permanently.

In the interval of quiet that succeeded the teacher's assent, the superintendent could hardly keep from screeching with delight. Of course, he already knew the Calvary that a public board-hearing is to a teacher. The teacher, out of his ignorance and innocence, supposed that a hearing would be like a trail in a court of law, with the judge's and jury's decision taken as final -- the innocent vindicated, and peace restored. But the superintendent knew that here was entertainment enough to satisfy the bloodlust of that segment of the population that thrives on excitement and strife for a long succession of days. If he could emerge as a popular hero, his re-election would be assured.

He was more than ready to supply the circus, if not the bread.

Meantime, we had to go through the motions of having school, while the "hearing" was pending. The prospect of the circus was enough to diminish interest in lesser forms of entertainment.

But at this juncture, the girls swung into action on a project that was designed to furnish ammunition for the school improvement committee to use at the "hearing."

The girls were busy taking notes, both on everything the teacher said, and on their recollection of what he had said in the past. One day a little girl came up to him and said:

"Mr. Porter, I've got a broken bra strap. May I go find a safety pin for it?"

The teacher replied:

"Step down to Mrs. Porter's room. She can likely take care of you."

At the hearing, an affidavit was read concerning the incident:

Pupil: "Mr. Porter I have a broken bra strap. May I get a safety pin for it?"

Teacher: "How could you expect a tiny little strap like that to hold up such lush, big, beautiful sweet things like those lovely titties of yours? Um-m-m-m-m!"

Concerning that blurb, one newspaper reporter wrote:

"The child concerned is a little girl eleven years old, and small for her age. Her breasts are about the size of marbles. The story is obviously a lie, on the face of it."

Back at the first of the year, the teacher had said to a little girl, just to vary his "good morning":

"Was that your mother you were walking with this morning? She seems like a charming little woman."

Later, at the hearing, an affidavit was read that rendered the incident thus:

"Was that gorgeous tomato your mother? Ooooh! She's a living doll!"

The woman in question had just been through the experience of having her husband divorce her and marry another woman, and settling down with her to live not far from where he had lived with her. The teacher's attorney brought out that fact on cross examination during the hearing -- to the vast amustment of the spectators.

One day during the first period after lunch, the teacher noticed a spot of bean soup on his trousers. Seated behind his desk, he tried to rub it off with his handkerchief.

The fact was reported by that same little girl in an affidavit.

There were perhaps half a dozen affidavits read at the hearing -- all designed to picture the teacher as a lewd, dissolute character. They had prepared half a hundred, but had to throw the rest out on advice of counsel. Even a mouthpiece of his caliber was afraid to introduce them at the hearing, they were so absurd.

The man who, as a high school pupil, had stolen the keys of the school bus, and his friend, the woman who had been expelled for delinquency, made a pilgrimage to Azurville, where the teacher had worked for three years just before falling into the Clear Springs hole. They walked along the streets of that town, entered business places and homes, introduced themselves, and asked whether the people knew the teacher. Nearly everybody did, since he had been a leading Methodist layman in the community, and prominent in civic affairs through his activities in the Civitan Club.

These good friends praised the teacher highly. Some of them, when told what the visitors had hoped to accomplish, had told them off indignantly. They returned to Ft. Digby considerably chastened.

While they were in Azurville, they visited principal birdsong, and asked if he could help them. He said he believed he could. He selected a little girl whom he believed they could depend on, and commissioned her to write a statement, putting everything in which she figured might injure her former teacher. Possibly they paid her for it.

The teacher was shown a copy -- mimeographed -- after the hearing. The fact that the blurb was mimeographed gives rise to the suspicion that hundreds of copies were run off and distributed to school administrators throughout the state.

In it, the little girl had told that the teacher smoked cigars in class, sent out for coffee, to be consumed in class, knocked down a boy with his fist and stomped his half-unconscious body with his feet. On one occasion, the letter stated, the teacher was taking the little girl home from school, when his improper advances became so insistent that she had to literally fight him off, and finally leave the car before she reached home.

But that scabrous document was never introduced at the hearing. The mouth-piece tried to introduce it, but the teacher's attorney sprang to his feet and called:

"One moment! Just one little moment. Counsel says this letter is an attack against the teacher's character. Is the writer of that letter in court?"

"No, she isn't," replied the mouthpiece.

"Then I object to its introduction!" snapped the teacher's counsel.

"Sustained!" intoned the county attorney, who was acting as judge in the proceeding.

That took most of the wind out of the hell raisers' sails. They were badly hurt, but they crippled along valiantly.

The teacher had to listen for four hours while that mob -- one after another -- took the oath, and proceeded to perjure themselves by reciting all the kinds of lying crap that diseased minds could think of. No clean, decent mind could have conjured up the statements that riff-raff produced.

One after another, they got on the stand, and poured out their perjury. Counsel for the accused cross examined, and made each of them wish he had died and gone to hell before he got on the stand. Each was made to contradict himself or herself, until each witness could have died of mortification.

The bulk of the testimony the dams offered concerned the deplorable physical condition of the paddled boys. As a result of all their efforts on the doctors and the hospitals, they could get but one statement: One doctor had found a slight bruise, less than half an inch long and less than a quarter of an inch wide, on one boy, and stated that it could have been caused by the pinch of a bicycle seat. The other boys were clear of marks.

Under questioning, one boy testified that after the first paddle blow, he had felt nothing at all.

One cross examination, teacher's counsel asked:

"You say you felt nothing after the first stroke?"

"No, sir" replied the boy. "I was numb!"

"You mean to say you never felt the next fifty blows at all? asked counsel.

"Fifty strokes?" repeated the boy, incredulously. "Hell, he only hit me six times in all! Where do you get fifty? Six licks is all he laid on any of us."

"Well, Mama," said counsel, "That pretty well knocks out the lurid story of the beating of the century, doesn't it."

After the first few witnesses had been reduced to absurdity, the others should have testified more carefully. But by that time, the members of the committee had imbibed enough whiskey to make them reckless. Each witness sailed in as if he or she were battling for the Lord. Each one, on cross examination, was reduced to absurdity, and retired to his place covered with chagrin and disgrace. They kept leaving the courtroom and taking long, unhealthy pulls at the bottle of Old Grandad, Old Crow, Seagrams, Seven Crown, and any other liquid they had brought along to keep them fortified through the ordeal, or what they had looked forward to as a few hours of Roman holiday. But it didn't turn out to be the Roman holiday they had expected. They had turned out to see a school teacher slaughtered. Instead, they were being slaughtered themselves. Their children, one after another, got on the stand and testified that they had been at fault all the way -- that their punishment had not been brutal or excessive -- that they liked, rather than disliked, the teacher -- that they felt no resentment toward him -- that they respected him for paddling them -- that they, in his place, would have done worse.

While this was in progress, their dams and sires were keeping up a procession to and from the rest rooms, and returning more and more glassy-eyed, as the hearing went on.

The shameful farce continued through four and a half hours. The committee was disastrously defeated, but the newspapers of the state were playing it up big. The teacher was receiving publicity that was highly damaging to him. Just the fact that he had been attacked was destined to cause him serious trouble on long as he worked in the state.

He should never have been subjected to such an ordeal. The superintendent should never have allowed it. Only he had to divert dissatisfaction from himself, and the principal favored the proceeding as a device to ease pressure on himself.

The officials adjourned, promising a decision for the following evening.

The committee returned to their homes to sleep off the effects of the alcohol they had guzzled during the evening, and the teacher fell into bed, exhausted.

The next day at school, we dealt with a quiet and chastened student body. They hadn't accepted defeat, but they weren't as cock-sure as they had felt previously.

The concerned parties met at the county school office the next evening, to hear the official verdict.

The superintendent came into the office where the teacher was waiting with a couple of supervisors who were friends of his. The school board, who had acted as jury at the hearing, had reached its verdict, but had made no official announcement.

Superintendent Lipton, who knew this, and knew what the verdict was, tried every argument he could think of, to spook the teacher into trading his resignation for a favorable verdict that had already been reached -- to Lipton's certain knowledge.

The teacher listened to his arguments and replied:

"No deal, colonel. If I'm found guilty as charged, of immorality and brutality, I stand dismissed anyhow. If I'm found not guilty, there is no reason why I should resign. No deal!"

Presently everybody was called into the board room to hear the verdict read.

When we were seated, the resolution was read:

"We, the board of public instruction of Putnam county, having weighed the statements made in this hearing, pronounce accused not guilty, because of total lack of evidence to support the charges made against him. The members concur unanimously in this declaration."

Before the hearing began, the teacher said to the principal, Mr. Schmidt, I expect you to attend the hearing and testify in my behalf."

"Oh, uh, uh, now, I'd rather not become involved in this trouble. Just leave me out of it. No sir, I'd rather have nothing at all to do with it."

When the teacher reported that shameful attempt at weaseling to his attorney, the attorney picked up his phone and got the principal on the other end.

"Mr. Schmidt, you are going to attend the hearing, and testify on behalf of your teacher. You are going to give me your solemn word of honor that you will be there, and will testify, or I'll slap a subpoena on you. Do you want it to go down in the record that you had to be forced to do the right thing -- the manly thing? Give me your answer right now!"

Putting the chips down like that brought the principal around to the side of the angels. His testimony carried lots of weight -- was probably decisive. But he had to be forced to do it. His natural instinct as a principal, prompted him to weasel out and let the teacher hold the bag -- face his traducers along.

Next morning's newspaper screamed:

"Education Board keeps Clear Springs Teacher."

Following was the blow-by-blow account of the hearing, making much of the fact that his attackers could bring no evidence to support the charges they had made.

On the editorial page, the main article dealt with the verdict, praising it and the school board that had handed it down, and ending with the hope that, in as much as the affair had been handled by lawful process, the losers would accept their defeat in the spirit of true Americanism, and would therefore refrain from further agitation.

But gentle reader, the editor didn't know how thoroughly and deeply the spirit of Democracy had stained that community.

Next day's headlines screamed:

"Parents Vow to Continue Struggle at Clear Springs."

That same morning we began the day with less than half the pupils in attendance. Many children had been withdrawn from school because they were the children of committee members; many parents had withdrawn their children under threats of bodily harm to themselves and/or their children if they didn't.

Some twenty women, dressed up in their dungarees, or shorts, or pedalpushers, and carrying banners bearing scabrous insults to the teacher, the principal, and the board of public instruction, shuffled back and forth in front of the school -- picketing.

In the Digby News Press, December 8, 1956, the bright and shining crusader, Mrs. Amelia Smart, the gal who had been expelled for delinquency only a few short years before, was quoted as saying, when told of the school board's action:

"We are going to fight until we get porter and principal Carl Schmidt out. I just don't know what to say. I never thought anybody could be that stupid" (referring to the members of the county school board.)

The board charged principal Schmidt "to see that the school is operated efficiently and with proper discipline."

The same paper reports that Mrs. Paul Kraut had "talked with a dozen people, and they're keeping their children out of school."

She said "arrangements are being made to send at least a dozen pupils to school in Ft. Digby and Frondisi. Several Clear Springs pupils are attending a Catholic school in Frondisi.

"Mrs. Smart, a leader of the attack against Porter, called the board's decision "an awful blow."

"I don't know what prompted the board's decision. You can't "Write" the expression on my face."

Another leader of the committee:

"We will fight as long as we have breath in our bodies and a dollar left in our pockets."

So they wiggled into their shorts and peddle puchers and dungarees and sneakers, and picketed the school. Later in the day, they felt they could do with a little ride, so they piled into several cars and drove to Ft. Digby where they picketed the courthouse. With their bandanas tied around their heads, they looked like a truly revolutionary group.

Now this p9icketing -- this carrying of scabrous posters -- this yelling of insults, occurred after the properly constituted authority, after due deliberation according to legal and constitutional process, had handed down its decision.

During this shameful demonstration around school, smoke was seen billowing from the house of a family whose children had not been withdrawn from school. The father and mother were both at work. The house was gutted by fire.

Testimony was given at the hearing concerning the weight of the paddle used in punishing the pupils. The outlaws agreed that the post-mistress must have weighed the paddle. The next day her little boy was waylayed and beaten, on his way home from school.

We went through the motions of running classes with half the pupils absent, while fifty adults milled and murmured outside. The same school board that upheld justice at the trial allowed some pupils from Clear Springs to be enrolled in other schools in the county, and the Catholic school at Frandisi welcomed other as long-lost sheep of the fold. The superintendent of the county worked hand in glove with the outlaws. If that dignitary had possessed the honor of a civet car, he would have forbidden the enrollment of those pupils in any other school of the county, and he would have charged each family three dollars a day for every day each pupil was kept out of school.

But these sterling citizens continued to "fight". They drove in solemn procession in front of the old principal's house, late at night, and pelted it with rocks.

One night a company of grown folks slipped into the principal's front porch and emptied a bucket of fish guts on the floor.

On another occasion, while the old principal was attending prayer meeting at his church, as was his custom, these gentry burned a cross in his yard.

The old gentleman happened to be hiding behind a shrub in the yard another night when a delegation drove up and pussyfooted up to the house. They began preparation to set fire to it. The principal opened fire on them with a repeating rifle -- not to kill anybody, for he was not a killer. he accomplished his purpose, though, which was to frighten the arsonists off. They skedaddled to their car. Some bullets entered the side and rear of the vehicle as they roared away.

Some days later, the sheriff of the county admitted, in the presence of the writer, that he had discovered the car bearing the bullet holes. No action was ever taken against the cowardly men who attempted to burn the principal's house.

Time was wearing on. The Christmas season was fast approaching. We were busy preparing the season's festivities. The program we prepared was quite elaborate.

When the evening came to celebrate, the building was decorated most attractively, and all lit up. The corridors and rooms milled with pupils and villagers. The auditorium was jam-packed.

When the program was well along, the lights suddenly blinked out. The principal rushed to the master switch in the back corridor and sure enough, it had been pulled. The writer took up guard duty at that master switch, and it was not tampered with again during the evening. But members of the school improvement committee and selected friends from among the adult population congregated in the back of the building and on the back steps and in the back yard, and howled and bellowed obscenities and profanity, while out front the children sang "Silent Night -- Holy Night."

Yes, state witnessed a complete break-down of law enforcement in Putnam county that year. The sheriff made no move to apprehend the arsonists. There was no curt refusal to enroll hoods from Clear Springs in other schools, as there should have been. No effort was made to enforce the school attendance laws. no police protection was provided against thugs during the Christmas festivities.

Memory flares up concerning an incident in which the principal was poetically punished for his "now, now, boys" attitude when teachers were desperately trying to get order observed in class:

During the progress of the year, pupils were steadily being added to the roll. Finally a sufficient number of new pupils had been enrolled to permit the engagement of an extra teacher.

Some re-organization was effected, whereby ninth grade English was taken from Mr. Porter and given to the new teacher, and the principal took ninth grade science. Mention has been made of the New Jersey boy who could entertain so interestingly by clog-dancing while seated. Well, the principal now had the comedian in class. The comedian now began to serve up to the principal the same dish he had forced upon the teacher.

123

The principal promptly gave him ten days suspension.

That afternoon the boy's dam arrived at school, accompanied by the boy and the county superintendent.

The mighty executive assumed his most highly judicial air, and spoke:

"Mr. Schmidt, these good people complain to me of your high-handed action in suspending this boy from school. Now, Schmidt, don't try to justify this injustice. There's no justification <u>for</u> it! We simply can't tolerate this sort of thing, and we <u>won't</u> tolerate it! Now, this boy is to return to his classes as usual tomorrow morning. And don't let me hear of more such inhuman conduct on your part! Come, folks."

And the great man turned on his heel and led the way out. While he had been speaking, the dam had been sneering out at the principal, and the boy had stood smirking.

After that, not even the principal had any authority in that school. We could understand more clearly than ever before, the secret of his former authority: The pupils believed that the principal was solidly backed by still higher authority. They <u>knew</u> that the principal was not backing the teachers. They had always felt free, therefore, to flout the teachers; but up to that time, they had been sufficiently cautious about flouting the principal. After the dishonest and shameful capitulation of the superintendent, joy was unconfined. There was <u>no</u> authority present in that school which the pupils were bound to respect.

There is no horror like that of a society, large or small, that has been given over to anarchy. How we lived through each nightmare day, I'll never know.

The writer tried to stop racing in the halls by appealing to the risk of injury that was being run, by such conduct. All he could get in the way of response, was a snarl or a derisive laugh. One afternoon, one of the girls was being wildly chased by one of the boys in the lower main corridor. The girl rushed at a glass door, and thrust her hand against it to open it. The glass broke and the girl's hand was all but severed at the wrist. She didn't lose her hand, but it was a near thing.

Those who insist that there are just some school people who "naturally" command respect, and some who don't, are talking nonsense. Law observance on the part of those who want to flout the law, whether it be school regulations, city ordinances, or what have you, is a matter, not of personal respect or lack of it, for some teacher or policeman, but fear of the power of enforcement.

Society doesn't say to a policeman:

"Now, Murphy, we depend on you to keep order on this beat. You must not make any arrests or say anything to a law breaker to which he might take exception, or which might make him feel humiliated. If any complaints come in against you, we shall have to punish you."

Society doesn't say to a policeman:

"Monahan there are no handcuffs for your use. There is no jail for you to lock up tough guys in. There are no courts to which you may appeal for judgement. We depend on you, Monahan, to keep order out there by exercise of sheer strength of character and good example. Just be dignified, and "all business," Monahan, and if you have sufficient dignity and strength of character -- if you are a sweet enough fellow, you'll have no trouble. You just be a sweet fellow, calm and dignified, living before these people, rather than talking, and nobody will want to do wrong. Nobody will drive at sixty in a thirty-mile zone. There will be no robberies, stick-ups, muggings, beatings, rapes. Just live before them, Monahan. We enforce mighty high standards on our officers." yet even the authority of the police is being undermined.

School administrators are saying the equivalent of that to teachers. They say, when questioned by laymen, (no teacher may ask a question of an administrator)

"Oh, now you've getting far afield. The police have to deal with the public!"

Yes, and the teachers have to deal with the public's children.

"Democracy" has so permeated American society that this age has been called by competent observers the "age of non-intervention." The courts are standing solidly back of the Communist conspiracy in this country. So loyally are the courts protecting thugs that the policy of Washington, D.C. the nation's capitol, are virtually ham-strung in their efforts to protect the public from the depradations of thugs and hoods.

In far too many instances, the laws of Congress that bring embarrassment to the commies are thrown out as unconstitutional by the Supreme Court. That august body proceeds to reverse the action of lower courts in which communists have been found guilty beyond the shadow of a doubt, of plotting the overthrow of this government by violence and force.

In school, we never had the authority to lock the pupils up, or levy fines. It was not necessary. But we did once have the authority to paddle a boy or girl for a boy's or girl's offense; we had the authority to restrict their freedom by detention after hours; in extreme cases we had the authority to suspend from membership in the student body.

But no more. Authority on every eschelon has been so consistently betrayed by the eschelon immediately above, that now there is no regulation that can't be violated with impunity by any pupil who can get the backing of his dam.

Where the policeman on the beat has no authority to make arrests; where the traffic officer has no authority to issue tickets; where the courts have no authority to impose jail sentences or levy fines, the public is at the mercy of hoods and thugs.

The teachers, if they exercise the authority still vested in them by laws that have never been repealed, are so shamelessly and so brutally punished by the very administrators who require them to maintain order in the schools, that they are hamstrung in their efforts to set up and maintain order in the schools, that they are hamstrung in their efforts to set up and maintain a learning-teaching situation in the classroom And the decent, law-abiding kids, who constitute 85 to 90 percent of every student body, are at the mercy of the hood and thug elements. They go pussy-footing around school, hoping to escape the notice of the thugs, or join them in sheer desperation.

It is time we faced up to this situation.

We had instances of plain and fancy harassment during the days following the "hearing." Men of the improvement committee would move on the school, just as they had seen quartettes of gangsters move into gin mills on the T.V., and pretend to inspect the plumbing, the drainage, or the wiring. They'd move around and through the building, stand together and confer -- looking at the teachers menacingly.

Women came practically every day, to "visit" the classes. They moved majestically into a class-room, took seats if seats were available, stood in a row at the back or side of the room if they weren't, pulled their lips back tight against their teeth, and glared at the teachers -- their eyes smoldering with anger.

We got so we rather liked having them come, because the kids behaved better while they were there. Evidently they had been given some training, somewhere along the line, about proper behavior before "company."

But these people were folks who operated under cover of darkness, beat up other people, and burned homes to the ground. They burned crosses in peoples' yards, and emptied buckets of fish guts on their front porches. Of course, daylight cramped their style somewhat, but in spite of the fact that the teachers were people of decency and courage, they felt uncomfortable, having people roaming around and through the school, showing an attitude that was unmistakably hostile.

We had been given ample proof that law enforcement in that county was a farce. We were hopelessly outnumbered , in case of a riotous showdown, and we had no police protection whatsoever, closer than twenty-three miles away, over a road that was being rebuilt at the time.

It took courage to go through the routine of teaching, under the conditions that obtained there.

Mention of the free use of the agony columns of the newspaper by irresponsible and uninformed correspondents has been made. However, toward the last, some people who still retained common sense and the spirit of decency and Americanism, began to writ in.

The Ft. Digby News Press published the following letter to the editor:

"Disgruntled Clear Springs parents have pawed the ground and believed threateningly. They have withdrawn their children from school and have been a public spectacle both as they picketed and at the public hearing in Ft. Digby last week. They have breathed fire and vengeance against the school, the teachers, and the board of education.

"They should be proud of their efforts when the scoreboard shows these results:

1. Children whose lack of home training shows in the excrement found on restroom floors at school; misuse and destruction of school property, and lack of obedience to, and respect for, their elders.

2. Their careless regard for truth and general lack of consideration for others is shown both in the kind of newspaper publicity they release, and in the attitude they showed at the hearing.

3. They have been hyper-critical of a principal and a teacher. Their critism was wholly destructive in character and they had no person among them who could qualify by education, training, or experience, to fill either position.

4. They have forgotten, if they ever knew, the request of Jesus: "Let him who is without sin cast the first stone." They look out of a dirty window instead of into their mirrors.

Pride should flood their hearts at the adverse publicity they have released in the state. This loud-mouthed group is a crowd of

"Johnnie-come-latelys who can do nothing better than engineer a fight and cause confusion.

Your school is exactly what you and your children make it. If your children have pride in their school, they do not abuse the building. If they are taught respect for adults, there will be no discipline problems.

Character education begins at home."

One day while classes were changing, the writer heard the raised, angry voice of one of the women teachers, followed by the sound of repeated blows to the face. He rushed out and found one of the New Jerseyites cuddling his face in his hands, while the teacher bawled:

"Don't you <u>dare </u>to run into me, and then start that baloney about being sorry, and running your hands over me! Don't you one time <u>dare</u> to lay a hand on me, in any way, shape, manner, or form, for any reason whatever!"

It was immediately after that that the writer insisted upon a look at that boy's record, and at the record of still another pupil whose conduct seemed to him to be abnormal. It was then that he found that those two boys had a history of mental and emotional instability -- that they had no business whatever in a public school.

The writer came to the conclusion that the game there was not worth the candle. With such organized and unscrupulous opposition, and in the complete absence of law enforcement, we were playing a game which we could not hope to win. When there is association with mentally and emotionally disturbed people, there is actual danger.

When the superintendent called in the writer and offered a position in another school for his wife, if the writer would resign his own job, the writer agreed. He had gotten his wife into that hell-hole, and he felt that he should get her out of it.

The 9th grade group had made a practice of hanging around the first grade room, pounding on the door, calling in to the first grade children, running through first grade play groups, pre-empting the play-ground equipment in the first-grade play area, and bothering the little children in every way they could, think of, and nothing could be done about it.

As the writer's wife was the first grade teacher, he was prepared, at all times, to kill any and all who might provoke her into protest and then subject her to assault and battery.

Accordingly, the writer felt that he was paying entirely too much for his salary. But conditions had gotten nearly as bad as they are in New York, New Jersey, Maryland, and Illinois, not to mention Texas, California, and Arkansas.

The writer's wife was given a transfer, and the writer was unemployed during the rest of that school year.

As he walked along the streets of Ft. Digby, he was accosted practically every day by total strangers who spoke appreciatively to him, and requested a hand-shake.

The story of Clear Springs draws to an end. A few weeks later, the Principal went on trial before the school board, on charges of neglect of duty, incompetence, and incapacity.

Again the hearing failed to adduce the smallest shred of evidence to support the charges brought. However, by that time, the board, influenced by the superintendent, had wearily adopted a policy of appeasement.

The superintendent had finally made good his promise to the leaders of the mob, to the extent of getting the resignation of the accused teacher; now if he could get the principal thrown out, he could claim the votes of the mob and their associates, as the pee-pulls' friend.

When the school-board-turned-jury voted at the end of the principal's ordeal, three of them voted to oust him. It was so ordered.

Right there, however, they ran into difficulty. The Principal had a continuing contract. He was in good health, although sixty-five years of age. There was not one shred of evidence to support the charges that had been brought against him, though other evidence of duplicity and premeditated action on his part in undermining his teachers could have been adduced, which would have brought merited punishment upon him. But that line of inquiry had not been introduced or pursued. The case, as it was, had not one leg to stand on.

The Principal and his attorney took it to court. There could be but one verdict. Contract had been broken without cause. The Principal was sustained. The board of public instruction was directed to continue paying his salary as if he were working, until he should reach the age of compulsory retirement.

This experience provides food for a great deal of thought on the part of every reader. Those committee members actually believed they had the right to interfere directly, to tear up a public school. They were deeply in earnest. They were stained through the through with the spirit of Democracy. They felt no reverence for representative government -- they felt no loyalty toward elected officials. They had no faith in the integrity of any school official or officer of the law, or in the law itself. They felt no responsibility about obeying the law. They knew no law but their own whim.

They knew that in union there is strength. When they had organized, they had no difficulty in finding a member of the bar who would act in their behalf. They won the victory, too. But the victory they won was not a victory over a school teacher. It was a victory over our country.

They constituted a vicious pressure group, such as exists in some form in every community in the United States -- in the offices of every large business corporation in the country, and in government. Right now, members of Congress are being pressured by the Administration, into supporting measures that both Congress and the Administration know are bad for the American people.

The law enforcement in the United States is breaking down. The "Wets," during the period of Prohibition, told us that enforcing the Constitution would cause disrespect for all law. Exactly the opposite has been our experience. It is so difficult to add an amendment to the Constitution that only twenty-two have been added during the whole course of our history." Before an amendment can be added, it has to have the support of almost all the people.

The Prohibition amendment had that support, or it never could have become a part of the Constitution. Yet close organization of a minority, ceaseless agitation, and brutal violence accomplished the first breach in the fundamental.

*Since this was written, three or four others have been added.

law of the land. Franklin Roosevelt saw his chance. By capitulating to the brass throated, murdering minority, against the Constitution he was later to swear to uphold and support, he added much-needed strength to his campaign.

Since 1932, the United States has disintegrated alarmingly. One reads of what happens everywhere in the newspapers and magazines, but it seems like something happening to some other folks, far away and of no concern to us. It is a fact that no day passes without the murder of teachers in their classrooms, and five sent to hospital in critical condition.

Down deep in his heart, the writer had not believed that such condition could ever touch him, personally. But after the Clear Springs affair, he had to face the truth: consciousness of rectitude, and the proven fact of it, is no protection to the citizen of the United States any more. If the improvement committee had happened to accuse him of murder, and he had been acquitted in open court, the committee would have changed to a lynch-mob, and would have murdered the acquitted man.

The law enforcement officers would have let them do it, too. Not that officers of the law are physically timid. Far from it. But the organization is too much for them. The double cross is too common. "Get the other fellow before he gets you" has been universally substituted for the ideal that once governed our behavior: "Do unto others as you would have them do to you."

CHAPTER 7

The writer labored under a paralyzing apprehension: he believed he had been blacklisted, and would be unable to obtain another teaching position. Throughout the remainder of that year, and through the ensuing his agent was unable to place him in another job.

In the meantime, his wife was teaching another first grade class in another school, form which the teacher had literally fled, as if pursued by the devil himself. She had attempted to launch a class of beginners who knew no law but their own whim -- whose dams had assured them of full support against their teacher -- who were possessed of leather lungs and brass throats. The principal of that school was determined to hold her job until she should reach age seventy, come hell or high water -- if it meant grinding fifty percent of her teaching staff every year. The teacher turnover in her school was notoriously high, even in a state in which all the school systems operate in a climate of fear.

But the two afore-mentioned supervisor friends practiced a little "Rank throwing" at this point. Each of them, at different times, assured the new principal that she was extremely lucky to have Mrs. Porter in her school, and they never ceased praising her knowledge and ability. The old woman was an astute politician -- and although she could never bring herself to the point of giving Mr. Porter any instruction, encouragement, or support, at least she was afraid to give her any opposition, with two supervisors plainly feeling the way they did.

The support of the supervisors broke the regular chain of brutal persecution between the dams and the classroom teacher, for the principal was afraid to attack this particular teacher.

Those little children were tremendously proud of themselves. They had run off the teacher they had started with. At the age of six, they were officially "holy terrors." They began to suffer the deepest chagrin when the first of their number got his bottom paddled until he screamed loudly and long -- then couldn't get the teacher punished because the principal was afraid to initiate the persecution. The dam suddenly ran up against a brick wall, as it were, and was given no encouragement at all. She went to the county office, and was caught by the general supervisor -- one of the friends, who advised her to try a method of helping her little boy get along at school that had never occurred to her: why not encourage the child to obey his teacher, behave himself, and follow his leadership? He assured the woman that there would be no punishment visited upon the teacher, and that cooperation was the only way to save wear and tear on the pupil's hind end. The supervisor told the dam to circulate the tidings among the other dams -- that the new teacher was going to stay, and that nothing could be done about it.

It didn't take long for the idea to imbed itself in their minds, and they quickly decided that Mrs. Porter was a worthy woman and a competent teacher.

The principal, however, was deeply embittered. If an error occurred in any report, she simply said there was an error in it, without locating it -- much less correcting it, as is the decent procedure. She turned it back to the teacher to find. This is one of the commonest injustices resorted to by principals who want to make life hard for any teacher. Also, this principal refused to clarify her orders to the point at which they could be understood by those who worked for her. Her secretarial staff and faculty continually walked into a dense fog of uncertainty. Mistakes galore were bound to occur, with resulting fatigue and despair among the teachers, who were crippling along virtually without leadership.

If she found two teachers talking together, she'd trot up and dismiss one of the, just like the young man mentioned before. Teachers in her school were treated as inmates in a prison.

Although Mrs. Porter was later found to have been suffering with pneumonia, she was required to stand on the play ground, "supervising" the children there, in weather that might have killed her.

The worst condition of the school was the principal's ignoring of the teachers, except when she pussyfooted up to the teachers' doors to listen to what was going on inside the room. If a teacher asked for elaboration or clarification of policy or orders, she was "cut off at the ankles" with frosty sarcasm and brutal insult.

That principal wanted to be known as a stern disciplinarian -- to teachers; and as a friend and protector of every little chee-ild. She stood between the teachers and the children -- her back toward the children, as it were.

No wonder her school was a howling madhouse. The principal conveyed the notion to the children that their teachers were mortal enemies, to be conquered at all hazards, and that they could always depend upon the protection of the principal.

When an adult appeared in the school, the little children looked up at him with eyes narrowed to slits -- little lips lifted in a snarl -- defiance writ large on every little face.

The remaining weeks of the school year wore on, and the year was finished.

When the writer left Azurville, he innocently thought that he had experienced the worst. During the year just closed, he had lived through outrage of a totally different kind, and had encountered conditions that were just as bad, but different.

Before we left Azurville, we both had been invited to teach at Ft. Lauderdale -- a county seat of the highest paying county in the state. The writer's invitation had to be cancelled at the last minute because the principal who invited him was suddenly transferred to another school, in which the faculty was complete. We had, therefore, gone to Ft. Digby.

At the end of the Ft. Digby year, the principal at Ft. Lauderdale who had wanted Mrs. Porter at the beginning was still clamoring for her.

We held a family conference. We decided to divide forces, Mrs. Porter to take advantage of the safety and security offered by a principal who liked her, I to go forth and work anywhere I could be employed.

We would go to Ft. Lauderdale, buy a home, move into it, and establish headquarters there. No more would we be under the necessity of moving at the whim of circumstances.

Of course, it meant living apart. But it seemed the part of wisdom to achieve some measure of security while the opportunity presented itself. We were past fifty, and it was high time to consider the future.

Accordingly, we did just that. The cost of moving was four hundred dollars.

At almost the last day of vacation, the writer was directing to apply for employment at key west, located at a distance of two hundred miles from his home.

Turning his car toward the nation's southernmost city, the writer drove down through the Keys. The route is a world-famous one, consisting of a road that extends across the islands (for the "Keys" are islands); and across bridges connecting the string of islands. One of the bridges is fully seven miles long.

Despite the novelty of the route, the trip seemed long.

Finally, the last bridge loomed before him, and presently the writer found himself on that romantic and storied island.

The people who live there call it Caya Hueso, (pronounced "Hak-yah Way'-so), meaning "Island of Bones." The "Bones" referred to in the name of the island were, or are, of two kinds: those of human victims of shipwreck and murder, during the ascendancy of the Spanish buccaneers, and the timbers of sailing ships wrecked on the coral reefs surrounding the island. Some of those wrecks were caused by storms; others by false lights set up by the natives of the place, on purpose to lure trusting navigators onto the reefs.

While the seas pounded the ships to pieces, land-based pirates rowed out from the island, murdered the crews and passengers, and stole the cargo.

In modern times, one of the finest lighthouses in the world was built there. It is one of the "sights" of the island --visited by tourists continually. There are luxury hotels and swank restaurants located at handy points through this city of thirty thousand population. There are magnificent beaches for swimming and loafing in the sun. Modern and medieval conditions and surroundings are jumbled together there. One of the most famous Catholic schools for girls in the Western hemisphere, dating back to the days of Spanish ascendancy in Latin America, is still going strong.

There are two forts on the island -- one an old Spanish structure, with thick roof and walls made of coquina, the coral rock of which Florida itself is composed -- impregnable to the ordinance of early days; and an American one, both abandoned now, except as museums cr4ammed with the tools, utensils and armament of by-gone days. It is possible to travel backward in time, three hundred years, in five minutes.

Driven into great rocks lying some distance out in the water, beyond the walls of the Spanish fort, are still to be seen, rings to which pirates chained prisoners at low tide. The unfortunate victims felt the tide rising about them; felt the nips of small fish with which those waters abound, as their flesh was slowly eaten off their bones. Thus they suffered, until death by drowning mercifully released them.

One element of the population -- those who own the land and other real property of the islands -- are said to be descendants of the buccaneers who once flourished there. They are known as "Conchs" and their speech, though peculiar, is intelligible.

Another group, of course, is composed of Navy personnel and their families, since there is one of the most powerful naval bases in the world there.

Most of the people are Spanish speaking immigrants from Cuba and other islands of the Caribbean. Key East, despite the presence of the Naval base, is an outpost of Cuba. The culture bears very little resemblance to that of any Anglo Saxon country. The people are clearly aware of all their rights, honors, and prerogatives as American citizens, but acknowledge no responsibility to the United States; nor do they feel any desire to become Americans.

The people have the swarthy, muddy appearance of natives of the Caribbean world, and Spanish is more commonly heard than English.

The schools are large and finely equipped. At the time of which I'm writing there was a new three-million-dollar senior high school. It is magnificent as a physical plant, though run entirely by hoods and thugs of the student body. The switch knife is the final and only authority. By outward appearance, one would suppose it to be a magnificent American school. The football team and other athletic activities are coached by the most competent young men and women who can be found. The "Conquettes" are a body of the most lovely-looking young girls one could wish to see, and they are highly accomplished dancers.

Going back, for a moment, to the Naval base, its presence on the island is largely responsible for the coming, year after year, of a sufficiently large crop of marriageable young women teachers.

That's why teachers can be discarded like last season's garments; the crop of replacements never sinks below the desired number.

But the girls are doomed to disappointment. Practically all the officers of the Navy are married the same day they graduate from the Academy at Annapolis. Far-seeing mammas have seen to that, and have seen to it that the girls are on hand to supply the young mid-shipmen with mates as soon as it is lawful for them to take mates.

The young teachers have not schooled themselves to marrying the enlisted men. So they are literally marooned on an island, with Miami a hundred and sixty-five miles away, and no access to that fabulous center except by automobile or plane. The teacher turnover, for that cause as well as many others, is very rapid.

With such a heterogeneous population, so closely packed into a territory which is definitely and absolutely limited, there is opportunity for infinitely varied social contacts and experiences.

There are churches of various Protestant denominations, besides the strong Catholic establishment. Voodoo is still commonly practiced.

Other primitive customs are to be observed. The writer was aroused on one occasion by a deafening and nerve-shattering racket caused by keening and chanting, and wailing and caterwauling, led by the spirited music of a hastily assembled brass band, playing "Johnnie Get Your Gun." He hurried to the stone wall enclosing his compound, peered over, and beheld a curious sight: scores of Caribbean mixed Indians and negroes, wildly beating drums and wailing.

By George, it was a funeral procession!

Burial, by the way, has to be on top of the ground. Graves can't be dug because of the closeness of water to the surface. So the burial plots look like a field covered by large loaves of bread.

On the writers first visit to the island, he interviewed the director of personnel, and was engaged to teach fifth grade at one of the large elementary schools. When he returned to take charge of the job, the director tried to get him to accept a job in the beautiful new senior high school.

Right at that point, the good luck that is the portion of children, fools, and drunks, interceded in the writer's behalf. Some instinct warned him to be content with his original assignment. As events developed, he had ample reason to be grateful for his choice.

Talking one day with the principal of the high school, the writer steered the conversation to school discipline. The principal squared his shoulders, (he was a Doctor of Education), threw out his chest, loosened his hard blue jaw, nonchalantly flipped the ashes off the end of his cigar, and spoke:

"It is our policy here for administration to keep hands off school discipline. We consider a teacher should be able to handle all trouble that arises in class. If he isn't, he just isn't worth his salt. Down in the front office, we don't care to be annoyed by anything that happens in the classrooms."

The principal and his staff arrived after classes had convened each morning. The principal ducked into his inner office, closed the door, and could not be reached in any way whatsoever. Anybody who tried to see his had to walk over the dead bodies of no less than three interceptionists. The office was criss-crossed by fences with locked gates in them. Security measures were as those at the White House. It is easier to gain access to the President than it is to get face to face with that Doctor of Education.

As subsequent events proved, that principal was a wise man. It was practically impossible to set up a learning-teaching situation in any class. All the practices described earlier were freely indulged in.

But the teachers tried. Most of them were not only new in that school (they always are, because the teacher turnover is terrific) but beginners in the profession. Superbly equipped and highly educated young people, afire with zeal and idealism, waded into the work. Each was presently in the same situation as a football player who is being opposed by both teams: the opponents' and his own. The moment he touched the ball, as it were, he was smashed to the ground and thrown for a loss. The loafers, comedians, and hangers-on simply made fun of their teachers. The teachers didn't know they had come up through the system, growing up like weeds on a manure pile, with no guidance, no direction, and no authority which they were bound to respect.

There are more than the usual causes of this.

A large percentage of these pupils belong to a mongrel race -- a mixture of Spanish and Indian, Spanish and Negro, Negro and Indian, Spanish, Indian, and Negro. Many came from homes in which there was no religion but voodoo. A great many were taught: "Now, honey, we live in the Land of the Free. All my life I've had to obey the white boss-man. But here, no son of a hog tells Grandma's baby what to do. If any white person bothers you, spit between his eyes. Grandma lived in the Island. But you were born in the United States. You are the equal of the best. You have rights, honors, and immunities. In this neighborhood, you outnumber the Whites several to one. The civic offices belong to us, because we vote together, and the white candidates for office are afraid of us. This is the land of freedom and plenty. Let joy be unconfined, and let freedom ring!"

One young teacher whom the writer knew was instructor in Spanish -- a highly refined, beautiful, sweet, up-Town little dame, just out of Vassar. There wasn't a trait of her character that would have brought unpleasantness to her among Anglo-Saxons. In the situation she was in, and among the people she was expected to teach, she was the arch-type of a civilization which is hated and envied, and despised by the people of Latin America. And there she was -- defenseless and helpless, among a pack of pupils, the majority of whom viewed her as the ideal victim of their inherited malice and hate.

The passion to dominate -- to stand forth as master -- is stronger as the incapacity, laziness, and brutality are more prominent, and as the beastial ignorance is more universal. The members of, and workers in, the N.A.A.C.P. don't want equality. They want dominance. They want to occupy the driver's seat, and swing the whip-hand. They can't surpass the white race in ability in the trial of ten thousand years, but by belaboring the Egalitarian dogma, and advancing it as Science (which it is not) they hope to impose their will on the white race by agitation and palavering everywhere from the waiting rooms of bus stations to the forum of the United Nations.

The American people have so firmly committed ourselves to Democracy, that we find ourselves denying obvious fact in every realm of human thought. Six negro colleges in the vicinity of Atlanta are disgorging graduates with the Bachelor's degree, that have fourth grade education.

But they want all the rights, honors, and privileges appertaining to that degree. They don't want to work. They want to wear patent-leather shoes, striped pants, swallow-tail coats, high silk hats and gold-headed canes, and work in the State Department or the United Nations.

The Spanish instructor was the first faculty victim. At the end of each nightmare day, she was in a state of quivering, weeping exhaustion. The soon had to resign.

We will mention only a few of the things that happened during that year:

One young man working there had his car-radio stolen out of his car in broad day-light, while the car was parked in the school parking area. The radio was never recovered, nor were the thieves apprehended. No effort was made in that direction. If the teacher had been a worthy man, in the judgment of the Administration, no pupil would have wanted to steal his radio.

A young woman teacher had trouble with her car. It didn't run right. She hadn't driven far before it stopped altogether. She had it towed in. Examination disclosed the presence of sand in her gas tank, that had ruined the engine and transmission of a new car for which she was obligated to pay three thousand dollars. Fortunately the car was insured.

Another favorite exercise was the slashing of tires.

The girl whose automobile was wrecked never knew who was responsible for the outrage. No effort was made to find out. "The city was not so large that she couldn't have walked to school. Parking in the school parking area was sheer carelessness on her part."

Another young man was knocked down and stomped nearly to death, in a corridor of the school building. He will never enjoy good health again. Nobody was punished. "If he had been a sweet-enough fellow, he would not have been subjected to this punishment, which, if the truth were known, he must have richly deserved."

Still another young man of that faculty happened to be a big bruiser -- a fighting man. Not many teachers, as we have observed before, are fighting men. But this one happened to be.

His mere presence was a challenge to the buckos.

Four of them lingered after the last class one afternoon. They shuffled forward in their best Marlon Brando fashion, trying to surround the teacher. Being a fighting man, the teacher stepped backward to a corner.

One young gangster asked one of the others:

"Wonder what could happen if a teacher got beat up?"

"Oh, I don't think anything would," he replied.

"What do you think we oughta do about this uncertainty?" asked a third.

"We oughta do it, and find out," chimed in a fourth.

Just then the teacher's fist smashed the face of the speaker. In quick succession, two of the others joined the first one on the floor -- one of them with a broken arm. The fourth rushed out of the room, straight to the Principal's office. He had no difficulty getting in to the Great Man. The interceptionists knew better than to stand in his way.

The principal said,

"Come in, son. Sit down. Now what's the matter?"

The boy told him that Mr. McCarthy had told four of them to stay after class -- that he had immediately begun to pound them and cuss them out in abusive language.

The principal snapped open his intercom and spoke:

"Mr. McCarthy, report to me at once," and snapped it shut.

When McCarthy reached the principal's office he was contemptuously ordered to "have a seat" in the waiting room. When he had cooled his heels for half an hour, the interceptionist graciously informed him,

"Doctor McBee will see you, now."

When he entered the presence of the Great Man, McBee said,

"McCarthy, I have just had the full, sorry story of your shocking, inexcusable behavior. No-no-no-no-no! don't try to justify it. The only honorable thing you can do. is resign. We can't tolerate this sort of thing. Just resign."

Thus ended another promising teaching career, before it had fairly started.

During succeeding days, the boy with the arm was a great hero. He had to miss one season of football, but he honors heaped upon him more than compensated him for that loss. His fame and popularity grew until he was able to get elected President of the Student Council.

One more instance will suffice to show how that school operated:

There was one young man on the faculty who was more richly endowed with the qualities associated with the high class teacher than any other whom it has been the privilege of the writer to meet, in a long time.

He was highly educated, and widely traveled. His development of mind, spirit, and ability in many directions had never been interrupted from his childhood. He had enjoyed every opportunity that good birth, distinguished ancestry, wealth and health could provide; and he had made the most of it. He was already a leader in the educational world by the time he had been a part of it but a few months. He was growing by leaps and bounds. His name and picture appeared frequently in the newspapers. He was often quoted in educational journals. He had a pleasing personality. Everybody liked him. He lasted into his second year. Then the blow fell. The whispering campaign momentum:

"Have you heard?"

"What?"

"They say Mr. Morgan is a homosexual!"

"No! Well, what do you think of that? Who would ever have suspected Morgan? Tch, tch, tch, tch, tch! It just goes to show!"

"Well, we can't have a man like that in our high school. The dirty bastard oughta be tarred and feathered. We ought to protest to the school board!"

"Aw, what's the use? He's in too solid to be pried loose."

"By God, the school board knows who put them in office. Old Man McCready is making a fortune, selling milk to the schools. If he lost his membership on the board, his business would be ruined, and well does he know it!"

When the "Committee of Citizens for Purity and Honesty" appeared before the board, and delivered their sorry message, the honest old gentlemen of the board were non-plussed.

"No! You don't mean to stand there and accuse Morgan? This is foul slander! You'll all be sent to the penitentiary for slander. This is outrageous!"

The Committee members slunk out. But the whispering continued. Pretty soon Morgan was stared at and sniggered at wherever he went. The gossip was sure to reach him finally.

At length the school board called him in.

"Son," began the old president, "you must have heard the stuff that's going around about you. All of us know it's a lie. But it has reached everybody in town by now. You can surely understand that your usefulness as a school man is ended. For your own sake, and for the sake of the schools, you ought to resign."

The stunned young fellow had already thought it over, and he agreed with them. He resigned.

Thus ended still another grand teaching career, before it had fairly started. Who could look for the needle in the haystack? Who could discover the instigator of that campaign?

No one, man or woman, who takes a teaching position in that town, is safe from this treatment. It goes to show the depth to which American society can fall, when our American-Christian heritage is not known and shared. How many American citizens under twenty today are familiar with the Commandment: "Thou shalt not bear false witness", or any other of the ten? There are a great many. But there are too many who are not familiar with them.

The writer duly reported to his principal - a man almost if not quite, young enough to be his son. Mention of that circumstance is made here because it figures in the story later.

The principal called the writer into his office and launched into the conference. He said,

"Mr. Porter, we're trying something new this year. you know this is a large school, having several sections each of grades one through five. Our new experiment is selecting the chief offenders against discipline out of all fourth grade sections, who also happen to have the lowest I.W. ratings, and who happen also to be Spanish speaking boys. Only two of the group speak English also.

"Now, we are lumping these incorrigible morons into one group, and we're turning them over to you because, well, er, ah -- because you are a man."

Wasn't that a glorious prospect? Wasn't that a bright and shining opportunity to "show stuff," as the coaches phrase it?

I assembled the boys' records. Not one of them had an I.Q. of eighty. Only two were as high as seventy-eight. Most of them were in the sixties; and one, whom I had to deal with during thirty of the thirty-six weeks of that school year, had an I.Q. of fifty-four. That one was built like a monkey, moved like a monkey, thought like a monkey, acted like a monkey, and had the temperament of a homicidal maniac. He was deeply stained by Democracy. "By God, he was 'as good as' any white son-of-a-bitch that ever lived."

I thought it might be an excellent idea to approach those problems as much as possible in their own language. My Spanish was something out of the far-off past -- halting and very slow. However, by getting my books around me, and first writing out the new lesson presentations, I was able to translate the bare presentations into Spanish. I couldn't hope to explain or elaborate or illustrate or particularize in Spanish, but just the presentation would help greatly, I felt, and I believe it did. It helped the boys to learn English, and it kept them from talking about their teachers in their own language. They knew my Spanish couldn't compare with theirs, but they could not be certain of just how much I didn't know. This uncertainty kept them within reasonable bounds.

With the help of the visiting teacher, I worked out a modus operandi that succeeded fairly well. It featured lots of drawing, coloring, and construction work. It served to keep the boys busy -- within the limits of the attention span nature had given them.

Now, the writer had boned up on Latin culture. He knew, for instance, that you can't slap or spank a Latin. It kills his soul. It is a punishment not to be visited upon a human, no matter what he does to deserve it. If corporal punishment of any kind is visited upon him, honor requires the murder of the punisher.

A case in point is this Che Guevara, who is now a highly exalted office holder in the Red government of Cuba. In his youth he was grossly insulted by an American sailor who was just drunk enough to be ornery. From that day to this, Guevara has wanted to kill all the Americans in the world. If he could deliver America to Russian slavery, he would unhesitatingly do so, to avenge himself upon that one turd-head American sailor.

The writer was familiar with the social organization and family life of these people. When a Latin man gets married, he takes his wife's name, just as women take their husbands' name in our society. Family descent is traced through the female line; consequently, a Latin clan is a matriarchy -- headed by the "little grandmother."

The "little grandmothers' of that city were deeply stained by Democracy -- in so far as knowledge of the rights, honors, and privileges of American citizenship are concerned. As to responsibilities -- there aren't any. "Just see to it that the God-damned Americans don't push you around, honey."

Our country has become a polyglot boarding house for all the rag-tag and bob-tail of the world. They immigrate to our country, gravitate to the company of the others of their national origin and cultural background, keep up the beliefs, superstitutions, languages, and associations and frames of thought and systems of belief, of the countries from whence they came. And hate the builders and maintainers of this country with a purple passion, and give comfort and support to anybody who has a plan to overthrow it.

Of course there are immigrants who come to us in good faith. They assimilate themselves to us by marrying among us, learning our languages, familiarizing themselves with our institutions, and obeying our laws. They try to throw off the old country and try their best to become Americans in spirit and in truth.

But these last are greatly in the minority. Any American who opposes having his country made a polyglot boarding house, or who would like to see immigrants make some effort to assimilate themselves to us and become Americans themselves, is a bigot -- a narrow, unworthy person.

Having become familiar with the extreme reluctance of school administrations to vex themselves with school discipline, the writer silently resolved to say nothing to the principal, no matter what happened in there. But the principal specifically ordered him to bring to the office those who fought.

The writer obeyed that directive, as he has always carried out his principals' directives, in good faith and to the best of his ability.

As for the rest, the writer had just been assailed by an organized mob a few months before, for paddling recalcitrants. The experience tended to make him a little cynical about school discipline. If no one else cared about it, why should a teacher get himself blamed for maintaining it to the point of levying corporal punishment?

No one who hasn't had the experience of being responsible for the program of a class, and had a class of morons, can quite understand what the teacher is up against. Exhaustive experiments have shown that children with I.Q.'s much under 90 are well-nigh completely unable to profit by the regular offering of instruction in the public schools. Yet the administrators and supervisors, knowing this, will ride the life of a teacher until it has been made nearly worthless as possible, because children down in the sixties, seventies, and eighties are not quietly and interestedly and successfully eating up the course of study which has been devised for normal children.

Pupils of low intelligence have an attention span which is much shorter than that of a normal child. The attention span of the average adult is much shorter than is popularly supposed. Any sermon which is longer than twenty minutes falls upon deaf ears.

Children learn by doing. Their ability to take directions determines their ability to do. When you have children who can't fix their attention upon any subject long enough to hear the directions through, you've confronted with real difficulty, even though your program has been especially tailored to fit their level of intelligence. Add to that, the language barrier, and you have a real problem on your hands.

That class should have been given to a teacher whose Spanish was easy and fluent. We had such teachers in the faculty, but the Great Educator in charge gave it to me "because I am a man."

Right there is another difficulty in dealing with Latins: they consider taking orders from a man as dishonorable and degrading. Throughout Latin America, it is almost impossible to get a building project completed. There are so many excuses to quit work that it takes forever and a day to finish a building. Workers will not take direction. That's why your windows can't be opened, nor your doors locked. That's why your plumbing won't work. A Latin who can show you a great many appliances is happy enough just to have them. He is apparently happiest when he announces that they have fallen apart. He is perfectly satisfied to leave everything in that condition.

The Great Executive must have known these people, surely, for he had been principal of that school for eight years. Of course, his Latin element in the whole school was not all he had: indeed, they were in the minority, considering the whole school. But there were enough of them to affect the program seriously.

Nor does the writer wish to imply that all Latins are alike, or that all are indolent and lackadaisical. We had a little Cuban girl who came to us in the Fall, without a word of English. When she had been with us seven months, her english was rapid, fluent, flawless, and spoken without a trace of Latin accent. She had taken instruction by the medium of English, and had mastered the subject matter of the fifth grade curriclm with a straight A average.

When your pupils' intelligence average around seventy, they don't have to be Latins to cause you plenty of grief and frustration. It helps, though.

Well, we crippled along for three months. The teacher was determined to have no run-ins with his little boys. One morning, one of his two English-speaking kids said:

"Hey! I'm being gypped! I paid such and such an amount, and you've given me only so many lunch tickets."

His teacher said:

"Come up and look at the record."

The boy came, and the teacher explained every figure of it to him. The boy only got more and more angry. He called his teacher every name he could think of. But his teacher was determined to resist being drawn into a fuss, or badgered into punishing one of those pupils. He said,

"Let's go down to the Principal's office. Perhaps he can explain this to your satisfaction."

So we went down. The boy pretended to be satisfied with the explanation he received, but he continued to regard his teacher as a cheat.

This same boy came to be known to all the teachers as "the champ," because he was often provoking a fight with some other child. If he couldn't promote a fight with some little boy in his own school, he would wait until the junior high pupils from down the street came by, and attack one of them. He was destined, later in the year, to attain great notoriety, have much fun, achieve great happiness, and chalk up brilliant success in bringing about the ruin of one of the teachers -- not the writer.

The administration in that school was truly admirable.

The schedule was perfect. Administration of materials and supplies was flawless. Extra curricular activities were woven into the program so neatly that we experienced interruption of the schedule hardly at all. The librarian, who, incidently, was so unfairly and unjustly treated, that she could not, in honor, remain to complete the term, was a young lady of extraordinary ability. She ran, not only the library service, but the audio-visual program as well, and conducted the service perfectly.

Before I go into that, however, I want to tell of the shake-up and redistribution of pupils that was effected at the end of the third month. The county officials ran a series of intelligence and achievement tests, and grouped the children according to the results. Of course, the county authorities broke up my group of special pupils. I drew a class of normal pupils, except that they were much higher in intelligence than average. From then on out, as far as my pupils were concerned, my year at Key East was one of the happiest and most rewarding of my experience.

To get back to the Audio-visual program: that young lady ran films that coincided perfectly with the other material we were studying - at the precise time we were studying it. All instructional activities and materials were coordinated with such perfection that nothing in that area was left to desire.

The plant was magnificent, except that no arrangement had been made to heat the building. That winter was the coldest in the history of the town. We were lucky in our room, for our windows were flooded by the morning sun. Our room was perfectly comfortable all day, because of that blessed morning sun.

The school was equipped with plenty of the best and most up-to-date teaching aids available, and the administration of them was perfect.

Worthy of special mention is the kitchen, the eating space, and the absolute perfection of the food served. The "hot lunch" of that school was so perfectly planned that I was able to eat it all year without gaining a pound in weight. It was tasty, attractive, satisfying, and non-fattening. I can't say the same for any other school lunch I've had experience with-even those lunch programs I ran myself.

I've a notion that our principal that year was a highly frustrated man. Perhaps he might have become as good a personnel director as he was an administrator, if he had been given the chance - though he pulled some tricks that were different from any the writer had seen up to that time, and more scabrous. Anyhow, his personnel management stank to Heaven.

And no principal will recommend any teacher whom he has wronged, and provoked into leaving his employ.

No doubt this policy will result in eliminating a great many qualified, experienced teachers from the service. Certainly, it contributed greatly to the one hundred seventy thousand shortage in the nation. This practice is national in scope. Not only is it practiced to eliminate teachers already qualified. It operates to keep competent young people from choosing the profession at all. For who wants to spend those years, that money and effort, to get into a life-work in which they must serve in one position for a whole life career, or be banished from it at the caprice of a principal? If prospective teachers had any idea what they are letting themselves in for, the supply of young teachers would be abruptly cut off, and the public schools would soon fizzle out entirely.

School administrators are deliberately misrepresenting the opportunities, wage scales, and intangible rewards of teaching. None of us ever become teachers because of money-madness, goodness knows. But now even the intangible rewards, spiritually discovered by young people inspired by the missionary spirit, have been choked out. But more about that later.

A circumstance obtained in that school that did much to cripple it. The head secretary was the widowed daughter-in-law of the school board president, and the apple of his eye. Some years before, she had begun gradually to take over ownership of that school, lock, stock, and barrel. She outranked the teachers and everybody else there. In fact, the teachers were under the authority of everybody. Positively nobody was there that did not outrank the teachers, even the few teachers who were sacred cows. the sacred cows outranked all the other teachers, but were themselves under the authority of the office stenographers (a company of high school graduates), the cooks, the scullery maids, and bus drivers, and the janitors.

The writer, up to that time, had never thought it possible that people could be so jealous of their petty authority. The school was highly organized. Perhaps its marvelous efficiency is attributable to that fact. But it must have caused a lot of grief to the principal.

At the head of the office staff (and the school), though carrying no responsibility, was the Daughter-in-law. There was a head-janitor, a head cook, a head scullery maid, a head but driver, a head playground supervisor, and three teachers of long service and strong political connections, who arrogated unto themselves the right to weigh the other teachers in the balance and find them wanting. The teachers were subject to all the other adults in the school, and also to the children. The children were not subject to anybody.

If a small fire had broken out, and somebody had shouted "Teach me that fire extinguisher," the auditor would just look to see whether the speaker had sufficient rank to ask her for a fire extinguisher. If she found he did have, after careful scrutiny and clear consideration, she'd reach him the fire extinguisher. If she decided that he lacked the proper rank, she'd leave the fire creeping toward the store of high explosives, and run to report to Big Daddy that that odious Jones, or whatever his name might be, had attempted to push her around, and she demands that he be called in and put in his place.

Big Daddy spent a lot of time putting people in their places, who had inadvertently offended the authority of someone of straw boss rank. As the teachers were subject to all others, and as the orders of the straw-bosses.

A thousand pardons! We mean custodial engineers! An engineer, of course, outranks a teacher, anywhere, and in Latin societies, anybody who pushes a wheelbarrow is an Engineer. sometimes were in conflict, the teachers were bound to find themselves in the wrong, no matter how the ball bounced.

And every time a teacher was "Reported", a black mark was added to his record. Pretty soon, he'd have enough demerits to amount to insubordination. It is very difficult to be satisfactorily subordinate to so many bosses, including the children. A teacher is bound to get in trouble sometimes with the 3rd assistant cook if he obeys the boss scullery maid to the letter.

The custodial engineers were hard task-masters, too. They drew a rigid line at the limit of things they'd do. If such and such tings were on the floor, the teacher had to do the cleaning. If he didn't clean neatly, he was reported to Big Daddy and admonished to do better in the future.

It is astonishing that children in a school should have the feeling that their teachers are their enemies, and the principal is their friend and protector. Earlier, we had the feeling that all grown folks were our superiors in knowledge, wisdom, and know-how; we felt that the grown folks laid down the law, and it was our duty to obey the law. If we conducted ourselves in harmony with our grown folks in charge, we felt that we had social approval, that we had done right, that we merited the best and highest and most satisfying rewards of life. In a word, we felt secure.

One of the loudest moans that go up from the young people of today is:

"I feel abandoned. I have no security. I am afraid of life."

No wonder children feel insecure! They come up through their first six years of life, seeing their parents acting to thwart, deceive, and out-do each other. They go on into school and quickly discover that the big person up front has to jump and humbly obey the quiet, deadly menacing voice that issues from the boss up on the wall.

It doesn't take long to find out that the owner of that voice is the source of all authority in the school. Pretty soon one or more of them witnesses the complete humiliation and depredation of their teacher. Principals snap at, and cross-question any teacher they talk to,l and ignore any question the teacher asks. Little children have long since learned to feel moods long before they have the vocabulary to name or describe them. In a situation in which their teacher is afraid - in which he has no respect shown him by the other grown folks - in a society in which he has no status or security whatever - a little child soon learns to ignore and down-grade that teacher to a lower status than his fellow pupils occupy. A child feels the prevailing mood very quickly, and responds to it readily.

In most schools, the teachers draw together into small groups of bosom buddies, and admire and respect each other, the members of their little groups. All of which is natural and to the good, if they didn't go ahead and make their association offensive as well as defensive.

In this particular school, it didn't take the Sacred Cows long to screen and judge the new teachers. Twenty-five of the thirty-five teachers there, were new. There was one other man besides the writer there that year. One sacred cow boldly announced one morning, in the teachers' lounge:

"A man has no place in an elementary school!"

The writer did not intend to accept condemnation and banishment right off the bat and by heavenly decree that had no connections with Heaven.

"How do you know he hasn't, Mrs. Flemming, he asked. "You seem to be at odds with some mighty prominent philosophers. It has been said by competent authorities, that children are grateful for the mere sound of a man's voice in a school; that they are unnerved by feminine voices all day and every day; that boys need the leadership of men; that there comes a time in the course of a boy's development, that he needs the example of a man to follow; that a child needs the influence and inspiration that only a man can supply. Anyhow, in this school, Mr. Grant and I were engaged to teach, and I believe he will agree with when I say that we feel as welcome and as necessary here as any woman on the faculty. I feel that your statement is dogmatic in the highest degree, without sanction in educational philosophy, nor is it backed by experience."

Right then the writer made himself an enemy who continued to claw at him throughout the year. She loved to issue orders to the other teachers, transmitting them from the principal. The writer didn't know it at the time, but he found out that she liked to snap out the orders without bothering to say they emanated from the principal.

The first part of her campaign consisted in organizing the silent treatment for the two men:

"We pay no attention to them, honey!" she'd say, with her face drawn into a grimace such as it would show on biting unexpectedly into a dill pickle. And any new teacher who accorded human recognition to either of the men was quickly made to feel the full weight of the Sacred Cow's displeasure.

Mention has already been made of peoples' bent toward conforming to the dictates of a loud-mouthed, militant, brutally assertive group. It is seen continually in the submission of eighty-five to ninety percent of the membership of a student body, to the assumed authority of the hood and thug element among them. So each new teacher struck out to feather her own next by attracting no adverse criticism from the Sacred Cows. The men quickly became the invisible, inaudible people around them.

It didn't help the school any at all. The children soon felt that they owed nothing to Nr. Porter, Mr. Grant, or any of the new teachers. If one of tem offended a pupil, he'd take out of the room like a bat from the Carlsbad Caverns, on his way to Big Daddy's office, to lodge a complaint against his teacher.

Instantly, the quiet voice, tinged with deadly venom, would come out of the box on the wall:

"Mr. Grant, report to me at once!"

The children had all seen one of their numver dodge out of the room. They all heard the voice from the box. They all saw the teacher trudge dejectedly to the front office, to receive his bully ragging in the shape of a nerciless grilling, and his brow-beating, in the shape of stern admonition.

Children, like the whole race of humanity,. admire and back a winner. The brow-beaten and bullied have no status with anybody, now especially with children.

The writer is a hard man to bullyrag and browbeat. He has been in the business too long, and knows it too well, to be impressed by people who try to misuse him.

One morning, during the first week of the term, "the champ" sailed into another child with customery ferocity. The writer took him by the arm and the seat of the pants, pulled him off the other boy, and made him take his seat. Another little boy raced to the principal. In less time than it takes to tell it, the principal's voice came from the box:

"Mr. Porter!"

"Will you report to me right away?"

"No, Sir. It will be ten-thirty before I can see you. If you will come to the cafeteria at ten-thirty, I can see you; otherwise, not until three-thirty this afternoon."

"Very well. See you at three-thirty."

Those little boys looked at me with respect. That one reply was sufficient to keep them from going entirely berserk during the three months they were there. They didn't settle down and behave entirely like humans should, but they felt that somewhere there was a limit beyond which they had better not venture. They didn't know just there it lay. They probed. But there was caution in their probing.

At three-thirty the writer met the principal in his office. The Great Man didn't attempt a grilling on the subject of what the self-appointed messenger of the morning had reported. He smiled sheepishly, and began:

"Mr. Porter, I know you're much older than I. But I do feel that you would do better to not call me "Son." To patronize the principal, especially in the presence of the children, makes for poor discipline."

The old teacher recognized a well-known gambit: "Make the teacher apologize for a fault he has not been guilty of; put him unfairly in the wrong. Get him off balance with a baldly-baseless accusation. When he indignantly denies it and attempts to defend himself, cloud up and rain on him until he's half drowned. Threaten him with dismissal, and send him out quivering with rage and fury, white and shaken. If the recipient of the treatment is a woman, send her fourth in tears. Whom the Gods destroy, they first make mad. We gods in the school offices would do well to make a teacher mad before destroying him. He is so much easier to handle, mad."

The old teacher smiled gently at the young principal.

"Mr. Madison, I'll bet I know why you believe I call you "Son." You know in my part of the country, we "Sir" all males whom we address. I "Sir" you when I address you, but the say I pronounce it, it comes out very much like "Son", especially over the intercom. I assure you that I have not thought of you in that relationship, and I'm going to give you a letter of explanation -- just as I have explained the error to you. Rest assured I shall not "Sir" you again. If you'll excuse me, I must meet an engagement."

The other new teachers didn't get the silent treatment from others of their number -- only from the Sacred Cows. But if one of them gave any measure of social recognition, seen in P.T.A. meetings, to one of the men, she was punished even by the other new members, so dreaded were the Sacred Cows.

We men were very much on our dignity, and paid off our persecutors in kind. It was lucky there were two of us to support each other. It made life easier for us.

Mention has already been made, of the relief that came to the writer as the result of the shake-up at the end of the third month. There was a class who were far above average, so that association with them was a pleasure.

The writer had no intention of losing face with his pupils by giving to any other teacher the slightest chance of insulting him, so he was careful to refrain from so much as a "good morning," to anybody, unless he was addressed first.

The precaution paid off. The teacher had good relations with his pupils. Being without friendship, except with one other grown person in the school, it was only natural that he should respond to any gesture of friendship, respect, or affection that might be offered by one of his fifth grade pupils.

Each day, each teacher lined up his class and led them out of the building, across the street separating the school from the two clocks of play-space provided for the pupils (and which was kept roped off from traffic), for a half hour of play or exercise.

After the period was ended, we lined up and walked back to the building, and to our room. Nearly every day, some little boy or girl would slip his or her hand into mine, and walk with me. Sometimes I'd have a little boy on each side - sometimes a little girl on each side; sometimes a little girl on one side and a little boy on the other.

Imagine my surprise one afternoon, when, on entering the lounge, I was directly addressed by a sacred cow!

"Mr. Porter", she said, "we have noticed something in your conduct which we look upon with grave concern, not to say suspicion."

"Well, Mr. Flemming, what is this thing in my conduct which you look upon with grave concern, not to say suspicion? I didn't know you or any of your friends were able to see me at all - much less observe my conduct. Do you care to elaborate?"

"It is this matter of leading your pupils by the hand, from the play-field to the building."

Tightening her lips against her teeth, she went on:

"It certainly looks bad. It just looks mighty suspicious!"

"Mrs. Flemming, just exactly what is it you suspect? I've noticed that the natives of this town suspect every male above the age of twelve of being a cockster, and every female over the age of twelve of being a whore. Is that what you suspect? If so, come right out and say so - then the next move will be mine. I'll keep you locked up for the rest of your life.

If you hadn't been so intent upon isolating me socially, perhaps I'd have less incentive to enjoy the friendship of the children. Besides, from all I've learned, friendship between children and their teacher is conducive to easy teaching for the teacher and rapid, successful learning for the pupils.

Now, unless you have something pleasant to say to me, I'd appreciate it if, so far as I'm concerned, you would maintain your customary silence."

Soon after that encounter, it was necessary to divide my class one afternoon. About half my pupils were summoned into the auditorium to take part in a program, while the other half remained in the classroom. I believed it was more prudent to stay in the room than to go to the auditorium.

Mrs. flemming dropped by, and curtly ordered me to go to the auditorium. I replied.

"Madam, I happen to be in charge of this class. Kindly attend to your own business, and I'll attend to mine."

Two minutes later, I was summoned to the office.

I saw Mrs. Flemming standing at the principal's desk - a mountain of flesh, quivering with rage. As I entered, she stalked out through another door.

"Mr. Porter," began the principal, "when I send out orders, I'd like to have them obeyed."

"Mr. Madison, when I receive orders from you, it is my great pleasure to carry them out instantly. Is there some trouble, somewhere?"

"Take my direction that all teachers should accompany their groups to the auditorium just now. You indignantly refused to do so."

"Ah! I understand now. You must have transmitted that order through Mrs. Flemming! She just didn't bother to mention that it was your order. If she had, You would have had instant compliance.

I can't help but believe that a messenger should transmit the principal's orders <u>as</u> the principal's orders - not as her own."

"There's another matter that I'd like to mention," intoned the young fellow, abruptly abandoning the matter under discussion. That is another gambit much favored by great school executives: abruptly change ground to another subject, leaving the one under discussion hanging in the air. It is intolerably insulting, and leaves the teacher desiring to slap the principal's face, then thrash the tar out of him.

"This matter of hugging and kissing the children," he went on.

So the kids' slipping their hands in mine, during the walk from the play-ground, had expended into hugging and kissing!

I laughed merrily. Suddenly breaking it off, I replied:

"No kissing, Mr. Madison. But when a child comes to me with a boo or a paper, I put my arm around the child just as instinctively as I breathe. I never knew a teacher who didn't. I don't know any now who don't. but no kissing at all, Mr. Madison. You may bank on it!"

"Well," sighed the Great Man, clearly much relieved, "I'm very glad to hear that. I told my informant that she must be mistaken, or exaggerating. I was morally certain there had been no kissing."

"Your purity of heart does you credit, Mr. Madison, and in this instance, it is roundly justified. I'd better get to the auditorium now. See you around."

There was a difficulty toward the end of the first six weeks period of that year, that vexed my sorely. It had to do with the grades that should go on the report cards. As my group was a most unusual one, in that they were totally unable to profit by the school's regular curriculum, I had had to devise, with the help of one of the supervisors, an entirely different program to meet their needs. Devising some method of evaluation was the problem.

I had attempted to take the matter up with the principal on several occasions, but each attempt had failed. The telephone claimed his attention, or I was interrupted by the secretaries on other matters, or other teachers butted in.

One evening, at the bowling alley, the director of personnel asked me "how I was coming." As we were good friends, I mentioned my uncertainty in the matter of evaluation. He replied that "certainly a fellow needs to thrash it out with the principal."

"But, Mr. Benny," I said, "Mr. Madison is so busy I can't get in to him."

And I described the efforts I had made.

"Why don't you make a dinner conference of it some evening? Invite Mr. and Mrs. Madison and the supervisor who has worked with you, and get at it that way? No time will be lost. You can decide together what to do, and a nice social occasion can be enjoyed by all concerned."

"Well, I'd like to. But I don't believe any principal would be the guest of any teacher at dinner. I'm afraid he'd think I was trying to get too close - trying to put him under social obligation to me. You're new in this state yourself, Mr. Benny. You haven't noticed yet what a great gulf exists between principals and teachers."

"Oh, come now! Surely you must be mistaken about that. Surely to goodness a principal wouldn't take that attitude toward a teacher with a problem! You just trust my instinct on this! It will surely work out!"

"Well, Mr. Benny, you seem confident. I don't believe the plan will work, but I'll try."

The next day I dropped into the office and told Madison,

"Mr. Madison, I'd like mighty well to have a conference with you on this evaluation problem."

"Mr. Porter, you'll have to excuse me now. In a few minutes I must attend a meeting at the county office."

"I know you're snowed under, Mr. Madison. I'm going to propose a dinner conference, at the suggestion of Mr. Benny. That way, no time will be lost. He suggested that you, Mrs. Madison, Miss Glover and I, discuss this thing at dinner some evening soon.

May I make so bold as to suggest it? Would this coming Tuesday at 7 o'clock, at Luigi's, be a good time and place?"

"Why, Mr. Porter, I think the idea is excellent. I think Tuesday would be satisfactory."

"Very well, Mr. Madison, we have an engagement. I'll see you or call you Tuesday afternoon, to remind you."

I reserved a table for four at Luigi's for Tuesday evening. Miss Glover had already accepted my invitation.

Tuesday afternoon I dropped by the principal's office and said to him,

"Don't forget our dinner engagement tonight, Mr. Madison. Luigi's, seven o'clock."

"Oh, Porter, dog-gone it, I had intended to tell you; at the last minute, Mrs. Madison found she had to attend a supervisor's meeting. She had to fly up to Tallahassee this morning. She'll be out of town until late tonight. We'll have to postpone our get-together."

I said,

"How about Thursday night?" The time was getting short. Something had to be done, or I would have to act by myself in the evaluation matter.

"I believe that will be all right. We'll say Thursday at seven."

I changed the arrangements, and supposed the matter was settled. Silly boy!

The time arrived. So did Miss Glover and I. But no Madisons. We waited forty-five minutes. Still no Madisons.

I called Madison on the phone.

"Oh my soul and body!" exclaimed the Great Man. I forgot to mention this to Mrs. Madison, slick as a whistle! She's gone to the movies, and I'm staying with the children! I can't possibly come! Tell you what. I'll drop in about the time you finish dinner, and we can talk some then."

"All right, Mr. Madison. We'll see you directly."

164

Rejoining Miss Glover, I told her of what had happened. We dined, and got better acquainted than all our working together had allowed us to do. We discussed educational philosophy underlying the special program we had devised for my class, and the methods I was pursuing.

Toward the tag-end of dinner, about the time dessert and coffee came, Madison dropped in. He could stay only a moment. He had his children out in the car, and he must rush madly home and put them to bed.

"Tell you what, you two drop by my house, from here, and we'll talk them."

He strode away, and we finished dinner. He wouldn't even stay for coffee - refused to sit down with us.

Soon after dinner, Miss Glover and I drove over to Madison's house - in separate cars, as each would need his own, later in the evening.

He opened the door, and exclaimed, cordially,

"Come in, Miss Glover. Mrs. Madison hasn't returned from the movies yet. Make yourself at home."

He didn't speak to me at all, or include me in his invitation to enter. I went in anyhow. Presently I ventured to mention the subject uppermost in my interest - the evaluation problem.

He carelessly waved it aside, without looking at me. He hadn't addressed me or looked at me since I had entered the house. I felt like the Invisible Man.

"We'll get to that some other time."

I say I wasn't going to get any help, and presently asked to be excused.

"Sure, Porter, sure," he said, not looking at me." "See you tomorrow."

I took leave of Miss Glover, and left.

The next morning, I appeared in the Great Man's office, but didn't get to say anything.

"Porter, I'm sorry. I just can't see you now. Just go ahead and make up your cards as you think they should be."

All right. But I still believed he should be consulted. Nevertheless, I'd do my best. I made out the report cards.

According to custom and established procedure, I left them at the principal's office for inspection, before they were handed to the children.

That day was a most exhausting one. I was positively limber when three-thirty rolled around. The cards were to be distributed the next day.

Classes were dismissed at two-thirty, but the teachers had to remain at school until three-thirty, "in case any parent suddenly developed an urge toward a conference."

I was just leaving when the box on the wall buzzed, and Madison's voice came:

"Mr. Porter, will you stop by on your way out?"

"Yes," I said. "See you presently."

When I entered the office, he carefully closed the door.

"Mr. Porter, these cards you left this morning just won't do at all! The grades are entirely too high!"

How did he know they were too high? What did he know about the standards I had graded by? What did he know about the philosophy according to which I had set up that standard?

I thought, but didn't say, "Oh! Bur-ruh-ther!" He went on:

"Now, I believe if all these grades were lowered one letter, they would present a truer picture. Suppose you just use my desk and write a new set of cards? We wouldn't want to have them messed up with alteration, would we?"

Of course, every instinct of my soul, but one, clamored for positive action. I wanted to give him the cussin' he so richly deserved, and if he answered back, give him a thrashing he'd remember to his dying day.

I had seen Miss Glover the afternoon following the encounter at Madison's house. I said,

"By the way, Miss Glover, do you remember the reason we had to postpone that dinner conference of ours? Mrs. Madison had to fly to Tallahassee for a supervisor's conference. I've been thinking: you have exactly the same kind of job as hers, and have exactly the same rank. Why didn't you fly to Tallahassee that day?"

"Phooey. She never want to Tallahassee. She didn't attend the movies last night, either. You had hardly left the house when she appeared from the back bedroom, and made one of the company the rest of the evening. This is a series of the meanest tricks I've ever seen pulled!"

Every instinct but one, clamoring -- the instinct of self-preservation. I had experienced trouble the year before. If I resented the dish that had been served to me during the last few days, openly, it would be curtains for me.

So I meekly sat at the principal's desk, worn out as I was, and worked until dark. I went to supper then, and it took 'way into the night to finish the job.

The Key East chapter wouldn't be complete without mention of the social side of life in that historic town.

I'll never forget the happy home-life-away-from home that was mine, that year. Of course, I would rather have been at my own home with my wife and my old invalid mother. But I would get home not oftener than every-other week end.

A circumstance arose in connection with those journeys to Fort Lauderdale: I explained my situation to Mr. Madison at the beginning of the first semester. To drive home took four and a half hours, necessitating a trip through Miami traffic, as it did. I asked permission to leave the school, every second Friday evening, as soon as the pupils were dismissed.

Madison gave permission, and on several Friday afternoons, I pulled out soon after two-thirty.

One Friday afternoon, as Grant told me later, Mrs. Flemming looked around the lounge and asked,

"Where is Mr. Porter? I walked by his room, and he isn't there either. Where could he be?"

Grant replied that likely I was approaching Marathon, fifty miles up the Keys road, by then, and told her why Madison had given mepermission to leave as soon as school was out.

Mrs. Flemming blew her top. "I don't see why he should enjoy special privileges around here. The rest of us have to stay. He's no better than we are. I'm going to raise hell 'til this foolishness is stopped!"

The others agreed that it was an outrage that one of their number should be allowed to begin a long journey an hour ahead of quitting time. This attitude among themselves is characteristic of societies which are repressed or ill-used. A Communist, believing in the Slave State, will denounce his own mother to the Peoples' Democratic Republic, and derive a feeling of righteousness from it. Teachers are only one group in our society, but they will denounce one of their number go higher authority at every opportunity, in the hope of improving their relations with administration. It is the writer's belief that teachers will not be treated as American citizens until we begin to throw off the slave psychology that besets us at present.

Getting back to life as it was lived between school dismissal time and bed time, I'll have to say that it was highly satisfactory.

When I inquired at the school office concerning the possibility of renting a room in some home as near my work as possible, I was given the name of Colonel Albert Pierce, whose lovely home was located only three blocks from the school. I had noticed the place - had admired it as the ideal location for me, but hadn't thought it possible that the people might take a paying guest.

The fact is, that colonel Pierce had only recently recovered, in some degree, from his first stroke. His health was poor; and inasmuch as he and his wife were elderly people, and living in that great house alone, they believed they would feel safer if they had a younger man to live with them. So Mrs. Pierce had asked the director of personnel to send them a teacher who needed a home. The director advised me to apply, and I did. I was accepted.

I was given a lovely room and private bath. The room was decorated in five shades of brown - a décor that struck me at once as the work of an interior decorator of unusual ability. Later in the year, after the elderly couple and I had become friends, it was hardly a surprise to me that Mrs. Pierce was, indeed, an artist of the first magnitude - that she had designed the stage settings for such famous showmen as Ziegfeld and the Schuberts.

The whole house was as beautiful as my room - furnished in excellent taste throughout. I was immediately given free use of the whole place, and trusted as a son, rather than a "roomed."

I shall not attempt a detailed description of the house and furnishings, for it deserves the efforts of one better versed than I in such matters. The place was simply spacious and palatial.

The elderly couple were both people of refinement and education. They had been everywhere, had seen everything, and had been on friendly and familiar terms with the great and famous of the world. All this came out, not suddenly, but gradually, over the year, as our acquaintance deepened into friendship.

There were pieces of furniture, each of which had its own story. One table of surpassing beauty had been the gift of the duke of Alva, when they were his guests in Spain.

A set of carved jade elephants were the gift of the Maherajah of Bangalore, and as objects of art, worth a fortune.

The chandelier in the dining room was a miracle of ornamental cut-glass, imported; and, I have no doubt, worth another fortune. the solid mahogany furniture and bevel mirrors of the dining room were magnificent, as was the silver tea service and china that filled the cabinets.

There was a magnificent library, and a hi-fi stereo record player that gave us much pleasure.

It developed that one of their sons was an alumnus of the University of Virginia - one of my colleges, and a grandson was at the time, a senior at Ohio Wesleyan - my alma mater.

The "Old colonel," as I affectionately called him, turned out to be a famous retired utilities tycoon and international sportsman with whom I had been familiar by reputation for many years, but had supposed dead. I believe there's no thrill like that of finally meeting and knowing someone whom you have read about and admired, but had given up as dead.

I had seen his two-thousand-acre estate in Virginia, as a boy, and had often admired his famous harness-racing horses which he bred there.

I found that the sumptuous yacht pictured in the living room was not just "a" yacht, but was "the" family yacht, in which they had sailed the seven seas, and which required a crew of twenty-two "able-bodied sailors."

These associations were made gradually, and largely as a result of a terrible accident that befell the old gentleman that winter: He suffered a broken hip in a fall, and had to undergo surgery and hospitalization for several weeks.

While I was alone in the house, brosing through the library, I discovered albums of clippings and roto-gravure pictures from newspapers that brought back into clear focus memories from boyhood and youth, of the man I had known then, only by reputation. There were writings of the sporting events in which he had figured, in yachting and racing; pictures of him in the company of other famous personages in the world of business, society, sporting, and royalty. He had been on first-name footing with the world's leaders, including Presidents Theodore and Franklin Roosevelt, and King George the Fifth.

The reader can imagine what full-bodied pleasure association with such a man, on the footing of full respect and equality which he accorded me, must have been! My principal could treat me as shambily as he knew how. It didn't matter to me - Colonel Pierce was my friend, and his friends were my friends.

Mrs. Pierce kept no servants in the house. She did the cooking, housekeeping, and nursing herself. She didn't board me, though I was free to do my own cooking in her kitchen. Often through the year, Grant and I cooked special treats for ourselves, and spread the results of our culinary efforts on that mahogany table in that palatial dining room.

Just living with those people, in easy comradeship, was a never-ending pleasure. The "Old Colonel" - he was Colonel of the 29th Combat Engineers, World War I, and also a veteran of the Spanish-American War - was able to bring the great world right into the living room, and people it with those who had bossed it for two generations. His wife was one of the most delightful ladies I have ever met, either actually or in literature. Hers was a sense of humor constantly alive and active. We shared a thousand laughs, as we cooked together, gathered supplies at the super-market, or just sat in the living room and talked.

Their friends included the most important people of the town, who were frequent visitors, and who, of course, became friends of mine.

One young man who became a special friend was amusing himself, among other ways, during the final months of his hitch in the Navy, by teaching the adult Spanish class, which met two nights a week at the high school. I had joined the class in order to refurbish the Spanish I had first learned as a young college undergraduate, but which had grown rusty and dim through the years.

Seldom have I met a young man so brilliant and versatile. He was only recently an honor graduate of Pitt. His interests took in every activity a person could engage in, in Key East. By virtue of his mastery of Spanish, his hitch in the Navy was a happy one, for Latin American dignitaries were forever being entertained by our top brass at the great Naval Base, and his presence as interpreter was in more or less constant demand.

He and a somewhat older career Navy man lived in the great house which for some years had been the home of novelist Ernest Hemingway. Our boy had gotten possession of the fuly furnished mansion through his friendship with Hemingway's son, who was then a medical student at the University of Miami.

Those fellows were the "partyingest" men I've ever met. And, of course, they had the most abundant partying facilities of anybody.

McCauley's diverse interests brought together the most interesting people who resided in town, or who visited the city. One never knew what famous personage of the literary, sports, entertainment, of military world he might meet at any time at McCauley's. The social atmosphere was truly a raridied one.

Among the people who became members of our set that season were Gloria Swanson, Sally Rand - both of whom were Key West girls, and had grown up there - and playwrite Tennessee Williams.

Mention of Williams brings to mind an amusing and instructive experience:

On one occasion, the boys had thrown a dinner party, served by caterers engaged for the occasion. Later on in the evening, when everyone was having a good time swimming in the pool, lounging around, dancing, or just "chewing the fat," the writer wandered into the kitchen. It was in a monumental mess. How in the world would those excellent fellows ever straighten it out?

I began to "redd up," as the boys kept no servants, beyond a negro woman who came in once a week. Presentlly some semblance of order emerged from the chaos, and I began to wash dishes. Somebody wandered in, found a dish towel, and began to dry. I looked over to see who it was. It was Williams.

He began to talk as we worked. I had learned long ago that the best way to please a big-time operator is to listen to him. And that was exactly the way I spent two golden hours - listening to one of the most highly gifted playwrites of recent generations.

When we had completed our task, the kitchen was spick and span, and I had enjoyed two of the happiest hours of my life. It was truly a red-letter day.

At school, each teacher plowed along at his own speed. It was my good fortune to have play-time scheduled for the last half hour of the day, the same time Grant brought out his class.

We would take our children over to the play field, where they were taken in charge by the P.E. instructor, then wander over to the shade, sit on a park bench, and enjoy, instead of a Chesterfield or an Old Gold - a succulent chew of tobacco. by that time n the afternoon, we would both be pretty dry for a chew. Those periods of comradeship compensated us for a day of being treated as outcasts by the Sacred Cows and their minions.

The gardeners who cared for the grounds were Cubans of more than average education and culture - perfectly dandy fellows. Being constantly interested in learning Spanish, I made the most of my opportunities of associating with them, during these periods. The friendship we enjoyed was highly satisfying to me.

Toward the end of the year, achievement tests were given to the fifth grade sections. I was delighted with the showing my pupils made. None had achieved less then two years' progress that year - and some achieved as high as four years' progress.

Then came an incident that ripped our school asunder for several days:

"The Champ" chased another boy (one of Grant's pupils) into the class-room at the end of a play period, belaboring him with blows at every jump. Grant ordered the pupils to their seats. All obeyed except the one boy who was lying in the floor with "the Champ" on top, pouring on punishment with his fists.

Grant jerked "the Champ" off his boy, and told him to get to his own room. Instead of going, "the Champ" jerked out of the teacher's grasp, circled him, and attacked the other boy again. That time, Grant gave him a resounding slap in the face, and "the Champ" fled from the room howling, cursing, and bellowing threats of mortal vengeance on the teacher.

Another little boy raced to Big Daddy's office with the news.

Of course, Mr. Grant was immediately summoned and placed on the defensive.

The writer, knowing as he did, the attitude of Latin's of low degree toward corporal punishment, and understanding only too well, the attitude of administration toward any teacher who is under attack from any quarter, was deeply apprehensive for his friend.

As soon as I reached home, I told the colonel the whole story.

"We're not going to stand by and allow a good man to get chewed up," exclaimed the old gentleman. "Reach me the phone."

I handed it to him, and he said to the operator,

"Young lady, get me State Senator Campbell on the other end!"

When the leading Lawyer of that part of the state answered, the old man barked.

"this is Al Pierce talking to you. A young school-teacher friend of mine is in danger of being professionally murdered."

And he filled him in, up to date.

"I want you to take charge and see that nothing happens to him. And bear in mind, he's my friend!"

"Will do, Colonel," replied the Senator. "Tell him to come to me at once!"

Grant dropped in, and was told of the measure that had been taken for his defense. He said that our principal had advised instant resignation, but that he had refused to resign, although at the time of his summons to the office, he was not yet aware that his defense had begun.

He and I went down town to the Senator's office, where we brought our lawyer up to date for a second time, as Col. Pierce had given only an outline of the situation. The Senator immediately swing into action. First, he phoned the principal, and had him report to his office. When Madison had cooled his heels for half and hour in the waiting room, during which time the Senator had called the office of the Board of Public Instruction, filled them in briefly and apprised them that he was taking the accused teacher under his protection, he was graciously informed that "senator Campbell would see him now."

"Good evening, Madison," greeted the Senator - without bothering to use "Mister." "We have an excellent young man here, who is not going to be sacrificed to mob clamor. Of course you agree, I'm sure, that he has acted in a highly commendable manner. It is my intention to back him to the limit. Your part in the defense will consist in making available all records pertinent to this action, and assuring all teachers concerned that they will not only testify but will do so without fear of reprisal.

"I have already talked to the superintendent and school board president, so that I can assure you that you too, are safe in supporting decent law enforcement and use of regular legal procedure, rather than meekly caving in before a howling mob. That will be all, Madison, for now. Hold yourself in readiness for action. I'll keep you informed."

It felt good to see Madison dealt with as he had always dealt with teachers. He had been a principal for ten years. It was his proudest boast, that in ten years as principal, he had never given a word of appreciation, encouragement or commendation to any teacher.

"The Champ's" father had listened to the boy's tale of woe as soon as he reached home. The "little grandmother" was beside herself with rage. She demanded not only the dismissal of the teacher, but his blood, as well. Her son, the boy's father, later strode into the office of the county board, which happened to be in session, pounded the table, and began to wobble his jaw and mouth threats to teacher, board, and general public. He talked with the easy fluence of one accustomed to having public officials cave in at his frown.

But the board had already been briefed by one whom they feared more than the Caribbean League. They soothed his ruffled feathers, telling him that they would hold a hearing in the matter, in two days.

The Caribbean politician, at the hearing, gave a glowing description of the indignation felt by the Island's immigrants. He casually brought up mention of one of the boy's uncles, who "weighed two hundred eighty-five pounds," and whose blood-lust had been thoroughly aroused. "Well, we could take if from there." He thus managed to convey his threat of bodily harm, without actually making it.

Grant spoke up:

"Since that man weighs two hundred eighty-five pounds, the fellow is bound to be a slob. I'm willing to bet I can thrash him standing, in three minutes by the clock. You're not scaring anybody!"

Grant was wrong there. He was scaring me out of condieraboe growth. I knew enough about these people to expect a whistling knife some night as we walked home across the mouth of a dark alley, or a shotgun blast as we approached the entrance to Grant's lodgings.

The innocent teachers, not knowing that we were playing with fire, warmly applauded Grant's swaggering sally. I felt chilly, for I knew the League politician, though sounding bombastic, was kidding us not.

The hearing got under way. Teachers had been given permission to speak, thanks to Senator Campbell's influence over the board and school officials. They proved that the boy was habitually in trouble of his own making - that he would be a dangerous person in the community as soon as he took on man's size and strength - that owing to the fact that nothing had ever happened to him as a result of his scabrous behavior, he evidently believed he bore a charmed life. They proved that his teacher had done right - that he had to assert and maintain order in the classroom. The boy had gotten exactly what was coming to him.

The decision of the board was not long in coming. Their verdict was "not guilty." The case was dismissed.

For the present, most of the teachers believed we had seen a triumph of right over wrong. But they hadn't seen school administration in action, goaded by persistent neighborhood clamoring and threats.

Those people were stained through and through by "Democracy" - this time, mixed with and motivated by, tribal Indian and African negro reibal customs. They had no reverence for law or orderly legal process. They "wanted what they wanted, and they wanted it right now." The hell with the outcome of the legal hearing!

Now, Grant was a Tennessee boy, raised according to the ideals and modes of thought of Andy Jackson, Davy Crockett, and Bedford Forrest. He believed that if one of these people wanted revenge, he'd walk up to him in broad day light, and challenge him to a fist fight. I knew different. They'd let it lay for awhile, then throw a knife in his back from some dark alley, or blow him down with a shot gun, from ambush, and their consciences wouldn't bother them any.

The next night after the hearing, I moved in with Grant. His home was a small house in the rear of a larger one, not far from my abode. As Grant was a hunting man, and ex air-force soldier, he had several guns. When we passed along the dark walk that led from the street to his house, I kept the area well lighted by a flashlight. We kept the doors locked at night, and slept "on our arms."

No longer did we walk abroad for our health. We drove everywhere - for our health!

As luck would have it, no attempt was made on Grant's life. I suppose the dispatch shown in making and presenting the case - the apparent fearlessness of the board in reaching a just verdict, and the fact that the defense was conducted by the most influential politician of the area, gave the leaders pause, to the extent of controlling their bank of half primitive followers.

Teachers make an awful mistake when they meekly knuckle to school administrative persecution. It is not true that teachers waige their right to protection of the laws of the United States, and of American legal process by becoming teachers. If Grant had yielded to panic, and resigned, when told to do so by our principal, he would have had his means of livelihood snatched from him in a trice. This way, he had shown all concerned that as an American citizen, he was protected by law. He probably literally saved his life.

But school administration hates to have a teacher conduct himself as a white male citizen of the United States. It wants teachers to be vassals - subject to Administrative whims.

No, his trouble didn't come form the populace directly, though it was instigated by them. It came from our principal and his secretaries. He was roundly blamed for every natural mistake he made in accounts or reports. Directives were issued to him too late for him to carry them out. His orders were deliberately delayed, so that he could be made to appear dilatory in the performance of his duties. There are a dozen ways by which the front office can give a teacher a black eye, and they used them all.

We were accustomed to being subjected to indignities. There was hardly a day that we failed to experience some petty indignity. Now there was initiated this deliberate campaign of persecution - failures on his part deliberately caused by refusal of administration to come up with their part of the team-work necessary to the smooth and efficient functioning of a school. These failures were all entered into his record, to be used against him to the end of his professional career.

The mob was exercising influence under cover - threatening the principal with all kinds of trouble - even to the ruin of his career, if he failed to "play ball" with them. Friends, he played.

There wasn't much time left in the school year, by the time this program began. So the young teacher didn't have time to feel the full rigor of it during those weeks.

The principal called him in, and told him he believed it would be better for everyone concerned if he didn't come back the next year. Being more innocent than an older and more experienced man would have been, he felt strong in his recent victory. He believed that now that he had been sustained, the administration at the county office would continue to sustain him. His triumph, he felt, might begin a new era in school administration in that town. But the affair didn't work out that way. It is easier to throw dog meat to a howling wolf pack, and have done with it, than to run our institutions according to law and legal process, and common sense, and justice and decency. It is easier to grind up a teacher, and pitch him out as appeasement to a clamoring throng, and hope to Heaven they'll be satisfied, and not attack the administrators. If the principal could get Grant to resign, he could asy to the tribesmen,

"Look! I proved that I'm the friend of the Pee-pull, I, Madison, Big Daddy - I'm the protector of each little chee-ild! Your best bet is to string along with me."

"The hell with the integrity of American institutions! Let this one last until the day of my retirement. That's all I ask. "After me, the deluge."

So Grant refused to resign. He returned for another year, and caught the whole weight of the persecution program. How the young man lived through that year, no one will ever know.

Not only did they make his life a misery for that year, they wrote up such an uncomplimentary record, that for two years, he was unable to obtain another position that he could keep.

He had chosen Florida as the scene of his labors, but he could not obtain a position in the state for the following year. His agent finally placed him in Maryland. He launched into that job - was getting along fine, until some enterprising stenographer, having despaired of success in chewing the wrinkles out of her chewing gum and needing something to do, sent to Key East for the records his enemies had hand-tailored.

When she received it, she was fiendishly delighted.

Right there is one of the glaring weaknesses in school systems. A stenographer who has barely finished high school, outranks all the masters of arts, science, and education in the system. Very soon after they go to work in a county education office, or in the office of some school principal, they stop being stenographers, and start being "secretaries."

Well, this secretary presented the hand-tailored "record" to her boss (or obedient servant) as the case may be, and the fat was in the fire. They fired the young man in the middle of the week, and black-listed him in the State of Maryland.

Now, this is not just one isolated case in the nation. Such deals are being handed to countless young people all over the country, who have dedicated their lives to teaching - have spent their youth and thousands of dollars, in preparation for teaching.

One wonders how much of the one hundred seventy thousand teacher shortage is caused by deals of this stripe?

It can only be urged that this prodigality in the destruction of teachers is mighty expensive.

The writer was also called in, at the end of that year. The Great Man was hesitant and troubled. After all, this teacher had done nothing to deserve this. The Sacred Cows, however, had spoken! "No man has a place in an elementary school!" He dared not refuse to placate them.

"Mr. Porter, I'll put my cards on the table. I believe it would be better if you didn't come back next year."

I replied, "I'll put mine right beside yours. We have already obtained a new position for me, for the coming year."

His relief was almost ludicrous. The victory had fallen into his hands like a ripe plum.

Halleluiah!

I left the royal presence with mixed feelings of relief and remembered anger.

Sometimes we had a faculty meeting. Madison had undergone throat surgery the summer before, so that he was unable to speak much above a whisper. His voice was ideally suited to putting people to sleep.

Couple that fact with my state of exhaustion at the end of the day, the heat in the room, the natural distaste and discontent I felt for the fulminations of the Sacred Cows, and the reader may well see how a person could pass off into that state of half-awareness that borders on sleep.

One such afternoon, the principal said that he was sorry indeed that it was so, but one of the teachers had been guilty of contributing to the delinquency of minors. That was his last topic, or announcement of the meeting. Then he dismissed the meeting, and called out,

"Oh, Mr. Porter, would you stay a moment? There's something I'd like to see you about."

Now, what did the other teachers infer from that? Why, the obvious! Mr. Porter had contributed to the delinquency of a minor!

I said,

"How dare you leave such an inference floating around? What minor are you talking about?"

"Oh, I'm sorry I approached the subject in that way. But you've been leaving your door unlocked when you take your class to the play field. That's an open invitation to any child who wants to, to come in and pilfer. I was thinking that pilfering is delinquency. I reckon that's what made me speak like that."

"You're going to clarify that by individual messages in the morning, or you and I will meet in court."

He did.

Packing, as we used to say in West Virginia, was a "short horse, and easily curried." A single man gathers only very little around him when he has only himself to look after, so the car was quickly loaded, and we headed north on U.S. 1, bound for Ft. Lauderdale and home, on the whole, pleased. I had put a successful year of teaching between me and the Clear Springs night-mare. I had successfully weathered the first three months, when I had been given an impossible assignment. I had lived to see a normal school group file into my classroom. I had enjoyed working with them. They had learned, too, as shown by their much-better-than-average scores in the achievement test. I had had a lot of unpleasantness during the first three months, but had gotten through without spanking any of the kids. I was leaving a great many good friends, but I was taking with me a host of pleasant memories. And, best of all, I was not only returning home, but was going to a job in the highest paying school system in the state.

I felt that I had shaken the Clear Springs experience like water off a duck's back. As I drove up the Key's road, I was a reasonably happy man.

The evening summer was one of satisfaction and relaxation.

That fall, I was assigned to a fourth grade class in a school that had never existed before. We were an elementary school with eleven teachers and eleven "portables", plus a "portable" to use as an office, and one to use as a toilet building.

A "portable" is a separate unit, built as a classroom of ordinary size, with the regular furnishings, but made strong and sturdy, so that wheels can be mounted on it, and the thing moved long distances if necessary, from one location to any other where it might be needed.

These had been placed in a sandy field rimes with scrub pine. When you stepped out of the portable, you sank to your shoe-tops in sand. Later there were walks between the buildings, made of big flat stones. There was no cook-house; we didn't need one. The kids and teachers brought their lunches with them in paper pokes, and we enjoyed the arrangement all right. Only one draw-back; as we had to be with the children every moment of the day. But that isn't an unusual situation any more.

At first, each teacher had a "free" period for planning the day's activities and preparing materials. I was always the busiest portion of the day.

The enrollment grew rapidly. We were located in a new real-estate development. Houses were selling like hot cakes; and each house-purchaser had enough children to fill it.

Soon we went on half-day sessions. That meant that one teacher and his class occupied a portable until noon - when another class and another teacher took charge of the portable immediately on the dismissal of the morning class. We had to stop up the speed of the program to get over the territory ordinarily covered in a whole school day, in half the regular time.

Each teacher was on duty all day. That gave you a half day to plan activities, prepare materials, and work up statistics and records. We were busy every minute.

When we began, the crew consisted of eleven teachers. Soon,. however, teachers began to be added, until we had twenty-three by the end of the year. The county had exhausted its supply of portables, so it was necessary to send in construction crews and build a dozen new ones in the compound. Throughout the year, we were never without the buzzing of saws, the slambank of hammers, and the shouts of workman.

Just twenty feet from my portable was the toilet building. Throughout the day, teachers were bringing their classes to that place. On arrival, the children set up a hullabaloo of shouting howling, and screeching that didn't stop until they had returned to their room. In a few minutes, another class would arrive, and the howling and screeching would be resumed.

Our student body had been gathered from all parts of the North, but most of the children were New York and New Jersey Jews.

We started out with a good crew, but soon there arrived a woman from New York's lower east side, full of advanced educational theory, having very few years of experience, and a voice like a rusty gate hinge, a penchant for attracting attention to herself, a positive genius for stirring up discord among her associates, a flow of talk that never stopped, and a determination to raise hell.

Our principal was a young West Virginian, tall, lanky, and lantern jawed, with deep-set large brown eyes, and a determination to be a Great Executive if he had to kill off all his associated. But that determination wasn't apparent at first. He looked a great deal like Abe Lincoln. That just made people like and trust him at first sight - a mistake not realized as such until too late.

I liked him at first sight. Also, he was from my part of the country, and I felt at home with him. I looked forward to a happy year, and hoped that year would extend to half a dozen.

I had already had five years experience in teaching in the lower grades, including one year as elementary principal. I had begun taking special courses in elementary education, intending to add "elementary" to my certificate. Most of my experience had been in secondary work, but I liked elementary, and was sure I could turn in a better performance than I had ever achieved before, because my wife, who had taught fourth grade for ten years, and had been recognized as one of the best, would be at home with me that year, and would ride close herd on me, to see that I committed as few blunders as possible.

I worked at that job as I had never worked before. I worked at it all day every day and half the night every night.

There were forty-two fourth-graders in my group. Three dozen of them were among the finest kids I've ever worked with. Five were little boys who knew no law but their own whim. It soon became apparent that their whim was going to prevail, too, because there was Big Daddy standing solidly back of them, scowling at me and flexing his muscles, as it were.

I had one little fellow whose mother was "secretary" to a lawyer in the neighborhood, who was also a politician of some local importance - a member of the lower house of the state legislature, in fact. As the woman was girl-Friday in his office, her little boy regarded himself as basking in the reflected glory of his mother's employer. And it turned out that he was kidding us not. He was the most important person in the student body. He delivered the last work and rendered the final decision on all points of school policy, and delivered the final judgment on pupils and teachers alike.

He was seldom in his seat. His voice - at full volume - was heard almost continually. He never listened to a directive or paid any attention whatever to instruction, or allowed anybody else to, if he could help it. Never, at any time, did he turn in an assignment. At the end of the year, he had not completed assignment number one. Yet such was the policy of the county, that his grades had to be high enough, through the year, to pass him to the fifth grade at the year's end.

We waged a contest for leadership of the class the whole time. He deserved a damned good paddling more richly than any child I ever knew. But I had learned how hard the parents of recalcitrants in Florida try to railroad any teacher to the penitentiary who paddles a child, no matter how richly he deserves it. The principal is still in possession of that authority, and I decided that if any of mine got paddled, the paddling would be done by an official who would not be called upon to pay with his life.

The hardest part of this child's behavior to bear was his easy assumption of the position of intermediary between his teacher and the principal. When the principal entered our room and asked the teacher any question at all, this child answered it. Then he'd shoulder in between us, and explain the matter in detail. The principal always turned from the teacher and listened to the child, respectfully.

This child got so he'd listen to a directive, then cock his head to one side, wisely, and ask,

"Are you sure Mr. Box would approve that? Seems to me I heard him say something else about that."

It surely took a grown person with iron control to ignore the little fellow, and go on teaching his class.

There was a little New Jersey-ite who was bent on "having fun." He came supplied with rubber bands, to propel his spit balls at the other children. If, at any time during the day, he was not badgering some other child, it was because he was busy rolling a new supply of spit-balls, humming to himself the while, in a rich baritone voice. He was the only ten-year old child I ever knew who had a deep, rich, baritone voice. The sound of it must have fascinated him, because he exercised it at all times except when he was sneaking along the floor, flat on his belly, toward one of the New York boys on the other side of the room, to ram a pencil or some other sharp instrument into the rump of the New York boy.

I kept as close watch on him as I could, but I couldn't watch him all the time, for I had the responsibility of teaching forty-one other children. Of course I was wrong - I should have forgotten altogether about teaching, and devoted my entire attention to him. How wrong I was, was borne in upon me later.

When the New York boy would feel the pencil jam into his rump, he'd jump, turn his desk over if he could, howl as if he was being killed, and kick the lad from New Jersey. Then the one kicked would scramble to his feet, stagger up front, grab the teacher's coat tail, and wail,

"Tee-cher, he Kee-icked me. Boo-hoo-hoo-hoo-hoo!"

After that act had been used several times, the teacher lost patience one morning. He led that boy to his seat and ordered him to stay in it, and never again to stick anybody.

That evening, the teacher was summoned to the office.

The principal leaned back in his swivel chair, his fingers locked behind his head, and said gently.

"Mr. Porter, Mrs. Whoosia told me that you spoke unkindly to her little boy this morning. Could it possibly be so?

"Yes, sir, it could." And I told him why I had spoken unkindly to the little boy. If I had paddled him, I suppose I would have been knifed or shot for it.

"We-el, now," said the principal in his best Abe Lincoln manner, "we must remember that these pupils are only kids. You're not teaching in high-school now. Don't let it happen again."

We had two New York boys who had organized a protective racket by the end of the first week. They collected and pocketed the other children's milk-money. They made a pretty good thing of it, until their activity was discovered and broken up.

One of the New York City boys had reached the fourth grade, after having already repeated both third and fourth grade - and still he couldn't read. Later, his father spent a whole session at school with us. At the end of the session, he said to me,

"Mr. Porter, you have a half dozen boys here that if I were in your place, I'd half-kiol; and number one on that list would be that boy of mine. Last night, when I was helping him with his arithmetic, I glanced up, and he was looking out the window. I presume he acts that way when you try to teach him."

"Yes, he does, if he isn't already busying himself at something else."

We had another little boy who was among the smartest. His grades were straight A. Only he was the life of the party. He could, and did, make the weirdest grimaces I've ever seen. The comedy act he could put on certainly vowed his audience in school and everywhere else.

Then we had a big girl, who suffered from cerebral palsy. She was nice-mannered and affectionate, but utterly without a sense of responsibility. Sometimes when she reached for her milk container, she could pick it up. The next time she reached for it, she was just as likely to knock if twenty feet, with the resultant mess. The janitor criticized the teacher roundly to Big Daddy for allowing this to happen.

When she was done with paper or anything else, she dropped it on the floor. At the end of one exhausting day, Big Daddy followed the teacher across the grounds to where his car was parked, and gently requested him to "just go back and look at the mess that little girl had left around her desk. The janitor had objected to sweeping the room with a pile of junk like that littering up the floor."

The teacher replied:

"Mr. Box, it will not be necessary to go back and look at the mess. You know that child as well as I do. You know that she shouldn't be trying to attend any public school. I don't have the authority to refer her to the proper officials, but you do. Why don't you do it? And as for the janitor's complaint, I shall have to continue to depend upon the janitorial staff to sweep the room.

The paraphrase Holy Writ, it was accounted unto the teacher for insubordination, and he was brutally punished for it, as will be seen, later.

One of the most stringent regulations of the school was the one which forbade the presence of animals, especially dogs.

One of our New York boys who couldn't read, or do anything else, had a habit of arriving at school a few minutes late. He's swagger in, greeting his classmates in a hearty, cheery voice, during the devotional.

One morning the teacher locked the door before he began the devotionals. He had hardly begun when the boy arrived, tried the door, was unable to open it, and began to pound and kick it, loudly demanding entrance.

At the completion of a devotional exercise carried on despite the hullabaloo, the teacher opened the door, and in staggered the boy, leading his large, surly dog by the collar. The teacher stepped around the corner to the office, and reported the situation.

Box scissored hastily back to the classroom, and thundered,

"How dare you bring a dog into class? You know as well as anybody that dogs are not allowed here!"

"Why Mr. Box," exclaimed that sweet, innocent child, "I never brought no dog here. I was only trying to lead him out!"

At that, half the children in the room gasped, and a half dozen voices esclaimed, indignantly,

"Why, you did so bring the dog in!"

"Taking him out, phooey!"

"How did he get in, if you didn't bring him in?"

"He wasn't in here before you came!"

Bid Daddy ordered silence. His eyes burned with stone intensity, and his lean jaw was menacing as his glance swept the class. He leaned forward, his gaze boring into one little girl who had spoken:

"Are you sure he was not taking the dog out instead of bringing him in?"

There was no mistaking the attitude of the principal; he was inclined to accept the apparent and bare-faced lie as gospel truth. There wasn't a child present who didn't know the boy's story was a lie - yet each and every one of them was awed and bullied into silent acceptance of the lie. The boy got by, and the teacher was placed in the wrong. The boy was triumphant when the principal had stalked out.

"I reckon all you jerks can see who throws the weight around here," he sneered. "Just try to stop me, and see how far you get!"

Soon after that shameful episode, he came through with another disruptive tactic - he brought a bottle of ink to class. About mid-morning, he and the other New York boy suddenly sprung up

- in the middle of a reading class, and throwing themselves into each others' arms, began to wrestle. In a split second, they had upset the ink bottle - with the resultant mess. Every activity had to be suspended while the mess was cleaned up. It took half an hour to settle the class to work again. The morning was spoiled.

During the next two weeks, that act was repeated three times more. It was a great success. It could be depended upon to spoil a whole morning session every time. Of course the teacher forbade the carrying of ink into the room by any pupil, after the first morning had been wasted. But, like the boy said, it was plain to be seen, who threw the weight around there.

The last time that trick was tried, the teacher nipped it in the bud, before it had been completed. He took the bottle of ink, emptied it in the sand, and threw the bottle under the building. That morning sailed along as all of them should. But if the teacher believed he had heard the last of the matter, he was doomed to disappointment. The boy went home and reported the incident to his dam, and the woman hurried over to Big Daddy's office. That evening, the teacher was summoned to the sanctum sanctorum. Big Daddy leaned back in his swivel chair - his fingers locked behind his head. His face wore a sweet, longsuffering expression.

"Mr. Porter, what's this I hear about your having taken a boy's bottle of ink away from him, emptying the ink in the sand, and throwing away the bottle?"

It was the end of an exhausting day. Every day was exhausting. The teacher was in no condition, physically or emotionally, to retract, explain, or apologize.

"I think you have the story straight. Only four times during the past two weeks, a bottle of spilled ink has been used to spoil a morning. The boy was forbidden repeatedly to bring ink to school. Yet he continued to bring it. The fifth time he appeared with it, I emptied the bottle, and saved the morning.

"Now, I think affairs have deteriorated to a rather low ebb when a child can flout his teacher like that, repeatedly - then when the teacher takes preventive action report him to the principal for discipline!"

Box smiled a weary, sweet, long-suffering smile, and replied, in a reasonable, tired voice.

"Now, Mr. Porter. I'm not disciplining you at all. I do think, however, that you, being an adult, should have been able to handle the matter in some less drastic manner. Taking the child's ink (the child was thirteen years old, in the fourth grade, and had an I.W. of 65) Surely, you could solve this problem with more finesse"

The expression on the Great Chief's face had grown stern:

"Just don't let a thing of this kind occur again. That will be all!"

The teacher wanted to say,

"I thank your highness for Gracious punishment!" But a man has to hold his job if possible. A teacher has to eat, if he can contrive to do so.

The principal had, of course, promised the pretty, pouting woman that he would certainly take action at her behest. She had complained that her "shawn" (son) had suffered anguish of spirit when his ink had been poured out, and had demanded that the teacher be punished.

Evidently, Box had been raised on the novels of Sir Walter Scott. When Lady Rowena found herself in a ham, or thought she had, this knight in shining armor pulled down his vizor, raised his lance, dug in his spurs, and charged into the fray.

"Fear not, liddle leddie! Dry them tears! Sir Galahad is on the job! The body of the villain will soon be stretched on the ground at your feet!"

Now he had made good. He had come through. He had dealt with the villain. Everybody was satisfied. The boy was free to mess up the school sessions as he pleased, and no skin off box's nose - he thought.

Up to that time, this same boy, thought completely independent of everybody else around there, had respected and obeyed Box. After that, however, he was independent of box too, and that didn't set so well with the Great man.

One noontime, box was on his way across the grounds when he noticed this same boy misbehaving in some perfectly scabrous way - I'm free to acknowledge I don't know <u>what</u> the boy was doing. When box called to him, he paid no more attention to the master's voice than he paid to anyone else.

Box brought him in, in high dudgeon. They could flouk the regulations; they could treat the teachers like dirt. But when they disregarded the authority of Big Daddy, buddy, there was hell to pay! His intention was clear. He intended to lam the daylights out of that boy.

The boy began to blubber and bawl, heartrendingly, before the wood touched him. But the principal's heart had hardened against him. It was all right for him to purposely to slop ink over desks and floor - it was all right for him to sink his fist into the stomachs of kids half his size, so deep as to push back his cuff. It was all right for him to keep up a constant disturbance in class. It was fine and dandy for him to bring in his dog and thus break up the morning's routine. But, by George, this was something else again. When he disregarded the voice of Big Daddy, his ass suffered - that was all there was about it.

Into the office they went - the boy blubbering and bawling. Over the desk the unfortunate, sweet, innocent child stooped. Wham, whang, bam, plap, slam, whang, whang, whang, blow, slam, whang whang whang, went the paddle. The boy couldn't come through with cries more heart-rending than he had emitted even before his punishment began. After a few wild shrieks, he actually became silent with wonder and unbelief that the impossible had finally happened! In six years he had frustrated the efforts of various teachers. He had bullied and abused his classmates. He had refused to treat anybody with human dignity. He had been cock of the walk, wherever he'd been. And now this!

When the victim became silent, the principal, his ego salved somewhat, and the first fury of his resentment somewhat dulled, desisted.

The secretary, an older woman with a boy of her own, suffered acutely. Her gre-a-a-a-t mother heart bled. She assumed that the writer, being the boy's teacher, had sent him up for punishment. (He had not. He had had nothing to do with the incident.) But the kind hearted old lady would see to it that the writer suffered. She maintained an icy silence toward the writer, herself, and she organized the silent treatment toward him on the part of the faculty. Henceforth, until the end of the year, the writer was the invisible, inaudible man.

Now, Box had petted that boy and others, at their teachers' expense, until the school was well-nigh beyond control. But he had the gumption to realize ultimately, there had to be some authority recognized and obeyed around there,, or it would be impossible for anybody to live there. He didn't care how much bluffing and frustration the teachers had to take; he didn't care how many brutal affronts the teachers had to suffer, just so his own sacred authority was respected.

No doubt he reasoned that if the other men and women were as worthy characters as he, they would be respected and cooperated with, as he was. The whole situation meant to him only one thing: the pupils could recognize a MAN when they saw him. Only one conclusion was possible for his mind to arrive at: he had the sheer, down-to-earth, one hundred percent, plain, dogged WORTH that it took to succeed. The teachers, and especially the writer, was a mere old woman, unworthy to associate with free-born Americans.

It never occurred to him that there was no benevolent authority standing back of recalcitrant pupils, scowling and flexing its muscles, when facing him. He never thought of the difference between his position and that of the teachers in the school. He forgot that, in the case of a disagreement between a pupil and a teacher, the teacher is always wrong, and his punishment swift and sure.

The writer began to notice the absence of the principal from school, in the afternoons. He was making a great many home visitations. He didn't know whom box was visiting, but he soon found out.

Now, the vast majority of the parents represented in the writer's class, admired and respected him as an efficient teacher and a gentleman. That had to be changed. If the murderous trick that had been conceived during the pro-planning period, that year, was to succeed, it wouldn't do to leave any friends or well-wishers of his in the neighborhood.

So Box circulated among those people, and used all the sweetness and suavity and smoothness of his personality; all the weight of his office, and the full majesty of his title and position, to put his message across.

What <u>was</u> that message? Nothing much to it. It was short and went straight to the point. It was deadly poison:

"Because of the fact that Mr. Porter is primarily a high-school teacher, the instruction your children are getting is of poor quality - definitely below standard."

At the end of the year, when the teacher needed the backing of friends, he didn't have any. That little detail had been taken care of. The ground had been cut from under him. The old lady who headed the P.T.A. and mixed more prominently in local politics than any other citizen in the community, and who had been a warm friend of the writer, and a fine professional admirer, and who had expressed the conviction that "teachers are not expendable," was sorely needed at the end of the year, when the trap was sprung. Did she gallop to the rescue? Gentle reader, she took a plane for Mexico, and stayed there until after the murder.

One day the writer received a message from the principal: would he please step over to the office? The principal had somewhat to say to him.

Of course the teacher would report to the office, when summoned, to hear what the principal had to say.

When he got there, the principal said,

"Mr. Porter, Dr. Van Swaringen has asked me to bring you into his office this afternoon. We are to ride in together in my car."

"I wonder what the good doctor has on his mind," I replied. "Of course, we'll go in and find out. But we'll have to go separately, and meet there. I have to go to Miami at four o'clock, and there isn't time to pick up my car after our conference with Van Swaringen. You just go ahead down, and I'll meet you there."

When we met at the county office, there were four of us present: there was Dr. Van Swaringen, the director of personnel, Mr. Johnson, a supervisor, Mr. Box, the principal, and myself. The odds against the teacher were mighty heavy.

The Dr. opened hostilities:

"Mr. Porter, Mr. Box complains that your performance as a teacher leaves much to be desired."

"Well, Dr., I have no doubt that there is a great deal of distance between the quality of my performance, and perfection. I've never claimed to be perfect. But I plod along, doing the best I know how, under the circumstances. What is Box's beef? What does he want?"

"He complains that you are insubordinate. He can't get you to obey him."

"I have carried out his directives in good faith, and to the best of my ability," I said. "Just how have I been insubordinate?"

Box spoke up:

"I asked you to keep your room quiet and near, and your class in line and orderly, on its way to the bath-room and to and from the play field, and you haven't done it."

One of my little New Jerseyites would break out of line and race to where we were going as fast as he could run. It was he of the bass voice.

The Dr. spoke again.

"I present you with this bill of particulars, Mr. Porter," he said. "Excuse me, now. You boys go ahead and thrash this out to a conclusion."

He strode from the room. Supervisor Johnson immediately began a gentle-voiced, subtle cross examination on matters that had not been introduced in evidence, and for which no foundation had been laid. While he said,

"Mr. Porter, what do you think of the advisability of beginning teaching of children from the point they've presently reached?" I had been scanning the first paragraph of the bill of particulars.

I answered,

"Eh? What's that you said, Johnson? I'm afraid I wasn't paying attention.

He repeated his question.

"Well," I replied, "I don't see how else you could teach, It's like going from one place to another in our car. You have to start from where you are. Taking the children at the point they've reached, one begins their training from there. It's considered good pedagogy in the most enlightened circles, I believe. Mr. Johnson, this document is so thick I can't read it now, much less reply to the allegations made in it. I'll have to attend to it at a later date. Right now, I must meet an appointment in Miami. If you don't mind, I'll go now, and see you later."

Why is it, that when a man gets to be a principal or school supervisor, he thinks the world lost a really great trial lawyer? He fancies himself as a cross-examiner who cannot be resisted.

It is at that point that the most scabrous bullying and brow-beating is indulged in.

The administrator forgets that the situation he has set up is totally different from a courtroom situation. He arrogates unto himself, the authority to cross-question the teacher, without being subject to the rules of cross-examination. There is no judge to preside, and hold him to the rules of evidence. The teacher is not represented by counsel. Indeed, it is carefully contrived that the teacher doesn't even know he is being tried for his professional life. He is led to believe that he is a participant in an Educational conference between equals, for the purpose of ironing out difficulties that rise in our work just as they rise in any other field of human endeavor. It isn't until the administrator begins to try to trap the teacher into what he regards as damaging admissions, that the teacher gets the wind up. But the greatest weakness in the teacher's position is his unwillingness to antagonize the administrator. He knows that the administrator holds the power of professional life and death over him, so he clings desperately to the fiction of the "conference" idea, and gives respectful consideration to the irrelevant, immataterial, and incompetent questions and statements of his prosecutor.

Some of the most important tricks of the school administrator are,

1. Get the teacher to admit that he isn't perfect.

Well, that isn't hard to do. Any Christian will freely admit that he isn't perfect. Then, hammering upon human imperfection in general, and gradually narrowing the idea down to the individual, the administrator presently has the teacher denying specific allegations that are ridiculous, and makes him appear feeble and childish.

2. Never allow a teacher to finish answering any question. Better down his self respect by firing another question at him, on another subject, and keep it up.

Generally one administrator doesn't trust to luck for this. He knows that the teacher is as well versed in pedagogical and administrative theory as he is, and can think as fast as he can, and express himself as clearly. So he has two or three administrators besides himself, surrounding the teacher, each peppering questions and statements, and lying allegations at him without a court stenographer to read back the statements of the accussed. It soon becomes apparent that the teacher is not in conference - he is on trial.

3. Handle the teacher "without gloves." Snap at him. Accuse him ridiculously. Snarl at him. Don't let him finish an answer. Shift ground constantly. don't allow him to ask any questions. If he asks a question any how, refuse to answer it. Tell him you'll ask the questions, and he will answer. Only don't let him do it.

4. Get the teacher angry.

Cause him to give you a good cussin, and tell you to take your job and go to hell. That way you've made him deprive himself of his own job, and you can write "insubordination" into his record, and so make it difficult if not impossible for him to find employment elsewhere.

That is what Johnson and box and Van Sweringen had planned for the writer. But Van Sweringen found at the last minute that he had no stomach for it, so he walked out.

Johnson and box elected to go ahead with it. But it didn't work out that way, because the writer had had the same training they had been through, and so was able to recognize the first gambit that was thrown out.

Now, these precepts are not written in text books on Education. The professors on graduate faculties don't come right out with it. Those of us who have knowledge of such tactics, get it around the table in discussions, and in bull sessions.

The writer is as able to make a teacher feel like a back-house rat as any administrator who ever tried it. He has read the ninth volume of Hawkins' Electrical Guide as carefully as any other graduate student of Educational administration, to say nothing of Graves' "Administration of American Education."

The course in Personnel Management is well remembered, because, from the beginning of that course to its end, the writer was in a towering rage. One would think, from the general tenor of interest, that the most important duty of the school administrator is the dismissal of teachers.

While this philosophy is being more and more widely promulgated, the professional standards which teachers must meet have been raised constantly, so that the building of a teacher has come to mean years and years of study, and thousands and thousands of dollars and expense.

These people are scratching their itch for personal power at the expense of banishing from the profession, thousands of teachers who are experienced and wualified, and who have paid the price of qualification. They have spent their teachers like a drunken sailor throwing away his savings ashore.

No wonder there's a shortage of teachers!

this penchant for weeding out teachers is especially harmful to men, because the men who now hold the positions of authority and relatively high pay are constantly on the lookout for men who might succeed them.

If, before the race starts, the opponents can be disqualified for running, they can win the race by default.

Administrators know this only too well. In Florida, and no doubt everywhere they have organized and closed their ranks so tight that a man who is qualified and experienced as an administrator finds it next to impossible to obtain or hold a teaching position, for fear he might aspire to one of their jobs. So they write "insubordination" on his record. When he applies for another teaching position, he is asked,

"Where did you work last year? Who is principal there," as has been explained earlier.

This practice will have to be broken, or the teacher shortage will get more acute rather than less so.

Of course, the teacher suffers. But the schools suffer, too. They are already suffering acutely.

And what remedy do the administrators apply to their sickness? They gather up housewives, truck drivers, and traveling salesmen, and confer complimentary certificates upon them, and so fill their teaching positions. It would be just as sensible to issue master's papers to landlubbers, and appoint them captains of ocean-going vessels, as to gather up housewives, truck drivers, and traveling salesmen and appoint them to teaching positions.

Now, the landlubbers may be estimable men, but they are not master mariners. The housewives may be sweet girls; the truck drivers and traveling salesmen may be worthy fellows. But they are not teachers.

You don't catch the Medical profession filling their ranks by indiscriminate appointment. A man may be a highly educated person; he may hold numerous university degrees; but if his training does not include that of a physician, he certainly is not given an M.B. degree, and licensed to practice medicine and surgery.

Yet laymen who have some college training, are being recruited as teachers, while experienced and professionally qualified teachers are unable to obtain positions.

To get back to the office conference: having declined to take part in the farce that had been planned, the writer took leave of the prosecutor and his aid, walked out to his car, got in, and drove away. The administrators were left with no one to work on.

That didn't stop the, though. In a few days the teacher was handed a letter from the director of personal, stating that the result of the conference of previous date, had resulted in the discovery that the teacher's philosophy of education had been found "to be at variance with that presently in practice in the county."

The writer immediately filed a protest, in writing. He flatly denied that his philosophy was at variance with that practiced in the county, and denied there was any evidence in his teaching that pointed to any such conclusion. He denied that such evidence had been addressed even by cross examination.

The protest didn't help any. The writer never expected that it would. He realized that he had been selected for slaughter, and he knew there was no way of saving himself, since he had nothing better than a one year contract. No appeal would avail in a set-up in which a teacher is not accorded even basic human rights, to say nothing of professional status.

It was not until the close of the day of the "conference" that the writer got time to read the bill of particulars. The document was so scabrous, so unfair, so distorted and altogether so wrong, that the teacher was stunned. Needless to say, he got no sleep that night.

After school the next day, he sought the Great Man in his office. He asked:

"Why have you compiled this document? What do you hope to prove? Whose idea is this? How could you pretend to be my friend during the first semester, at least, and occupy yourself with the production of this masterpiece - for it goes back to the preplanning period last fall."

Even as he spoke, the teacher remembered a circumstance that had arisen during the first weeks of the school-year, that went far toward answering the questions he had just now put to his principal:

At the beginning of the term, the writer had been asked to have charge of all devotionals at faculty meetings, P.T.A's, etc. After a few devotionals, the principal had asked the writer to see him for a few minutes after school, one day. Of course, the teacher stayed.

The principal came to the point at once.

"Mr. Porter, about these devotionals you've been leading - you know we have a large proportion of Jews represented in our student body. It is offensive to them to hear Christ mentioned so prominently in the devotionals. Couldn't you plan devotionals without the mention of Christ?"

Well, the writer is a Christian. He's no Holy Joe, but he is a sincere believer, and a constant tryer. To say that he was bowled over by the request is expressing it mildly.

"Mr. Box," he replied, "this is a Christian country. It was founded upon Christian faith. It's institutions are grounded in Christianity. This is a school in a Christian country. It is a melting pot, a great deal of the duty of which is to receive a heterogeneous student body, and turn them out as Americans. To be an American in the highest sense means the same as being a Christian. Judaism, Mr. Box, was all very well in its time, when it was serving as the seedbed for Christianity. But Judaism just hasn't got the plan of salvation for the individual, or for society. It has passed away. We are no longer bound to Judaism, nor do we owe it reverence or obedience. No. Mr. Box, as long as I have charge of the devotionals, they will be Christian devotionals."

I'll have to be fair to Box on this. He couldn't wait for me to reach the office next morning. He trotted out to meet me in the parking area. He said,

"Mr. Porter, I've slept on the matter of Christian devotionals, which we were talking about last evening. I think you'r right on that. Your stand is well taken, and I want you to keep right on with it, as always."

Parenthetically, a Miami judge has since ruled that the festivals of Easter and Christmas may be celebrated in the public schools, just so no mention of Christ is made.

Atheistic Communism is certainly growing strong here.

Box opened a drawer of his desk and took out an official-looking slip. He handed it over to the teacher. it was a directive from the office of the director of personnel, dated Aug. fifteen, the beginning of the pre-planning period. It read:

To all principals:

"Look over your faculty and select those whom you believe are not going to be satisfactory. Begin building your case against them from the beginning. Keep a careful running record against them that shall be air-tight, so that, at the year's end, they may be discharged."

The writer remembered the camaraderie with which he had been treated. He remembered the friendly, thoroughly professional discussions which the principal had participated in with him. He remembered the times the principal had consulted him on questions of school policy, during the first semester. Most clearly of all, he remembered his attitude toward the principal, during those months - how he had never at any time, offered advice - giving it only when the principal asked for it; but when it was requested, giving freely of what he had learned form his life-time of study and experience.

He remembered that it had been on his motion that the faculty had requested the board to make box's appointment permanent.

And now he realized that all this friendliness and co-operation at the beginning had only been motivated by the desire to lull him into a false selse of security - to lower all barriers of reticence - to gain his confidence, for the purpose of destroying him when the time came.

The writer is going to include that document in this book, that the prospective teachers who read, may know what can be done to them after they've begun their careers. he is going to take that case, item by item, and comment upon it, since he never had the change to reply to it at the time it was presented, or rather, sprung upon him. There was no hearing of any kind - no opportunity to defend himself against it.

This indictment was presented to the county office judges, the teacher was tried, in absentia, and secretly, on the basis of it. Then he was called in to hear sentence pronounced.

That is the way teachers are served.

Following is the indictment, omitting the introductory paragraphs:

Mr. Porter is a very sincere-talking gentleman of the old school (54 years of age) with seemingly high ideals and standards. He is a devoutly religious person, and has a vast store of textbook knowledge. He can expound upon any subject, and be very convincing of what he can do. However, in actual practice, I find that he is unable to handle children and has a complete lack of understanding of the growth and development of elementary school children.

He isn't really sincere; he only talks sincerely. The statement that he is a gentleman of the old school is made only as an introduction for the statement that he is fifty-four years of age, an appeal to the well-known policy of having no teacher who is over fifty at the time of first hiring. If the teacher is under fifty at the time of hiring, he can stay until he reaches the age of compulsory retirement. The writer was hired at age 54 by mistake.

His ideals and standards are not really high. They only seem so.

His store of knowledge is only rote stuff that he has memorized from his textbooks, and not classified, digested matter that, mixed with thought and experience and wide study, has emerged as a philosophy of life or education.

He can expound on any subject, and be very convincing as to what he can do, but don't be fooled. It is all mere talk. When it comes to a show-down, he is unable to handle children, (sic) and has no knowledge or understanding of them. But box, without one-fifth the study and experience, possesses a perfect, full knowledge of children. The teacher was "handling" three dozen of his children all right - only the half dozen wreckers in the class were not handled, and even their parents had thrown up their hands in helplessness. They couldn't "handle" them either. (And by thunder, they didn't intend that any teacher should succeed where they had failed. If the teacher showed any remote in his efforts, they would sail in and wreck the teacher.)

Mr. Porter is certified in the secondary field and in administration and Supervision and is now working to complete his elementary field. He has taught 30 years, with 25 of these in the high school.

that five years in elementary work was almost as long a period as the principal's entire career, up to that time. Yet he had gained nothing form those five years, whereas the principal had clossomed out as a full fledged expert - fully qualified to sit in judgment on the old teacher.

The writer strongly suspects that it is the presence of Administration and Supervision on the certificate that rendered him dangerous to the principal, as it's a safe bet that the principal did not have those items on his own certificate at the time. Very likely he thought the teacher was learning the ropes, getting ready to succeed him the next year. he would fore-stall this possibility. It accounts too the gusto with which he obeyed the directive to "select those whom you believe are going to turn out to be unsatisfactory".

Miss Louise Bears came out and helped him find his reading groups, but I found him extremely uncooperative about their grouping - his attitude being "that is all right for you to do that, but it won't work for me." He has worked quite closely with the other fourth grade teacher, and tries to get her to do as much of his work as she will do. During the pre-planning adys of school, he simply made copied of all that she did as far as orders, schedules, etc., were concerned.

One morning Miss Bears appeared, for the purpose of finding the reading groups. The teacher was making the milk order, and collecting the milk money. While Miss Bears busied herself asking a dozen questions and arranging a circle of chairs in a small open space in the back of the room, the teacher completed the collection of money, made up the order and the report. He excused himself for a minute or two, to step around the corner to the office to hand these in. He was gone not longer than two minutes. But when he got back, Miss Bears was so angry that she was fit to be tied. She launched into a denunciation of the teacher that was a masterpiece of vituperation and abose - in the presence of the children. bit Mama surely showed the children just how low their teacher stood, in her estimation.

The allegations that the teacher was uncooperative in this grouping, that his attitude was one of "this won't work," is ridiculous. Any teacher knows that grouping according to ability, intelligence, interest, and degree of accomplishment, is necessary if any success at all is hoped for. May, more; it just happens that the teacher in this instance had been trained by the same world-famous authority who had trained Miss Bears.

She was simply deliriously angry because the teacher had left the room for a couple of minutes. She promptly trotted to Bid Daddy and demanded the teacher's blood - and got it.

Mr. Porter worked quite closely with the other fourth grade teacher: true. They shared the same classroom. It was the best educational procedure possible, to insure uniformity of instruction for all fourth grades.

Getting the other teacher to do his work consisted in her taking over the aty instruction of his class. She was a specialist in art, and her taking over the art gave the children the best instruction possible in that area. The principal noticed only that Mrs. Berman was teaching his art; he didn't interest himself deeply enough in what transpired, to know that Mr. Porter was teaching Mrs. Barman's arithmetic and spelling. He was too intent on making a damaging case against Mr. Porter to notice this.

In the matter of schedules, reports, etc., Mr. Porter participated fully in the work, but Mrs. Barman, being a fine typist, typed up the copy that was handed in; whereas Mr. Porter, who didn't type at all, would have had to hand them in, in long-hand.

That Fall, there appeared an article in the State Journal of Education, urging exactly this procedure in trading work - assuring the children the best instruction possible - by teachers who happened to specialize in some branch of the work. This procedure is being used in the best schools, from one end of the nation to the other, with most satisfactory results.

To return for a moment to the grouping, not only was the grouping accomplished, but reading consultants were sent out to help the slow ones, twice a week, for twenty minutes. They met those pupils who have already figured so prominently in this narrative, two or three times. Then they didn't come any more. They reported:

"These pupils have I.Q.s that are just too low! I wouldn't attempt to teach them to read."

Shrugging their shoulders, smiling, turning out the palms of their hands, they said,

"They just don't respond. They can't or won't give attention to instruction. Send them back to Mr. Porter. I can't be bothered with them."

So they turned them back over to Mr. Porter.

I have found him inconsiderate of other teachers, in that he smoked cigars and spent most of his free time in the teacher's lounge puffing there while his feet were cocked up on the sofa. His personal habits are not to be recommended either; he often cleared his throat, rinsed the tobacco from his mouth and expectorated in the drain of the drinking fountain. Several of the other teachers complained of these habits, and when I asked him to be considerate, he exclaimed that the puny women just couldn't take much.

We had two teachers' lounges in that school, during the year. The first one was a narrow space partitioned off at the end of the office portable. It had a window at each end, under which sat a teachers desk of the ordinary sixe, which filled the space from wall to wall. There was a double row of straight chairs along that space - so little space being left between the rows that all the teachers had to sit with their feet "cocked" up on the chair opposite, because there was insufficient knee space for a grown person to sit whit his feet on the floor. We had to write on boards held in our laps, during half the day, as we were on duty all day, and teaching half-day sessions. All were busy at all times, as we had to write our lesson plans, prepare our materials, and work on our cumulative record folders. The impression that Mr. Porter was loafing, that box is so careful to leave, just wasn't so. The teachers' "Lounge" was the only piece he had to work.

As for the cigars, every woman on the faculty who shared that space with Mr. Porter, was a chain smoker of cigarettes, which was as offensive to him as his cigars could possibly have been to them. He never thought of such a thing as protesting the use of cigarettes by the women, and they never objected to him about the cigars. If they had, Mr. Porter, being a "gentleman of the old school" would have discontinued using them.

His mention of the use of the drain-pipe of the fountain is sheer brutality. One could, with as much reason, fulminate against Box for allowing his own bath water to wash down the drain pipe of the shower.

The "weak women" bit was spoken, not by Porter, but by Box himself, on the occasion of his asking Porter to tote out his cigar butts and bury them in the sand. Porter listened to that unreasonable and cheeky request, then promised to comply. He should have complied only on the promise that the other smokers would bury <u>their </u>butts in the sand. But this little incident occurred early in the year, and the old teacher was willing to submit to the petty indignity, if that's what it took to get a passel of whining women off the young principal's back.

Feeling ashamed of the indignity he was heaping on the teacher, the principal smiled one of his gentle Abe Lincoln smiles, and said,

"Those weak women just can't stand much."

During the early weeks of school there was of necessity several notices and bulletins from both the control office and our own school office, directed to the teachers. Many of these asked for replies. All the teachers complied except Mr. Porter. His mailbox was always stuffed, and he apparently had not read anything in it. Any records handed in were usually wrong. He always makes the simplest task of a monumental one. He has often told me, "I just don't know when I'll get time for this. I teach like forty all day long."

During the early weeks of the school year, Mr. Porter had just one repository of records, bulletins, and other papers: his mail box. He didn't even have a desk in the room where he worked. Box saw only the stuffed box, and jumped to the conclusion that the contents had not been read. He was so young in the business that he would suppose that a teacher would ignore requests from the office for information. Porter was well aware that administrative details are the most important part of the school program. He knew that failure to comply with demands for information was tantamount to suicide. He would, therefore, as soon have but his own throat, as ignore communications from any office. Every one of them was read, and complied with promptly. Sometimes he'd say, "I don't know when --" etc., just as one person would say to another - "looks like tain."

"I teach like forty, all day." boy, that was bad, wasn't it. Here is a teacher whose chief interest was teaching! Have to see that he's punished. We can't have that.

Any records handed in were usually wrong.

By that, he means that some errors in the monthly report were discovered. It is standard procedure, the nation over, to subject the monthly reports to checking and re-checking. The principal or his assistant regularly goes over every monthly report of every teacher, checking for errors. When the reports go into the county office, they are checked again. Plenty of errors are found in the reports of most teachers. If teachers' reports were commonly free from error, this procedure would not be established, nation wide. To say that errors were found in a teacher's reports is not saying that he is different from other teacher. But blurting out that statement looks good when you're writing up a case.

Mr. Porter has been observed on several occasions to date. His outbursts of yelling at the children is very upsetting to them.

My impression was, that he was just trying to be louder than they were. I talked with him about it, and he agreed that he must stop.

After the fiftieth time a teacher observes a little boy snaking across the floor on his belly with a sharp pencil to stick in the rump of another child; when he has told another, for the twentieth time, to get in his place and stay there, only to look up and find him somewhere else, trading pocket knives with another pupil, he's apt to raise his voice! And the little fellow is upset! And his dam wiggles into her shorty-shorts, buckles on her bra, thrusts her feet in her sandals, shakes her curls loose, hangs a cigarette on her lip, and repairs to the office of Big Daddy, where she pleads, with her voice liquid with duffering, that something be done to stop that evil old man's yelling at her shawn, "what just isn't any way to talk to my shawn (son)!"

"Fear not, liddle lady! Sir Galahad will see that the teacher is properly rebuked! You may rest assured!"

Sure, the teacher agreed that he must stop. He didn't yell because he wanted to. He yelled for the same reason all the other teachers did, because they all had to yell to keep from fursting. And we all yelled. One would think from reading the report, that Porter made all the faculty noise. He only made his share of it. Only he was written up for it.

Talked with Mr. Porter about what he was expected to do in the classroom in relation to the total school program.

Booswah! Read that statement again. It is mere educationist jargon - not intended to mean anything. As if a veteran teacher and principal didn't know what to do in a classroom! One of the most pernicious conditions in schools today is the conviction in the minds of building principals that they have to draw teachers up and lecture them about the "total" program. The writer was professionally concerned with school programs before this principal was born.

A carpenter or plumber serves his apprenticeship, then he is no longer an apprentice. After he has worked at particular jobs for a few years, he is a master carpenter or plumber. A physician graduates from a medical school, and he's a doctor of medicine. After he has served his internship, he's on his own - a full fledged doctor. Not that he doesn't keep on learning as long as he lives. But he is not regarded as standing in need of supervision. He writer his prescriptions and makes his diagnoses independently and on his own responsibility. In some cases he seeks a consultation with another physician, or with more than one, but on the footing of equality. Only a teacher is a life-long apprentice - made to undergo careful elementary training at the feet of each youthful Gamalial he happens to work with.

If anybody believes that children don't sense the principal's lack of confidence in, and respect for, the teacher, he is tragically mistaken. This lack of confidence and respect is communicated to the, causing them to yield to the ever present temptation to appeal to higher authority, over their teacher's head. This touching cybow of special respect and confidence toward them, flat hers the ego of a great many principals - makes them feel big and powerful. But the advantage they gain, is bought at the high a price. No one person can run a school alone. Whenever any principal cuts the ground from under any teacher, he is contributing to the breakdown of his school.

Talked with Mr. Porter about all the misbehaviour of his pupils on the way to the toilet and back. He reported that he just could not do anything with them on the outside.

Earlier in this chapter, mention was made of classes being harded to the toilets - twenty feet from the writer's room, and of the howling and shrieking indulged in on those occasions. If Box ever badgered any other teacher about the behavior of the pupils, this writer never heard the fact mentioned. Certainly no teacher's effort to quiet his or her group, if made at all, ever had any effect upon their behavior. Their noise was one of the treatest crosses this teacher had to bear, but he lodged no complaint about it, because he understood the total helplessness of the teachers to stop it. Of course, if Box had stood at the entrance of the toilet building all day, the children would have been quiet and orderly, since his was the only authority recognized.

There's the rub. Any time a principal fosters the notion that he is the only fellow who must be obeyed - that disobedience to a teacher is a matter that can be discussed and arbitrated - he is taking on a load of responsibility, greater than any one person can carry, because obviously he can be at only one place at any one time. Any principal who attempts to carry the whole burden of authority in the conduct of his school - who is unwilling to delegate as much authority as is commensurate with the responsibility he eagerly loads upon the teacher, is proving that he is not principal material.

Responsibility and authority go hand-in-hand. Teachers are loaded with responsibility, but denied authority completely.

I asked Mr. Drainer to visit Mr. Porter and he reported very poor planning, or at least he was not carrying out a well-planned program. His plan book is actually pretty good. Mr. Porter talked with me after school about Mr. Drainer's visit. He resented it very much. This recalls a comment at the beginning of school when Mr. Porter stated that "You will be just like the other principal's I've know. You won't let a teacher alone." He has repeatedly told me that he just wants to teach five more years, and he wants to teach them all at Driftwood.

Yes, the writer well remembers Mr. Drainer's visit. He arrived exactly three minutes before the class was taken to the playground. We were winding up a period of instruction in arithmetic. I maintain that three minutes is not sufficient time to find out whether a well-planned program is being carried out. That statement is some more educationist jargon. He didn't take time to find out about the program from observation. The plan book was "pretty good." So it was all he had to judge by. He conveniently ignored the written, detailed statement of the program. He just delivered his pontifical pronouncement without the slightest basis in fact. But when your only object is to destroy a teacher, it doesn't really matter how you do it, just so you get it done.

Drainer was invited to accompany us to the field. He came along - and occupied the whole time we were out there with a searching cross examination of the teacher on his qualifications, what grades he had taught, where he had worked, how long he had served the trade, and what were his plans for the future. At one point, he screwed his eyes almost shut, pursed his lips, and said, in the same voice he would have used to a youngster if he told him, "You little rascal, you've been in that cooky jar again,'

"Mr. Porter, I'm afraid you're using this position as a stepplng stone."

It was then that the teacher tried to re-assure the Great Man - tried to convince him that he represented no threat to anybody's administrative or supervisory job:

"No, Mr. Drainer. This is the last stepping stone I hope to stand on. I hope I can finish my service right here, and retire when the time comes. I've had a belly full of glory, and I have no ambition to move up. I only want to keep my job, and turn inas good a performance as anybody could.

At that moment, it was time to return to the room. I invited him to return with us, but he thought that wouldn't be necessary. And it wasn't. He had made his visit. Now he could cast his vote, which was all he had come for, anyhow.

When you read that statement again about "all you principals are alike, etc., it sounds like the joshing of one friend by another, doesn't it. And it happened at the beginning of school. This was near the end of the year, but it was clearly recalled to mind. When people are arrested on suspicion of murder, they are warned that anything they say may be used against them. But teachers are not so warned. My young friend, as he appeared then, was treasuring every idle word to use against the teacher, should it ever be needed.

Of course, when a principal is directed to "select those you think are going to turn out to be unsatisfactory" before school starts, he uses every method possible to build his case, doesn't he.

Mr. Porter's room is a terrible mess. I talked with him about having the children be neat and orderly. He said he would have pupils clear it up.

The mess the Great Man mentions was mostly in the vicinity of the little girl who was a cerebral palsy victim. The afflicted child wouldn't clean it up and neither would the others.

"I didn't make that mess, and I'm not going to clean it up."

Democracy again. And a wild, free authority to pay no attention to the teacher's orders. The teacher appointed a neatness committee, but it would not serve in such menial capacity. It was beneath their dignity.

"It is not your duty to clean house, honey. That's the janitor's job. You're as good as anybody else. No menial labor for you. You're there to learn, not to clean up the room.

Visited Mr. Porter's classroom again at noon. No clean-up today. Had Mr. Porter go back to his room to see that pupils cleaned it up. You couldn't take a step without hitting a piece of paper. Also, you couldn't see the waste basket - it was piled over with scraps.

Visited again at noon. The pattern of procedure emegges quite clearly. Big Daddy was certainly holding the teacher's nose to the grind-stone, wasn't he? He selected his time judiciously, just after the pupils had had lunch. It would have cost him less wear and tear on his nervous system to have ordered the emptying of waste baskets by the janitorial staff, at that time of day. But no. Had the <u>teacher </u>tackle the job. At that particular time of day, he could have sound substantially the same condition any place in the school. But he didn't. His object was to discredit Porter - not clean up the school. He needed a juicy entry for his record.

Looked for phonograph records in Materials Center. Found them all in his room, scattered on the shelf.

Another juicy item. Had he waited until the end of the day, he could have found them in the materials center. But he didn't want to find them in the materials center. He wanted to make it appear that Porter was hogging the materials.

Helped Mr. Porter operate duplicating machine. He had wasted at least 100 sheets of paper. He stated that he just couldn't learn to operate it.

Helped a teacher operate the machine! Boy, that was bad, wasn't it? It is entirely beneath a principal's dignity to be concerned with trivialities. The machine had caught a sheet of paper crookedly, and had thrown out a hundred, or or twenty, or a dozen, before the teacher could stop it.

"Just couldn't learn --"

A man makes some embarrassed remark when some mishap occurs. Ordinarily, box would have taken no notice of the incident. But it was a juicy item for the record - not to be passed up.

A parent came in with three dresses belonging to her daughter. She stated that boys had torn them in the classroom and on the playground.

Oh, what a weak teacher! To allow a boy to tear a little girl's dress, anywhere! If it come to that, why didn't Box prevent the tearing of the little girl's dresses? Or President Eisenhower? Either could have done it as easily as any teacher could. How could any teacher be expected to prevent the tearing of dresses when children are at play? But it makes a juicy item for the record.

What do you think of a woman who will wrap up three little dresses that have been torn at school, and trot into the principal's office with them, demanding punishment of her child's teacher? And what do you think of a principal who will inflict punishment on a teacher because some little boy tore some little girl's dress?

Were those little dresses the only garments that were damaged in that school that year? If not, were all the teachers censured when a child's garment was damaged? Oh, no. Records were not being compiled on the other teachers. When garments of children in other classes were damaged, no notice was taken of the incidents.

Report cards were turned into my office for checking. They should have been in yesterday.

Did the other teachers turn theirs in yesterday? If so, he had as many as he could possibly check yesterday. If not, Porter was no worse than anybody else, was he?

I had to take fourteen cards to him for correction.

How many did he have to take to the other teachers for "correction?"

Most of his grades were given without reference to the child.

What then, in Heaven's name, <u>were</u> they referring to - if not the child? Now does he know they were not given tin reference to the child?"

In most of these cases, the grades were all A's, all B's, all C's or all D's.

He means by that that the cards were not cluttered up with plusses and minuses.

Talked with him about this. He can see no differences in children.

How unreasonable can a man get? Does he mean to imply that the teacher is deaf, dumb, blind, and feeble-minded? Shame on him!

Had several calls about report cards from parents of pupils in Mr. Porter's room. One got straight A's and the mother couldn't understand, because child had had difficulty before. Others had D's and the child was supposed to have been a good pupil before, according to the parents. Of course, there is the transition between one grading system and another.

Nobody can grade a pupil except his teacher. His principal can't do it. His dam can't do it. His sire can't do it. In this area, the spirit of Democracy flares up as bright as it ever shines anywhere: direct intervention in the workings of an institution by the mob. Those people trotted to headquarters, and caused trouble for their childrens' teacher, over the grades their children made, without consulting the teacher at all.

One little boy got straight A's. He could not have experienced an awakening, on entering fourth grade, could he. He could not possibly have a better teacher than he had had in the first three grades, could he? His interest couldn't possibly have been awakened by an inspiring teacher, could he? For remember - three dozen of the forty-two pupils in that class were in there pitching - liking their teacher, and cooperating with him, in spite of everything that was being done to destroy him influence.

One little boy was supposed to have been a good pupil - according to his parents! Up to then, he had received nothing in the way of grades except "S" for satisfactory, and "U" for unsatisfactory. Not much leeway there, is there. Up to that year, allowing that the little boy <u>had</u> been a good pupil - he had been learning to read. In the fourth grade, he had to read to learn. But this lad is the one who never turned in assignment number, the whole year through. He was so busy being Assistant Principal, that he had found no time for his studies.

At 8:30 in making my rounds, I found Mr. Porter's children running in and out of the classroom, with little concern for the teacher. He was sitting at his desk, collecting milk money. School begins promptly at 8 A.M.

We had begun promptly at 8 A.M. We had had the devotional and the Bible story. That had consumed twenty minutes. Now the teacher was collecting milk money. The children were lining up, a row at a time, paying their money, and returning to their seats. That was the "tunning around" inside the room. One of my six chased another of the six out the door and back. The one doing the chasing had been jabbed with a sharp pencil - the other was the one who did the jabbing - whose dam hardly missed a day, trotting to the office to lodge some complaint. Could she have been smitten by the handsome young principal, and did she have to have frequent conferences for that reason?

But the incident, though it had to be blown up out of all proportion to its importance, made a juicy item for the record.

Had a long conference with Mr. Porter concerning playground activities of his children. Other teachers complain that he just brings his children out and turns them loose. They ignore other pupil groups and run through game circles, and so on.

Mr. Porter's games were planned before the class left the room. The teams organized , and each pupil knew what to do and how to do it. When a group of pupils are to play a game of soft ball, you can't hold their hands. You have to turn them loose.

Of course, there were a few who refused to participate in group activities. The pupils who were most troublesome to other groups were my bigger New York boys - the same ones who organized the protection racket early in the year, and he of the belly-snaking, the pencil jabbing, and the beautiful dam.

I observed many activities not becoming fourth graders.

Any school that continues to promote pupils to fourth grade, after having had them repeat second, third, and fourth, and possibly the first grade too, is going to have some pupils in fourth grade who should be in seventh grade, had they been normal children. Instead of being sent to fourth grade again that year, two at least - three, counting the little girl suffering from cerebral palsy - should have been referred to the proper authorities for special treatment. One of the two New York boys mentioned before, had already had psychiatric treatment; the other should have had. But Mr. Box only observed their activities. He was so intent upon perfecting his case against the teacher that the idea of taking the right action toward these children never occurred to him.

One child was struck in the eye with a pine cone; another child crawled under the portable.

Throwing pine cones was expressly forbidden. In fact, the principal's express order stated that "the throwing of anything except the ball - and that on the playing field - is sternly forbidden." Mr. Box had made this announcement to all the children, repeatedly. The teacher had cautioned the children about it, yet members of "my six" continued to do it. Mr. Box observed them doing it. Now, the teacher is forbidden to even raise his voice against the flouting of regulations, much less resort to any other, more drastic form of punishment, as will be noticed hereafter. Mr. Box <u>observed</u> them, and, though having authority to punish, merely <u>observed</u>. Yet when one of the children got his eye so seriously injured that it was touch and go for several days, whether he would lose his sight, no one was punished for it except the teacher.

The child who crawled under the portable was the one who was going in to retrieve his ink bottle, which had been thrown there on purpose, to discourage him from wasting another morning by slapping ink over a portion of the room and furniture.

Mr. Porter sat with his back against a tree, with about ten girls blocking his sight. No concern on his part.

A game of prisoner's base was in progress. The girls were using that tree as their base. but to read Box, one would suppose the teacher was playing "harem." The other teachers weren't sitting with their backs against trees - they were occupying chairs, carried out from the rooms. But having one's back against a tree - Man! that's a geinous drime!

How does he know there was no concern on the teachers part? He doesn't need to know. Being possessed of the title of principal, he ahs second sight, Divine inspiration, feminine intuition (half his ancestors were women - that makes him unique) and extra-sensory perception.

His room had nine pieces of play equipment today, leaving little for other rooms.

Yes, and he had six boys and one girl in there, who were unable to do anything in the way of school work. They had to have play equipment, in the desperate effort the teacher was always making to keep these pupils occupied, so that he could go on with a normal program with his three dozen normal pupils.

Did the teacher even get recognition of the fact that he was saddled with one sick child and six incorrigibles with the I.Q.'s of low grade morons? Was he even accorded the privilege of using the school's play equipment?

The teacher even asked for separation of the two New York boys. Was his request even considered? It was not. No. This teacher is a man - so he should take this situation in stride. Did the principal lend him the countenance of his special support? No. He only wrote him up in the record, and left a situation that would have properly taken six teacher to handle, for him to deal with, single-handed. The Great Executive was motionless.

Even the reading consultants - who could have met those children individually or in a small group of six, for two periods a week of twenty minutes, thus giving the teacher a paltry two periods of twenty minutes' rest from them each week - refused to touch them with a ten foot pole. They would have nothing to do with them at all.

No. Knock the teacher down, and stomp him to death! Load him that way - then write him up as a jack-leg teacher - having no skill, knowledge, or ability. See to it that the situation is regarded, not as one concerning the school, but as one brought on by the teacher's unworthiness and incapacity. Leave the unworthy one to wrestle it alone!

Right at that point, Mr. Box demonstrated that his common sense - his philosophy of education - were so weak and narrow as to be totally inadequate to the position he held. Here was a chance - nay, a manifest duty for him. Instead of standing on the sideline and criticizing, he should have been in there with clear understanding of what his teacher was up against, and busy giving encouragement and practical help.

But no. He was Observing - swinging his official weight - not on the side of help for his beleaguered teacher, but against him, and against his school.

He is the kind of man who would hitch a horse to a load too heavy for him to budge - then get on top of the wagon and lash the horse to within an inch of his life.

According to the child who was hurt, Mr. Porter had not asked him to play! So he fell to battling another innocent child with pine-cones. That was sufficient excuse to break one of the most stringent of rules!

The teacher didn't ask a fourth grade boy to play, at recess! Oh, fie! What is a poor, overworked principal to do with a teacher like that?

Mr. Porter stated that he didn't see it happen, since his back was turned!

Teachers should be equipped with eyes all around, so they can see all forty-two children at the same time!

But the situation is plain, by this time. Operation smear was in full tilt.

Mr. Porter was asked by the custodian to move his car from the driveway because it was in the way of the garbage truck backing in.

Mr. Porter's car was not in the driveway, nor was it in the way of any garbage truck backing in. There was plenty of room for the garbage truck to back in - it had the whole field.

He refused to do so, and the Custodian asked me to have the car moved.

The custodian was a retired civil engineer, so he was an Aristocrat. If anybody didn't jump when he said "frog," he wanted to kill him. Also, he regarded his job as degrading. On top of all that, he is a Britisher. How dare any stupid Colonial hesitate when he is addressed by the Voice of Authority? His whole career had been made in India. Whenever a breech-clouted native had failed to obey the Sahib instantly, he had been led out and given twenty lashes.

Now, the only thing that could be done was to appeal to higher authority. The British Aristocrat lost no time in trotting to Big Daddy.

I explained to Mr. Porter that it was in the way and the truck might hit it.

Yes, I explained, as if Mr. Porter were a half-wit, and in the presence of his children, and in a voice and with such a manner as one would use in admonishing a half-baked child.

Neither the Engineer-turned-custodian, nor the Great Executive himself, offered to move the car for the teacher. No. The teacher had to be brought under the made to obey. It was necessary to break him before his class.

At this point, too, the principal demonstrated his lack of capacity to grasp the total situation. Just let any person at all complain against any teacher, and Bid Daddy grabbed his club and started swinging.

Mr. Porter has been very careless about letting children leave anywhere from five to fifteen minutes early.

What is a teacher going to say to a parent who walks in and says:

"Mr. Porter, if you'll let me drive away with Little Prunella right now, I can miss the crush. It's raining cats and dogs, as you know, and soon there will be a thousand automobiles here."

The teacher knows that if he refuses permission to this pupil to leave, the parent will trot over to Bid Daddy, and Big Daddy will charge forth, into the fray. If he lets the child go, he gets reported in the record. By this time, the game had settled into a grim situation of "heads I win - tails you lose."

He is not helping to train the children to be considerate of other classes.

He had three dozen normal children whom he was teaching successfully. But the special six had had no training in that area or any other, for twelve or thirteen years. With his load, and without any authority of his own, or any backing from administration, he had very little chance of succeeding where everybody else had failed for twelve years.

He tells me he has a half dozen pupils who will not mind him.

He wasn't alone in that complaint. Their parents joined in it. The children wouldn't mind them, either. They wouldn't mind the police.

It is a mistake to think it is wrong for adults to impose guidance upon children. As they develop to a physical size of one hundred ninety-five pounds and six feet two, while retaining the mental and emotional level of little children, they constitute a social menace.

The established practice of punishing teachers at their parents behest has sown the wind, and we are reaping the whirlwind already. In the streets of our nation's capital city, it is no longer safe for a man to walk along the street after dark. "Wolf-packs" roam the streets armed with blackjacks, lengths of bicycle chain, and switch-blade knives. They beat, rob and murder citizens at will, and are not punished simply because they are not twenty-one years of age.

The present writer doesn't need to do into the consequences of this situation in homes and schools. J. Edgar Hoover has already done it.

The reason we have the deplorable situation we suffer is because Delinquency is defended by school officials, parents, and society at large; and delinquents are backed by the full power and majesty of the law enforcement agencies of the nation - local, state, and national.

Just as a teacher who tries to maintain order in his class gets fired from his job, so any policeman who dares to incur the displeasure of a thug who happens to be under age, finds himself fired from the force.

He continues to bellow at them at the least provocation.

Well, I think Big Daddy is broad minded there. He could have denied that there was any provocation at all. But he doesn't do that! He admits there may have been some small modicum of provocation!

Mr. Porter became very irritated because he was asked not to leave cigar butts in the teachers' lounge. He was asked to bury them, but has not fully complied with that request.

This is the second time in his document that he deals with the question of cigar butts, in a feminine society of chain cigarette smokers. He hasn't fully complied. Oh! The horrible, nasty man! Please Mr. Superintendent, take away his means of livelihood! He no longer deserves to live! Remove from us, Oh Loed, this scourge of humanity! We beseech Thee!

I observed Mr. Porter's classroom from the outside between 1:25 and 1:38 P.M. They were going to the playground for Phys. Ed. Mr. Porter was standing in one place, waiting for the children, giving no directions. Some children were still in the classroom; some were on the way to and from the toilets. It took thirteen minutes before they all arrived at the place they were supposed to play. Had a conference with Mr. Porter about this action, and he stated again, "They won't listen to me."

Before we went out to the play field, the children were taken to the toilet. The toilet was located twenty feet from our classroom portable. There were forty-two children. Not more than six children could get into the toilets at one time. But those who had to go, went. And then lined up to do to the play field. Some of the Six, or all of them, were punching, striking, and kicking each other, and jerking each other's shirt tails out, etc. But we got lined up, and we accomplished all of that in thirteen minutes. Hadn't the children been given directions for that maneuver a hundred times. Did he expect the teacher to bellow all the time, when he so heartily disapproved of bellowing at all?

No. This is just another item for the record. Mr. Porter's class, as a class, was no different from any other class in the school. Of course, the little boys whom the principal had learned to depend upon, rewarded his vigilance as usual.

Is it not strange that they would behave that way in the presence of the principal. standing there with his watch wrist raised, and his eye upon it? Did he expect the teacher to run up and down the line, giving instructions which the children already knew by heart, and which three dozen of them were obeying to the letter?

Visited with Mr. Porter in his classroom from 10:10 to 11:35. He was having arithmetic when I went in, and was seated opposite his desk, with his feet on another chair.

His feet were on another chair! That seems to be the capital crime. And he was seated! For his information, many teachers carry on some parts of the program seated.

He was reading reasoning problems, but only two or three children listening.

A bare-faced lie. Three dozen members of my class were in there pitching. The truth of this is proved by their grades on the achievement test at the end of the year.

One boy was drinking Koolaid, another was playing with a toy, and one was taking a cigarette lighter apart. Two girls were writing in their notebooks.

One would think those children would have honored their principal's presence with an appearance, at least, of attention to instruction, wouldn't one!

Only seven arithmetic books were visible!

The turd-head! Not even seven should have been visible, since the teacher had ordered them put away. The exercise was one in listening, then telling what process should be employed in the solution of the problem.

He came to a very simple problem, which the class couldn't work out, and he said "Frankly, I don't know how to work it either."

The teacher remembers that problem. "If I have fifteen marbles in a bag, eight red ones and seven blue ones, how many attempts will it take, picking out one marble at a time, to lift out all the red ones?"

If he hadn't been so young on Educator, he would have known that when a teacher doesn't know the answer, the honest, decent thing to do in frankly confess his ignorance. Nobody but a fool pretends to know it all.

He next went into a health class and had three children read and the same three answered the questions.

We merely finished up a lesson we had almost finished before. Those three were the only ones who had not already participated. But the Great man wouldn't think to inform himself - he was getting an item for the record.

I noted that three children, being newcomers, didn't have a single book in their desks. There were plenty of copies in the book-room.

The teacher wouldn't have left his room for five minutes at the mercy of The Six. He had to attend to such things as books, at the end of the day. He always wondered why a child couldn't have been supplied with books at the time of enrollment, instead of waiting for his teacher to look after the least detail. If I had gone out to gather a set of books for three pupils, he would have had another juicy item for the record: "pupils climb walls while teacher shilly-shalleys around, compiling sets of books."

After health class, he had a second writing period.

The writer's pupils always learned to write legibly and beautifully, whether at that school or at any other in which the writer taught. He can find no fault to a second writing period.

He explained to me after class that he was combining Science and writing, as he had had the class copy a summary page from the Science book. He did not take up the papers at the end of the period.

What better way to fix the contents of a summary in the pupils' minds, than for them to write it? And why should the papers be collected at the end of the period, since the exercise was one in copying? He writes as if these procedures were sinful, or something. They seem to the writer to be perfectly sound procedures.

Lunch break came, and when the bell sounded, the whole class made a mad scramble to the door. There were three boys outside before he could get them seated and dismissed with some semblance of order.

Again one wonders why there wasn't better behavior displayed in the principal's presence. The writer's experience over a lifetime is, that pupils are one their best behavior during the principal's visit. Probably he would have witnessed a "mad scramble" in any other class in the school.

The behavior of people, whether school children or grown-ups, depends upon their life-time training and habits. The occurrence Mr. Box should have noticed is not the mad scramble, but the fact that the teacher did get them seated, and he did dismiss them with some semblance of order. But to have commented upon those facts, would amount to giving up a juicy item for the record.

At the principal-teacher conference at the end of the day, we again discussed elementary school methods, techniques and philosophy. I gave him many ideas of how he could control his class, and suggested that he call upon me for help as he felt the need.

Yes, there was a principal-teacher conference at the end of the day. At the end of an exhausting day, the teacher who had been an established school man when the principal was a little boy, had to discuss elementary methods, techniques and philosophy. But the principal was serving his first year as a purely supervisory principal, so he had to impress the teacher with his knowledge of Educationist jargon that added nothing to the teacher's wide knowledge and rich experience, and which did nothing to correct the basic conditions obtaining in that class.

He urged the teacher to call on him for help, as he felt the need.

The teacher called on him for help in the incident of the dog. The reader remembers how that turned out. The boy was sustained, and the teacher was put in the wrong. He didn't need the principal or anybody else to tell him how to do his job. He needed the young man off his back. He needed him somewhere else than in the vicinity of his portable, his eye peeled for misbehavior of the Six, and his ear bent to catch him saying something wrong. The best and most help the principal could have given this teacher would have been to let him alone.

Somehow that principal managed to convey the idea to The Six, that when he was around, they were in the presence of a friend and protector, and that the teacher was under critical surveillance. As the year progressed, one wondered how the principal got anything else done at all - he was so alert for trouble at the fourth grade portable, and so constantly on the look-out. A principal can't do worse than be continuously breathing down a teacher's collar.

Of course he was also making a case against the other fourth grade teacher, whom he smeared as ruthlessly as he smeared the writer. So he was really gathering evidence against two.

That's the worst sort of supervision that can be imagined. It cripples the teacher, and it misleads the children. It is indulged in for destructive reasons, and supervision is not intended to be destructive in its results.

The writer would not have the reader imagine that he was scornful of the young man's knowledge, or unwilling to profit by it. But the quotation of the principal's actual report shows that the principal's motives were not to help, but to supply himself excuse for banishing the teacher from the profession.

A parent came in complaining about the disorder and lack of learning in Mr. Porter's room.

Allowing, for the sake of discussion, and for the moment, that there was some disorder and lack of learning in Mr. Porter's room:

How did that parent know there was? Was she a heroic figure, "coming in to complain" about disorder that her own child contributed to, in larger measure than any other child in the class? She could have lifted a large part of that load by just stopping her own little boy from exercising his rumbling voice all day long. She could have stopped him from snaking across the room on his belly, and ramming the other boys in the rump with something. She could have increased the amount of learning accomplished here, by having her boy pay some attention to instruction, instead of busying himself breaking up the learning-teaching situation which the teacher strove to maintain. She could have ordered her boy to line up with the other children and move with them from place to place in an orderly manner. But no. That procedure never occurred to her. Her method was to trot to Big Daddy and complain.

Then Big Daddy, for once, believed he'd better now always show up as critical of the teacher. Up to that time, his positions had been anti-teacher. Maybe he'd better improve redord a little, by a slight change of pace, so:

In defense of Mr. Porter I explained that the class load was heavy and that "perhaps" the child was making a mountain out of a mole-hill.

If his intentions had been honorable, he would have let that woman have both barrels concerning the conduct of her own child, and her responsibility toward the child, the teacher, and the school.

Of course, he was a young man, and relatively inexperienced. But he made the mistake so common among school administrators: he adopted an apologetic attitude. If you're running a grocery store, it's all right for the customer to be always right. But a school is not a grocery store, and any attempt to conduct it as one, is bound to bring on destruction.

Too many parents will stamp into a school office and demand punishment of a teacher for his attempts to train a child in the way he should go. And the principal, acting on the assumption that the parent is a customer, and that the customer is always right, adopts an attitude toward the pupil and his teacher of "now, now, boys!"

He calls in both teacher and pupil, and in the presence of the parents, sets up court, with himself acting as impartial judge, in a civil action, between two litigants of equal position, age, interests, prejudices and motives.

Actually, the status of the teacher and pupil is not equal. One is a child - the other an adult. The true interests of the child are not at variance with those of the teacher. The teacher is not "against" the child - he is "for" the child - just as truly as his parent is. The teacher is not playing a game as a contestant trying to win some advantage over his child opponent. He is recognized in law as being "in loco parentis" - in the place of a parent. We teachers don't want children punished. We merely desire their cooperation in maintaining a situation in which will be most conducive to their welfare, happiness, and rapid development. We want to see them increase not only in stature, but in wisdom, and in favor with God and man.

The child sits where and advances his "case" - prompted and helped by his parent - enjoying the sympathetic attention of the principal. He hears the teacher cross-questioned, belittled, and browbeaten. He hears his teacher, in extreme instances, actually threatened by loss of employment, or with bodily harm. He hears his principal apologizing, and promising that the teacher will be a better boy in the future.

Reader, such an experience is not helping to prepare that child for adult citizenship. He's getting a slant on all the relationships of life, that is not going to do him any good at all.

A little later, when he is cited for speeding, he's going to be cruelly disappointed when the arresting officer is not presumed to be a liar. He's going to be vastly put out, when mama is no longer able to make other people defer to him.

For the love of reason, let school administrators look at schools for what they are - miniature societies in which pupils learn, and teachers teach. Let us discourage manifestations of Democracy - the unwarranted interference of individuals in the conduct of this most important institution. Let us regard teachers, not as people who must be held in line, but as leaders of youth, having lofty ideals and pure motives.

Again the principal had a long conference with Mr. Porter regarding his Phys. Ed. period, classroom technique, lack of order, grades, and comments on his grade cards. It was recommended that he thoroughly plan every class period. We went over all we had talked about in previous conferences.

One has only to read the record to see that this highly efficient young man was in there pitching; he was on the ball; he was on his toes. Oh, how he struggled to make a teacher out of this old traveling salesman, who quit school in the third grade!

As a matter of fact, he had stated earlier in the record that Mr. Porter's lesson plans were actually "pretty good." He had stated orally that they were the best he had ever seen.

He had at least one other teacher on the faculty who flatly refused to make lesson plans. One one occasion, that teacher had ripped the plan book to shreds, and flung the pieces on the principal's desk.

But he "suggested" that Mr. Porter "thoroughly plan" every period. Mr. Porter "thoroughly planned" every period, and did a better-than-average job of it.

His phys. ed. periods, his "disorder," was taken care of by The Six. There was no form of punishment or plan of correction possible for the teacher to use against those morons. The teacher was heart sick at their behavior. The specialists, meeting them singly or in a small group a couple of times, flatly refused to deal with them at all. But these "conferences" with them as subject, got more and more frequent. Almost every day, the teacher was hauled up on the carpet, and subjected to humiliating grilling and admonition concerning them,

Of course he knew, by this time, that he was being purposely harassed out of the school, and out of the system. The knowledge is the only factor that kept his heart from breaking. If he had supposed that the programs was honestly motivated, and that the principal was in earnest in his activities, he would have been fairly on the road to a nervous breakdown.

That Christmas, the other fourth grade teacher planned and carried through, with the children, a wonderful Christmas program (from which Christ was not omitted, by the way.)

During the rehearsals, with our lack of facilities, it was necessary for the writer to keep all the fourth graders who were not rehearsing, at any one time, in his portable. One afternoon, he had seventy-eight pupils in a room built to accommodate thirty. (There were three fourth grades by that time.)

One can imagine the crowded condition of that room. During the period, one of the thirteen-year-old New York boys rammed his fist in the stomach of a little fellow not much bigger than half his size. The teacher, or course, did not see it happen. Would a practiced and experienced school gangster do that so the teacher could see him?

The little fellow said nothing to the teacher, fearing further punishment from the moron. But the boy's mother reported to Big Daddy.

The writer will give the reader three guesses as to who got the blame for that outrage!

Well, we ploughed along. At our school, we had no auditorium facilities, so it was arranged to give our program at a school two miles down the road.

On the gala evening, a classroom in the other school was designated as a dressing room for our kids. The reader can imagine how busy all three fourth grade teachers were.

When the room was virtually deserted, the New York boys, aided by others of The Six, went into that room, and tore up books, ripped note-books, and destroyed decorations. One took a wrecking bar and pried open the teacher's desk drawer. In the drawer he found a small sum of money, which he stole.

When the depredations were discovered, indignation knew no bounds.

Reader, guess who got the blame!

Big Daddy decreed that for one month, all privileges were suspended in our group. No access to the fountain - no access to the toilet, during the day. The teacher had to dismiss have-to cases to the toilet, singly. No play periods, no nothing. My three dozen good, smart, kids were cooped up all day in there, and so was their teacher, for one month, as punishment for the wrongs committed by two or three juvenile hoods, against whom, however, there was no conclusive proof.

Many parents thought the mode of handling the situation was an outrage.

Reader, whom did they blame?

Right again.

In that incident, Box again proved that as a principal, he is sadly lacking in capability. There isn't a shave-tail in the army who doesn't know that mass punishment is seldom, if ever, justified.

Concerning grades and comments on his grade cards.

One must not tell the truth to the parents, in the grade card comments, unless the comments are complimentary. If a pupil is breaking up his class, or entertaining them while the teacher is teaching, the teacher must not let the parent know.

In these conferences, the fact that little Johnnie had run through somebody else's game ring was breathlessly and scandalously reported, or little Jimmy had "said something perfectly awful!"

Mr. Porter, how long will you permit these outrages to continue? And so on, and on - Ad infinitum and an naseum.

The teacher was worn down more by these end-or-the-day "conferences" than by the work of the day - by the outrages, the frustrations and the humiliations.

Checked on Mr. Porter's room at lunch time, and you could hardly wade through the books, papers, pencils, and clutter in general.

We straightened up <u>After </u>lunch instead of <u>before</u>, just as everyone did. He could have found any room in school in need of straightening at that time of day. But Porter's room was the only one he was interested in. To read his record, one would get the impression that the principal's entire interest lay in checking "Mr. Porter's" room, and with "having conference" with Mr. Porter after school. Toward the end of the year his program of badgering was stepped up, and intensified to such a degree that the teacher had all he could do to keep sane.

Talked again with Mr. Porter about dismissing from ten to fifteen minutes early each noon period. I explained to him that it was unfair to fellow teachers who were keeping within the proper schedule.

Now he's back around to that "early dismissal" bit. Explanation has already been given: early dismissal was not for the class - it was only for individuals whose parents picked them up on rainy days. All the teachers dismissed a pupil when a parent asked for him. The teacher explained this to Box, which he didn't need to do, as Box knew about it without being told. But if it can be made to appear that Porter is being slack in his administration and unfair to the other teachers, it makes a good item for the record.

If the teacher had refused to let a parent have his child when he called for him, the parent would have trotted over to Big Daddy's office, and that afternoon the teacher would have faced even worse than he did for dismissing the pupil. This thing had long since degenerated into a game of heads I win, tails you lose, like we said before.

Three boys got into a fight in Mr. Porter's room. He stated that he did not see it. However, later in the conference he did admit that one of the boys had reported that others were hitting him, and Mr. Porter's reply was, "Maybe you're setting a bad example." Mr. Porter did nothing to the boys, and they were punished in my office. Again he reiterated that he could not control the rowdy children in the fourth grade.

The rowdy children in the fourth grade! Oh, what a weak unworthy man, to be unable to control the rowdy children of the fourth grade!

Every time that woman's "shawn" with the bass voice rammed a sharp pencil into one or more of the other boys, the injured boy hit him, and he had it coming. It wasn't a "fight;" the first boy provoked the blow, and the other delivered it.

But that was no way for her shawn to be treated. Her shawn should do as he pleased, and the other kids should like it. However, when Big Daddy listened to that husky voice of hers, liquid with tears, he didn't try to think any more. He tore into action - both against the boys who struck back, and against the teacher.

Some child was continuely retaliating against some scabrous offense which that little boy had committed against him, for he busied himself with little else than his program of disruption. And he could think of a great many ways of disruption.

If the teacher had punished every child whom that boy demanded punishment for, he would have done nothing else but punish the other children.

It was a game with planned procedure: you jab a pencil into me. I'll howl, and strike you. You run to teacher and demand punishment for me. If teacher spanks, mama will have him fired - perhaps sent to jail. Boy! Ain't this fun?

Another conference with Mr. Porter: subject - disorder on playground.

Conference! Almost daily. Complaint. Conference. Chiding. Admonishing. And mostly about nothing of consequence - nothing beyond that which happens when forty-two children are at play. Children in other classes were having the same troubles - no better, no worse. But the principal had found solid ground upon which to stand while belaboring the teacher. Take forty-two people of any age, anywhere, and turn them loose at games, however well supervised, especially when three or four of them are outlaws, and there will be some irregularities.

Recommendation: that he stay with his pupils at all times - giving no noon break to the children until Christmas. The principal was to give Mr. Porter a mid-day break from his children.

Mr. Porter was with his pupils at all times. But this mass punishment was the first exercise of it, preceding by some time, the instance already described.

The principal did take over a few times, for fifteen minutes, but he soon got too busy at that time of day, to appear.

Second recommendation was to arrange seating; to separate trouble-makers.

Of course, the teacher, having had no more than thirty years' experience, had never heard of such a device! Seating is a poor, weak remedy to apply to children who are amusing themselves by breaking up a class. Four of these six should have been in reform school. They had no more right to be in a public school than a dog has to be on a grand jury. mention has already been made concerning the attitude of the specialists toward them. The principal, writing his report, was intent only upon condemning the teacher and at the same time, covering up himself.

He wanted the officials at the county office to think, "My! What a sharp young principal we have out there! Boy, he's drawing that teacher up on the carpet nearly every day! Isn't he on the ball, though? And how business-like he is! How veddy, veddy professional! Recommendation number one, Recommendation number two! And now, recommendation number three:

He was to plan every minute of the day's work, so that there would be no lag in the childrens' time, thereby giving them no chance to get into trouble.

Every moment of the day had already been planned. And three dozen children were cooperating. But no amount of planning is sufficient to control a half dozen disobedient morons. There was no work they could or would do.

One of them would smile into the teacher's face, hold up his pencil, and deliberately break it in two, before the teacher's eyes, and the teacher was not empowered to slap the taste out of his mouth, or turn him across a desk, take a paddle, and make him wish he had died and gone to hell before he broke the pencil!

Pencil-breaking was only part of the fun enjoyed by these miscreants. They couldn't use the equipment, so they destroyed it.

It's a terrible thing to turn little boys like that into a class of children. God help the junior high and high school teachers who will have that group to deal with later on! The teacher is responsible, but he has no authority whatever to deal with these people as they should be dealt with.

As the year wore on, the principal found that they wouldn't obey him, either. So he swung the paddle more and more freely. They got so they feared him sufficiently to obey his orders - at least when he was in sight. But he had sufficient authority and status, so that he didn't have to go on trial for his professional life and physical liberty, for paddling a pupil.

The State Superintendent, some time ago, stated that he wouldn't think of taking over the principalship again, without the paddle in his hand.

Well, by the time a ten or twelve-year-old child has waited until the end of the day for his punishment, likely he has forgotten all about the offense for which he is being punished. The time for correction is now, and the proper place, here. And the proper hand in which to place the paddle is the teacher's. As for a child thinks, his teacher is the school. And the authority of the school should be the teacher's authority.

If the writer could have paddled that kid with the bass voice, and his dam threatened with jail when she interfered, ninety percent of the trouble he made would never have been made.

But, then, this teacher had been selected as one "not likely to be satisfactory" before the year began. He had begun with two strikes already called on him. The presence of these hunks of reform school meat was fortuitous. They helped like sixty, to accomplish the pre-planned slaughter.

He should also plan to have each child work on his own level in the basic subjects.

How veddy, veddy broadminded and professional! Bless his heart, all these provisions had been made at the beginning of the year. But, like the specialists reported, they just didn't respond. Their I.Q.'s were so low that attempting to instruct them in the basic subjects was like beating your head against a wall. They would have none of it. turn them back to Mr. Porter. He has only three dozen normal children to teach. A half dozen wreckers shouldn't worry him any. He's a man!

And believe it or not, the teacher could have ridden even that situation, if it hadn't been for the interference being furnished by dams, two or three other teachers, and that jealous young man in the office! At the time this trouble was being experienced, the teacher didn't know he had been selected for slaughter before the beginning of the year. It would have helped him greatly, if he had know.

Another parent reported that her son had been hit in the chest and stomach by another boy in Mr. Porter's classroom. When I asked Mr. Porter about this, he said he didn't see it.

It was the same gangster who had helped organize the protection racket. Does anyone suppose he did things like that openly, so he could be seen? Policemen seldom, if ever, are witnesses to gangland murders. If that young man, the principal,

238

had been chief of police, and a murder had been committed in his city, he would have fired the policeman on the beat for not having seen it.

Another mother came into my office in an emotional state, saying that she had just come from Mr. Porter's room, where she had overheard him scream at her son, "What in God's name do you want?" because the boy had asked a question of him about the gift exchange.

Yes, the incident occurred. Directions had been given, over and over. This particular boy would say:

"You've told the class. Now, tell me."

He had traded two or three times, already. When he interrupted still again, the teacher's patience had worn thln. He had straightened him out a dozen times during the Christmas party he was giving for the class. it was he of the bass voice.

Had that woman volunteered to come and help with the party? She had not. She dropped by just in time to witness the cracking up of the teacher's patience. She never did make an appearance at the portable. She trotted in to Big Daddy, to be soothed and appeased. Probably her emotional state was triggered by a fuss with her husband, before she left home.

She also stated that her son said this was a common experience.

Very likely this beloved shawn experienced rough replies, quite commonly. Whenever there was even one other person around, he demanded the complete attention. And a teacher with forty-two pupils can't give much attention to any one pupil. If a child can't take group instruction, he should have a tutor.

Mr. Porter told her that he was not permitted to allow books to go home.

Such was indeed the truth. He wasn't.

She also stated that she asked Mr. Porter to have her son make a copy of his spelling words so that he could learn the, and

Mr. Porter had replied: "I have more important things to do than to see that your boy learns to spell a list of words."

Now, that isn't very likely, is it. I would be shorter and easier to say, "Why certainly, Madam. Be glad to."

As a matter of fact, that's about what the teacher did say. And that's what he tried to get the boy to do. He made one list, promptly converted it into spit-balls, and from then on, he just made the spit-balls, without bothering to write the spelling words on the paper.

Why didn't she have him bring home a copy of his spelling words?

That boy's father appeared at school one afternoon, much concerned about his boy's learning to spell. He intimated pretty broadly, that if the boy had a teacher who was worth a pinch of snuff, that he would have no trouble learning to spell. He said if I would let him have a spelling book, he'd be responsible for getting it back to school.

Monday evening he was back with the book. I asked him how he was getting along. He said, slamming the book down on the desk,

"I drilled and drilled and drilled that punk on those twelve words, until he could spell them perfectly. Early the next morning I had him try to spell them, and the dammed sap-head couldn't spell one of them! Brother, I begin to see what you're up against!"

Mr. Porter's class now numbers forty. Entirely too many, but he is trying to carry out his plan; however, he is having great difficulty.

The two I lost did not include any gangsters. They were all back, as they used to say, "with bells on."

Mr. Porter missed his music period because he was on the playground when the music teacher arrived. The schedule had been in effect since October.

If the weather was rainy, the music teacher's lounge. At other times, she would get on a weeping jag that would last all day. She would just lie on the couch in the nurse's office, and cry.

That's what we were all used to, from her. Sometimes she put in an appearance at the portable when she was due - sometimes not. She must have been late that day, instead of entirely absent. Anyhow, when she hadn't come by music time, the teacher concluded that she was probably on another crying jag, and maybe she was. Only that time, she dried her eyes, and went to Mr. Porter's class, and horrors! He had his children on the play ground!

Better trot back to Big Daddy and report. Always report, partially, anyhow. Never miss a chance to report!

Mr. Porter did not attend the Area Teachers' Meeting at Hollywood Central. His reason was, "I just forgot."

How did he know Mr. Porter had not attended the Area Teachers' Meeting? Chances are, that little bird with the voice like a rusty gate hinge, told him. Anyhow, it is true. I forgot. That's a chestnut on me. Now, fellow citizens, that is a juicy item for the record. That one really has substance!

Still waiting for a cumulative folder I asked him for yesterday. He said, "Why can't you wait until Friday?"

The teacher had tried to complete that record for mailing, using the counter in the secretaries; office. He had been curtly ordered to move on.

He had tried to work on it in the nurse's room. He had been curtly ordered out of there, with a muttering under the breath - something about peeping Toms."

He had tried to hold it on his knee and complete it. Not much success too many papers.

He had no desk of his own.

He hated to work at it during school time. Of course, he knew that his duty was to drop everything and complete that record. But this occurred earlier in the year, and he supposed, silly boy, that account would be taken of the special circumstances obtaining then. Of course, he didn't know he had been selected for slaughter before school began. As it was, the incident was just another item for the record. Insubordination.

In checking text-books prior to the division of classes, we found forty-seven books missing. Thirty-five of these were in Mr. Porter's class. He didn't know who had lost which books.

Brief mention has been made of the fact that state-owned texts were not allowed to be taken home.

The writer had been directly bearded on that subject by the chronic complainer herself one afternoon, in the presence of the principal.

He explained that home work for little children was seldom necessary or helpful. If the parent does the home-work, what's the use of sending it? If the child doesn't know how to do it, home-work is only a vexation of spirit. If he does know how, he doesn't need it. If a child will pay attention to instructions and follow direction at school for seven hours, he will learn as much as his capacity will allow. At the end of seven hours of quiet regimentation, a child's interests are elsewhere than on study; and his body cries out for exercise; his soul needs freedom. It is an outrage to assign him a second shift, to pre-empt his free time.

Most parents agitate for home work for a purely selfish reason: they want their children kept quiet while they are at home. They want the teacher to be responsible for the children's activities not only at school, but also during the waking time they're not at school. Not that they want their children educated or trained. They just want somebody else to bear responsibility for them.

Home work that isn't checked and graded is vain. For a teacher to spend his evenings and week-ends grading home-work, is another outrage. The very parents who cry as insistently for home-work for the pupil to toil over (after work hours) and the teacher to check, grade, and record, (after work hours) would be the first to protest an extra, unpaid shift for themselves.

To get back to textbooks: teachers were forbidden to allow the pupils to take them home. The chief complainer complained to the principal that Mr. Porter wouldn't let her shawn bring home his speller.

The principal stood there and heard the teacher berated and abused, and accused of unworthy motives in keeping the books at school - and then said he saw no reason why the books should not go home!

Well, we allowed the books to be taken home. Soon we found ourselves short on some books. It was very annoying to try to keep the program going without enough books to go around.

Finally Bid Daddy made us account for the books, and the fat was in the fire.

The teacher appealed to the children to bring in the missing books. He sent mimeographed appeals to the parents to send the missing books to school.

Finally one little girl scraped up the courage to report that one of the New York gangsters - he who was so fond of delivering the belly punches - had a number of books at his house. He wasn't delivering the teacher's notes to his parents, and they, as usual, were paying no attention to his activities. This particular little girl felt safer than most, and better protected, so she dropped by the gangster's house, asked for all school books, and came in, staggering under the weight of fully half the books that were missing from our class, although the boy couldn't read any of the.

The other children delivered the books they had taken, and the crisis was met.

He was asked to bring the cumulative record up to date for the children who were transferring to the new teacher's classroom. This, being a work day for teachers, he should have had plenty of time for, because all books and materials had been moved the previous day by the children.

The enrollment had expanded to such a degree that we had organized another fourth grade class, draining off surplus enrollment from the other two. Did Mr. Porter get relief from any of his good time boys? Were some of them transferred, so that well-established procedures of shattering the peace in his class would be disorganized? They were not. All were left with Mr. Porter. It would have been an outrage to ask any other teacher to take any of them. No sir; no madame! Only his best pupils were transferred.

He had ample time to bring the records up to date, and did so.

But oh, what a lazy, unworthy lout he turned out to be! He had the books and materials toted over to the other portable by the children! He should have performed this coolie labor himself!

Classes have now been divided. Mr. Porter has A.M. session, sharing a classroom with another teacher, who had afternoon session. A question was raised about the condition in which he was leaving his classroom.

What enterprising genius was concerned about the condition of a house during a moving operation? Has anyone ever seen a house clean and orderly while moving is in progress? But Mr. Porter had to be chided and admonished. By this time he couldn't even be trusted to keep his hands out of the fire.

I spoke with him about this, asking him to be considerate of the children and teacher who must follow him.

Big hearted Daddy! So gently and sweet and considerate of everybody except the teachers he was harassing out of the school and out of the system! Please, Mr. Porter, will you turn over a new leaf, and, just this once - be an ordinarily decent human being?

I observed him having the children clean up the room the next day.

Old eagle-eye caught him in the act! The lazy poltroon was having the clean-up performed by the children. What an outrage! - to have the children performing janitorial duties! He should have performed that labor himself: Had he been worth a pinch of snuff, he would have sent the children out to wrestle, tear dresses, and pelt each other with pine cones, while he remained in the room - sweeping and dusting.

Ye gods! that I should be plagued by such a character!

I asked Mr. Porter once more for the cumulative folders, and he said, "I don't know when I'll get time to do them."

The teacher had already completed the cumulative folders, and delivered them to the office. At first, he thought the principal must be joking. So he fell in with what he thought was a joke, and replied that he didn't know when he'd ever get them done.

Over and over again, through this masterly document, the point is made that Mr. Porter was criminally lax in delivering administrative information when called for. The higher administrative officers down in the county office would be specially sympathetic toward a principal whose teachers were lax and neglectful in that area. I assume he made the same point in the cases of the other two teachers whom he had had no opportunity to "screen" himself, before he went to work. I haven't seen the documents he prepared concerning them, but it's a safe bet that they were hum-dingers. There were three of us who had been appointed before he was; therefore, he felt that we three were not beholden to him for our jobs: ergo, we would feel independent and defiant. He'd feel that way; he could see no reason why we wouldn't.

We worked under every possible hardship that could be imagined, yet we all pitched in and supported him loyally and efficiently, in the overall program of the school. Three of us he black-listed in the county, and made it extremely difficult for us to obtain employment anywhere else. The others tried to get away from him on every pretext they could invent.

I asked Mr. Porter to see that the cumulative folders were in my hands by Monday.

This was two days after the first mention of cumulative folders, and he had not discovered that they had been in his hands all the time.

Four days later, we still do not have Mr. Porter's cumulative folders complete, which should have been finished for the new teacher some days ago.

If there were incomplete folders, they belonged to children who had shipped out after the first completion. To assume that the whole file was incomplete is to commit an error.

I feel that Mr. Porter's attitude is adverse on ideas presented to him for improvement in his classroom. He has not carried out our plans for improvement satisfactorily, even though he always approves of them during our conversations.

Our plans for improvement were sensible plans, and worthy of putting into execution. Our three dozen normal children profited as much as it was possible, under the circumstances prevailing. But the Six maintained their own program of disruption - specializing in their misbehavior on the playground, thus earning the disapproval of the other teachers as well as their own. The principal showed, by his hauling Mr. Porter up on the carpet on every charge imaginable, at the behest of anybody and everybody who had a grievance or imagined she had one; by his constant surveillance, and obvious lack of respect and confidence, that despite the frequent conferences during which he spouted his newly acquired educationist jargon, that Mr. Porter was, in his estimation, outside the pale of educational respectability.

It is astonishing that the old teacher was able to accomplish anything at all. Yet his pupils scored unusually high in the achievement tests given at the year's end. This is a matter of record, and cannot be successfully questioned.

He has yet to ask for help, except in disciplining three or four children.

Asking for help, gentle reader, is regarded by administrators as a confession of weakness and incapacity. Administration does not regard a school, or a school system, as a social institution, nor teachers as a body, working as a team. Each class is regarded as a separate entity, and a large school is still seen as a collection of little schools, all operating under the same big roof. Administration doesn't want to be bothered by troubles in the classroom. "Any teacher worth his salt can control his class."

The incident of the gangster whom the principal picked up off the playground one day, and paddled, has already been mentioned. That punishment cost the teacher total social ostracism in that school, organized by the first secretary, who was so deeply moved by the gangster's bawling, crying, howling, and pleading, and moaning.

The teacher had nothing to do with that incident, nor with the other two paddling incidents. But he caught the brutal punishment anyhow.

He well knew what punishment would be meted out to him if he punished a gangster himself, or brought punishment upon him; so he studiously avoided doing so. But, like I said, he caught it anyway.

He is using secondary methods and techniques with fourth grade children.

Simply more educationist jargon. It is only during the last few years that such a gulf has been discovered between elementary and secondary methods and techniques. How can anybody draw a clear line between elementary and secondary? The lines are being drawn at various points along the educational trail. Most systems draw it at the end of the sixth grade. Secondary education begins at the seventh grade, in those systems. The writer worked in one system in which the line was drawn at the end of the fifth grade, and the sixth grade was included in the secondary set-up.

Some years ago, elementary school included grades one to eight. Secondary education began at the ninth grade, and continued through grade twelve.

In Western Europe, secondary education ends at the eighth grade, and higher education on the college level, starts at grade nine, and continues for six years, through what we know as junior college.

Our own famous private schools, such as Groton, Philips Exeter, et al, are conducted according to the same system.

Is one to use "secondary" methods and techniques in the seventh grade class, the members of which are reading on the fourth grade level?

"He is using secondary methods and techniques with fourth grade children!"

Oh, the ignorant, slothful lout!

But it is a disastrous indictment. It throws tremendous weight as an item in the record.

He gives many lectures over the heads of his children, while they just sit and do nothing.

How does he know the lectures were "over the heads" of the children? Did somebody tell him? He must have been told, because he never heard any of them himself. Was he told by the woman with the husky voice, whose "shawn" was listening? If so, any instruction whatever went over that lad's head, and over the heads of a few others. Why couldn't the principal's informant just speak for her own "shawn?" Certainly no one could speak for the whole class.

He is a great story-teller, according to his children.

Those stories were not reported to the principal as crosses which the children had to bear. The reports were happy, joyous recountings of delightful classroom experiences. The children loved them, and profited greatly.

The writer seems to remember that the Greatest Teacher of all used stories in his teaching, such as,

"A sower want fourth to sow --"

He loves to tell stories of his youth, stories about his family, etc. This is all well and good, but he needs to build background for these childrens' future training. This is my basic reason behind this report since I am directly responsible for these children and their futures.

Oh worthy, conscientious yount feller! How keenly he feels the responsibility resting upon him! What a devoted, forward-looking young principal! Gentlemen, what a jewel of a young man we have down there! Let us bind him to us with hopps of steal!

The writer knows no better way of stimulating interest in the school subjects, particularly the Social Studies, than stories about real people.

Begin a presentation to children with the statement , "far away and long ago, when I was a boy (or a little girl) --" and your children are all attention. You can hear the dropping of the proverbial pin. What better way is there, for building background for their future training?

Where are too many young Americans losing out on gaining a code that will do to live by - a code that makes them develop into responsible, decent adults? What is the reason boys of high school age are roaming the streets armed with bludgeons and switch blades, knocking down old women and stomping them to death?

I submit that these gentry have been given no knowledge of the cost of their country in blood and sweat and tears. Their education has not included an acquaintance with George Washington, except as the victim of a snearing, snide remark, "he couldn't tell a lie," or with Benjamin Franklin except as a dissolute old character who played at flying his kite on Sunday. Recently there has been some effort to reintroduce Davy Crocket, Buffalo Bill, and John Mosby, the old Grey Ghost. There were generations of American boys who admired the clean, decent characters so thrillingly described by Moratio Alger Junior. Boys of the type of Dave Porter and Frank Merriwell were heroes.

In the days of Theodore Roosevelt, boys adopted, as their guide to conduct, the simple, manly code of the President.

So this is his reason for his document.

I submit that he had a quite different reason. He had been handed a directive: "select those who are not going to be satisfactory." He was out to prove himself equalto the task of doing his part in creating the reign of terror being set up in the schools of the county. Because that directive went out to all the principals, and all tried to pomply. The system is operating now, under a reign of terror. Everybody connected with it is afraid.

So the old teacher, and many of his colleagues, were without jobs.

CHAPTER NINE

Some weeks before the end of that nightmare term, it became apparent that the writer had no reason to think he would be re-employed there. He asked the Director of Personnel what he should. The Director said,

"No. I wouldn't resign, I'd make formal request for a transfer to some Jr. High or High School position. I understand that your principal's main complaint against you is, that you are miscast as a grade school teacher, and that he has no objection to recommending you for a secondary job."

So the writer made formal application for a transfer to such a position. To get appointed, it is necessary to make the acquaintance of the principal you hope will give employment, gain his favor, if possible, and obtain appointment, or recommendation for a position in his school.

The writer compiled a list of Senior and Jr. High principals in the county. He visited the high school principals first, beginning with the most desirable high school in the city.

"Is the principal around?" he asked the secretary, on entering the office.

"It all depends on what you want," replied that dignitary. "If you want a teaching position, I can tell you right now, that there's no use to see him. There aren't any vacancies."

"I'd like to meet him, anyhow, in case a vacancy should develop. I'd like to establish contact with him. Will you tell him, please, that Mr. Porter would like to see him?"

She smiled a superior smile, shrugged her shoulders, and disappeared into the inner sanctum. Presently she returned, and said,

"Mr. Jones will grant you a few moments."

The writer entered, introduced himself, shook the hand of the Great Man, and was invited to be seated.

"We have no vacancies on the faculty at this time," he said. "However, your coming in is appreciated, and making my acquaintance can do no harm."

He questioned me concerning my secondary teaching field, my experience, educational philosophy, etc. We had a satisfactory interview.

"Now that I've met and talked with you, I can visualize a man instead of a mere dossier, should I need someone in your field. Thank you for your interest. Should the occasion arise, your will be the first folder I'll examine at the county office."

Nice feller. I left with a feeling of satisfaction.

During the summer I visited every secondary principal in the county, and though courteously received, got no satisfaction from any.

Late in the summer, a vacancy in my field did develop in the first school I had visited. I called there in high hopes of getting a job.

The secretary answered the phone, and when I gave my name and stated my business, she exclaimed,

"Oh, Mr. Porter! Didn't you know? You are not to be employed anywhere in this county, at any job, at any time. Mr. Box's document has been placed in your folder at the office, and has been made a part of your record. Of course, anyone who reads it would hardly desire to employ you."

I was stunned, but not for long. It was necessary to get that mustard plaster document out of my record.

I called the Director of Personnel. He could not be found. I called various other officials, but could get to none of them. Finally I reached the first assistant superintendent, and he finally consented to an interview.

We sat together for an hour - he with a copy of the document in his hands, and I with my own copy. I went over every item in it, and exercised my first and only opportunity to answer allegations made in it.

At the end of our hour, I asked that the thing be taken out of my record, so that I might be able to obtain employment. He agreed, and ordered the thing destroyed.

He was the first and only official I found who possessed enough manhood and common decency to listen to my defense, and take proper action. If I had been given opportunity to defend myself, I would never had been black-listed in the county.

However, the object had already been accomplished! The knowledge the secretary had given me was shared by all the secondary principals. I was not to be employed, and that was that!

At this juncture, a very great misfortune befell me: my mother died.

On our way home from her funeral in West Virginia, we were nearing the border of Florida, but were still in Georgia, when my wife said,

"There's a roadside telephone. Why don't you use it to call the county school office in Jacksonville. Maybe you could get a job."

Sometime previously, I had asked the director of personnel in our county if he would recommend me for a position elsewhere in the state. He had replied that he would. So I stopped the car, got out, went to the phone, and placed a call to the Jacksonville office.

After some delay, I reached the Duval County personnel director. After a few questions concerning my teaching field, certification, etc., she said yes, they needed somebody. If I would call at P.S. #14, in 18th Street, Jacksonville, the principal would be there, and she had no doubt we could deal.

We continued on our way, and presently we arrived in the city, and searched until we had located P.S. #14. The principal was indeed in his office, and after a short interview and examination of my papers, the young man hired me.

"One warning," he said. "Under no circumstances are you to paddle any pupil. Just simply put the idea out of your mind, if you ever entertained it. No one punishes any pupil but me."

I assured him that I would respect his wish in that area as in all others, and took leave - promising to report for work the following Monday. We drove home to Ft. Lauderdale, and the following day, I returned to Jacksonville, ready to go to work.

In P.S. #14, and elementary school, two seventh grade classes had been retained, to ease pressure on the local Jr. High. The rooms occupied all day by these pupils, were located in a smell frame building back of the main school, and connected to it by a covered walk. A small vestibule separated the two rooms.

I took charge of one group, while the other was taught by a little Jewish woman from Brooklyn who said she was thirty years old, but looked fifteen. My group numbered thirty-one pupils.

Of the thirty-one, twenty-five cooperated with me in a highly satisfactory manner. Five worked some, but insisted upon conduct wholly unacceptable in a class room.

Those boys talked incessantly, in tones varying from full voice conversational to full bellow. They stood up and threw wads of paper, erasers, pieces of chalk, etc., at each other. They wrestled, on occasion. They refused to enter the building when the bell rang. they wanted to stay in the yard and pitch just a few more baskets, or knock just a few more flies. They would roll balls under the buildings then take a half hour to locate and retrieve them. Then they needed another half hour to wash up, and brush their clothes.

One boy emptied a large box of chalk in the floor, then stomped the sticks to powder, and ground it into the wood floor with his feet, scattering the mess over as large an area as he could.

A second boy sat and amused himself by pulling the strings out of the Venetian blinds.

Still another returned to the building after school had been dismissed, found the bolt of the door lock shot, and stood and slammed the door until the lock had been torn out of the wood.

Once a week, I took the class to the library in the main building, which was located in the back of the auditorium. There was no librarian, so I had to act as librarian myself. While I was so engaged, these fun loving pupils chased each other up and down the aisles, and up and over, around the through, the stage scenery. They engaged in wrestling and fist-fighting, and in every activity they could think of, which might annoy or aggravate their teacher. When not racing through the auditorium, they wanted to keep the path to the bath-room hot. They wanted to run along the hall, yelling, laughing, and whistling. Of course, they were a pain in the neck to all the teachers in the main building.

I was caught on the so-called horns of the well-known dilemma: if I road herd on my fun lovers, I couldn't act as librarian, and the books would be disarranged, and lost. If I acted as librarian, my fun lovers disrupted the whole school.

One afternoon, one of the boys urinated on the floor of the library. Of course he didn't do it in my presence, so I didn't see him. But a little boy from another class, who was there on some errand, saw him, and reported him to the principal.

When taxed with the dirty deed, he looked up at the principal with his big blue eyes, and said, guilelessly,

"Why Mr. Dumkopf, I just didn't do it!"

There was the pool, and the stream running from it to a lower part of the floor. There was the eye witness. But the principal couldn't punish him, because it was a case of the other pupil's word against him.

Who got bawled out? You've guessed it! The principal snarled that is the teacher had been a worthy man, the boy would not have wanted to urinate on the floor! Why hadn't I seen him? What was I doing? How could a thing like that happen? What did I mean by allowing such conduct?

I was glad when that day finally ended.

The mother of another pupil wanted her boy to behave. She and his father had decided that he should be a doctor, and she wanted him to have a thorough education which would fit him for medical school. All of us together were able to pressure him into quiet, law abiding conduct, but his heart wasn't in it. He sat back with a sneer on his face that never left it. Formerly, he had been a laughing, care-free prankster, but now the world had shut down on him, and he was a quiet, morose, noncoroperative, scowling, sneering specimen.

His father drove a bread delivery wagon, and his mother was a stenographer in the office of one of the local doctors. One evening she called me on the phone, and said,

"Mr. Porter I am highly displeased with your performance as a teacher." (As if I were a stable boy, employed in cleaning out her stable.)

I replied,

"How do you know you are? Have you ever heard me teach?"

She went on -

"I don't have to hear you. I can tell you're a poor teacher, from 'way over here. I can tell because you don't assign enough home work to my boy. He races through your assignments in a couple of hours, and then spends the rest of the evening running me nuts.

How, is that any way for a teacher to let a boy act? You ought to give him enough work to keep him busy until bed time!"

There was an element of humor in the situation. I had signaled the principal to listen in, and he was on the line. I walked to her for eighteen minutes, sketching the high points of the most enlightened attitude toward homework for a seventh grader. Finally she finished off the conversation and hung up.

The principal patted me on the back and exclaimed,

"Bully for you! I never heard a situation handled more smoothly and satisfactorily. I couldn't have done any better myself, and --

The phone rang. He answered it -- grunted, and passed the receiver to me.

"For you, again."

I said,

"Get on this one, too."

It was another mother.

"What kind of a sadistic brute are you, anyhow? What fat-head has kept that phone busy all this time? I've been trying to call you for half an hour!"

I said,

"Well, here I am at last." (My ear already felt like it had corns on it.) "You got grief?"

"Well yes, I've got grief! What do you mean, giving enough homework to keep La Mar and his Daddy and I, all three, busy until midnight? Do you think that's all I've got to do - just working at homework?"

Shucks! Sometimes you just can't win!

I suppose no group is complete without a fat boy. We had one in that group. He was fairly smart - a good worker, and a thoroughly good citizen. But somehow, the half dozen fun lovers regarded as just good clean fun, the exercise of stuffing the fat boy into a large waste can in the boys' toilet, in a sitting position. That way he was doubled up so tightly that it was difficult for him to breathe. In such a position, he was helpless. Someone would finally help him out of the can.

One day the fat boy's mother appeared in Big Daddy's office, and told him the sad story, asking, with her big blue eyes filled with tears, and her voice chocked with emotion, if something couldn't be done to stop the practice.

Big Daddy called the teacher on the carpet.

"Why do you allow such scabrous practices to go on?" he asked. "Why don't you forbid such rough-house tactics?"

"Why, it's the first I've heard of it." replied the teacher. "Why don't I accompany the fat boy to the toilet? It's about the only way I know of preventing this thing."

"All right, go with him, and protect him. This is outrageous. We can't have that sort of thing at all!"

So the teacher accompanied the fat boy to the toilet, from then on. Only another complication developed: the other boys wouldn't go to the bathroom while the teacher was there. They stayed outside, and shinnied up the columns that supported the covered walk. From there they could walk all over the roof of the main building - and did.

Old Man Thompson, who lived across the street, and had nothing else to do besides observe what went on around school, promptly made a bee line to the principal's office, and made the shocking disclosure that some boys were on the roof!

Once more, the teacher was summoned to the carpet.

"Mr. Thompson reports that some of your boys got on the roof yesterday. Great guns! Why do you allow such things to happen?"

"Well, if I go to the toilet with the fat boy, that protects him from annoyance, but leaves the other boys free to climb to the roof. If I prevent their climbing to the roof, they go in and annoy the fat boy. I wonder - could you be out there for five minutes at that time, so that we could supervise both ends of the line?"

"I have more important duties than that! Things have come to a fine pass, when a teacher can't control his own class! What have I got <u>you</u> in the job for? Must I do everything myself? My God! When I hired you, I thought I was hiring a MAN!"

Well, I tried to be both places within the time limit. Sometimes I was too late. A couple had reached the roof before I got there to make them come down.

Of course I couldn't paddle them for it. I couldn't keep them in after school - they had to catch the bus. I couldn't subject them to fines or imprisonment. But I <u>could </u>give them F in deportment - I thought. In fact, I did.

Again I was called on the carpet.

"Mr. Porter, what do you mean - giving these boys F in deportment?"

"Well, Mr. Dumkopf, it's the last thing left for me to do. Certainly their conduct is far from satisfactory."

"Now, Mr. Porter! No child is a failure. Surely they deserve better than F. Surely you can do better by them than <u>that</u>!"

"All right, I reckon its impossible to please everybody. But I try. Always give every situation the ol' College try."

One day my fun lovers fell to bending sheets of paper into a spear-like shape and sailing them about the room - only they had invented a refinement: they stuck pins through the front, so that their sail-planes were really formidable weapons.

I stormed the castle. I explained how one of them could deprive a classmate of his eye-sight, after one of them had skittered across a boy's breast, and left three or four pricks that bled a drop.

The boys were impressed. they promptly stopped the practice - and permanently.

But the end was not yet. The boy with the breast - two days later - shoed his wounds to the principal, and told how they were caused. The principal's wrath knew no bounds. I saw him coming along the walk, carrying his paddle. He burst into the room - panting. He thrust the paddle-handle at me, and demanded.

"Do you want this?"

I said no. I had no use for it at the moment.

He then asked about the paper-sailing. I explained that I had already dealt with that, and that it wouldn't happen again.

But he wasn't satisfied. He said,

"Stand up - everybody who had a thing to do with this sail-ship thing, whether making, or throwing them, or both."

Five boys stood up. He grabbed one by the collar, and snarled,

"Ben over that desk!"

He proceeded to paddle that boy - thirty strokes. Three strokes are considered a hard whipping, and it is. The boy was badly hurt, though he stood it like a man. He could hardly straighten up.

The other four received similar beatings - until the principal's anger was appeased. Soon afterwards, the time for dismissal came. I figured that young man would experience repercussions from that day's work.

Silly boy! There were repercussions, all right. But against whom were they directed? You're right the first time! After classes the next day, the telephone began ringing. It was for me.

Mr. Porter, some days ago I was appointed to the chairmanship of the membership committee of the P.T.A. As I couldn't serve, I declined the appointment. Yesterday my boy was beaten black and blue because I wouldn't accept the appointment."

At that point, the sweet girl burst into tears.

"Mrs. Whosis, I didn't know you had been appointed - didn't know you had refused. And I didn't beat your boy, or cause him to be beaten."

"But you, being an older man, and supposed to know better - stood by and allowed it to happen. I hold you strictly responsible!"

"Mrs. Whosis, Mr. Dumkopf is the boss. I only work here. And though your boy was paddled more severly than he should have been, I'm satisfied he richly deserved it, on a dozen counts. How, he isn't injured, and I advise you and the others to forget it. There's no percentage in agitating the matter. And I assure you that your refusal of the P.T.A. appointment had nothing to do with the boy's paddling. That was rooted in another matter. you'd better take my advise and let it rest there."

I knew that the county administration would support the principal, though that support does not extend to teachers. There is no backing for teachers. Any woman in the neighborhood can prefer any charge that suits her fancy against a teacher, and have him or her discharged. The doesn't have to prove anything. Her unsupported charge is sufficient. When a charge is made against a teacher, the principal calls him in. He generally has the superintendent there, and a supervisor or two, for support. The teacher looks at the faces around him. The supervisor who so cordially supported and warmly approved his performance earlier in the week, wears a blank expression, and evoids his eyes. The superintendent who so kindly welcomed him into the job only a few months ago is an impersonal stranger. The principal who exchanged jokes with him at lunch that day, has now become a stern judge. Their game is to cross question, badger, abuse, and browbeat him until the super-human self control he has built up over the years finally snaps, and manhood asserts itself. The teacher cusses them out, invites them to take their job and ram it. And if any or all of them would like satisfaction for anything he's said, they can all step out and he'll fight them one at a time or all at once. But they can't want any further satisfaction. They're satisfied sufficiently. They're rid of him. And he has fired himself. That's the beauty of their game. He quit. Nobody fired him. He has no one to blame but himself.

Well, those women tried, but they were bucking a principal, and got nowhere. If the administration would decently support teachers, that way, the mouths of women who have nothing more thrilling to do than tear into a teacher, would be silenced, and our schools would no longer be blackboard jungles, but educational institutions.

In the other seventh grade class, across the hall, there were four boys who worked up vaudeville acts, perfecting them by careful rehearsals, for presentation at school. They had been given unmistakably to understand that their own teacher was strictly off limits, and was not to be badgered.

As I had charge of their class for their play period, they tried them out on me. I had to procure a double set of equipment to employ both my boys and these others. The rub came when we needed a double space on the play-field. Space was strictly rationed, and the other teachers felt that our group was preempting more space than we were entitled to.

Our game that Fall was softball. Some of the boys were big, dexterous and skillful; some were smaller, younger, less experienced and lacking in skill. My trouble lay in getting the good ones to allow the others to participate in the programs. Even with two teams playing, there were a few who had to await their turn.

These wanted to amuse themselves by strolling through the corridor of the main building, looking into the rooms, and greeting friends there.

Of course it was impossible for me to be with the boys on the field and ride herd on the others at the same time. The others could slip away without my knowing, and they did.

One afternoon the principal came striding across the field with two of my loafers in tow.

"Mr. Porter," he bellowed, "here are two of your boys whom I found making a nuisance of themselves in the main building. I can't understand why you permit this! Why don't you plan a program that will keep everybody busy?"

"Yes, Mr. Dumkopf, we will endeavor to keep these boys from annoying others."

But it was a large order.

I tried to explain to the boys that this wasn't just a ball game, but a phys-ed. program in which all the boys were expected to participate. But the leading boy of the afore-mentioned four thought differently.

"Phys-Ed." Don't make me laugh! This is a ball game, and By God, I'm in it to win! If these little awkward squirts horn into it, I'll beat them up, on the way home!"

He'd do it, too. The kids were well acquainted with that thug. I told the principal what we had, but apparently it was easier to shame and berate their teacher than to take measures against the thug.

One day, in class, I told one of my boys that he was a disturbing element. When he got home, he told his mother that I called him a scurvy elephant.

Well, that was name-calling, and name-calling is cursing. She reasoned that way, being a preacher in one of the fanatical sects. She got on the phone and called a hundred parents represented in the school - fulminating like a fishwife.

Than she laid siege to the county office - berating everyone she could get on the line for employing a teacher who "cursed" in class. They endured for a short time - then decided to rid themselves of annoyance by making the accused teacher pay. No effort was made to determine whether they had a profane teacher. Just call him in, and brow-beat him into tendering his resignation!

The first I knew of this tempest was when the principal met me one morning with orders to report to Mr. Bing at the county office.

I drove down there to the county office, and inquired for Mr. Wing. After cooling my heels in his waiting room for half an hour, I was shown into The Presence.

Mr. Wing leaned back and pursed his lips. He said,

"Mr. Porter, you are accused of cursing in class. Now, we can't have such behavior on the part of our teachers. We have very high ideals of honor and honesty and purity in our county. Now, there are three courses open to us. We can fight; we can transfer you; or you can resign."

"What do you mean by fighting? How do we fight?"

"We can ask for a hearing for you before the school board."

I remembered a previous school board hearing, during which I had endured the vituperation and abuse of abandoned, unprincipled, drunken rogues for four and a half hours, with full newspaper coverage.

I had imagined I had outlived that experience. I just didn't realize how the vilification had unnerved me. At the suggestion of a repeat performance, I found the game not worth the candle.

"How about the transfer?" I asked.

"That's out, I'm afraid. I haven't a thing to offer."

"The trial is out of the question. Being tried on such a ridiculous charge is totally beneath my dignity. There is left only --"

Just then the "secretary" poked her head in.

"Mr. Wing, Mr. Whosis would like --"

Whosis came bustling in, and I was ignored. One visitor after another came, and finally Wing went away with one of them, and it was nearly noon when he returned.

During those hours while I was waiting for Wing to return, I thought the matter through. I remembered all the circumstances of the job.

At first, I had been cordially received by the other members of the faculty. Then I began to sense a coolness developing. Finally those teachers had taken to acting as if they were deaf. They ignored a "good morning" when addressed by name. I had well-nigh become the invisible, inaudible man around them.

The principal sat behind his desk, reading the financial pages of the morning paper. It was necessary to pass the door of his office on the way to the teacher's room. At first, we exchanged greetings on my arrival, and the time of day. We used to chew the fat a little. lately he had not bothered to look up as I paused at the door.

I needed his assistance on the other end of the line, for a few moments each day. He was never there. I wasn't allowed to punish recalcitrants - he reserved that right for himself. yet at such times as someone did something he felt deserved a paddling, he snarled at me as though he thought I should have done it - as if I were somewhat less than a man, for allowing him to paddle pupils who so richly deserved it.

If he was going to insist upon being the only authority in his school, he ought to bear the unpleasant duties as well as the pleasant. He had the notion that no teacher should swing any pupil into line unless it was his own pupil. That way we didn't have a school at all; we had a large number of one-room country schools under one roof.

We had to consult him on every point. None of us felt free to go ahead with any part of the program on his own responsibility. It was strictly a one man institution.

Our P.T.A., as an organization, was crippling along with only a small percentage of the parents taking part. Yet there were parents bustling around and through the school, like bees in a hive. Gossip flowed freely.

When I needed the principal for consultation, he was generally in conference at the county office.

Our neighborhood was full of gossipy, sharp tongued women who had nothing as juicy to talk over as school affairs. I've heard teachers say perfectly scabrous - really devastating things about their colleagues. They couldn't do much real harm, though, because most of them had worked there from fifteen to twenty years, besides sitting on continuing contracts. We had two other men on the faculty - young fellows who had never taught before, who were preachers in the same sect as that served by my fish-wife mama. Many of the families represented in the school were communicants of that same church. The P.T.A. members who were such familiar figures around school - they spent the major portion of each day there - monkeying around at something - gurgled and cooed at these young men. "Deah brother Formaldehide - deah brother Benzine," Until those boys got the idea that they were big-time educators. Actually they were marking time as teachers until their church could send them out as missionaries to Peru.

They called me in and lectured me concerning the conduct of my business until it was a real thorn in the flesh, enduring them. If one of my boys knocked a ball into their territory on the playground, they reported the incident to Big Daddy, and I was called up on the carpet and reprimanded. The vaudeville actors in the room across the hall - not being allowed to misuse their own teacher, were working on me in increasing intensity. As I was not allowed to punish them in any way, I was the kind of punching bag a hood dreams about.

Now I was falsely accused of cursing in class, and presumed by the administration to be guilty - without any inquiry whatsoever being made.

I came to a conclusion: they could have that job back, and welcome. It was the only time I ever walked out of a job during a long career. But I had been crowded into an untenable position.

Bing had acted like a top-drawer bastard. When he finally came back, I gave him my resignation - which was exactly what he wanted.

If ever a game becomes not worth the candle, that one had.

I drove back to school to report to the principal - give him the report cards, which were due that day, and turn over to him the records, etc. Also I wanted to pick up a few personal belongings at the room.

When I arrived there, the fun-lovers were in full career. The substitute was desperate. She said to me, "Mr. Porter, I certainly don't blame you for resigning this job. I wouldn't have it at a hundred dollars a day!"

At mention of the word "resignation," a chorus of protests arose from the class.

"Oh, <u>please</u> don't quit!"

I made a little farewell address, thanking those who had stayed in there and pitched - appreciating the majority of the class who had worked with me.

By mid-afternoon, I was long gone.

CHAPTER 10

The following summer my agent placed me at Ft. Baltic Beach, in the Pensacola area. The town had been recently described in a T.V. show as a frontier area, left in the back wash of westward moving settlement. At the time I knew it, the population was around twenty-five thousand. Rapid growth had been caused by the location of Elgin Airforce Base, nearby.

There were three handsome boulevards, several attractive residential sections, and a business district down town. The school was located about three miles out of town, on the Race Track road. We had sixteen hundred pupils in grades seven to nine, and our faculty numbered fifty!

The classes were organized on the departmental basis. Each teacher taught only one subject. I had five sections of Geography, seventh grade.

I was very much pleased by the children in my classes. Many of them were the sons and daughters of air force personnel. They had, a considerable number of them, been reared chiefly in foreign countries.

A peculiar condition began to emerge from that circumstance. Those children were not citizens of the United States, but of the

United Nations. Their sympathies lay with the country they had spent the greater portion of their lives in; and they entertained all the prejudices against their own country that one finds abroad.

I had children who could converse rapidly and fluently in German, French, Spanish, and various other languages. Several of them had fine sets of magic lantern slides, made in the country each had lived in so long.

Each Friday, one pupil would get excused from all his other classes, and run his slides for all my Geography sections, giving a lecture on the places, manners, and customs of those countries.

Again, 85 to 90% of the student body were good kids making a conventional effort to learn. Ten to fifteen per cent included our hood and thug element. But five or six years before my coming upon the scene, the hoods and thugs had been so bold and powerful that teachers and administrators could no longer conduct the school according to the philosophy that had been in the ascendancy up to them. common sense had to be restored in school administration, or they faced the necessity of closing the schools altogether. The paddle has been replaced in the hands of the teachers, as well as those of the principal and his assistant.

The principal, however, was extremely uncomfortable under conditions in which the teachers were not bullied, and made game of. Whenever he could, he defended the hoods and thugs against the teachers - just like the other principals everywhere.

But mainly, the teachers were in the saddle, instead of the thugs. When a hood's cup of iniquity was full, we took him out front, to the office of the principal or assistant principal, and raised him one and a half inches with each paddle stroke.

No hood ever stood up and invited the teacher to make him - his mouth streaming profanity, obscenity, defiance and threats. Our assistant principal was a young man skilled in boxing and wrestling, and every hood knew that when told to, he'd go;

otherwise he'd be carried. but arrive at the front office he would. So when told to "come on," he rose without a word, and came.

But on the way, he could make up a case for himself that would make black appear white; right, wrong; guilt, innocende; and up, down. The few hoods I took out front that year excited my warmest admiration by their mental bymnastics, their quick thinking, and their nimble wits. Of course they'd had a dozen years experience pitting mama against papa, and papa against mama, and teacher against principal, and principal against teacher, and teacher against teacher. But in this school, it didn't work. Mr. Cowan, the assistant principal, was an expert at cross-questioning a hood - a skill he never practiced against a teacher - and the hood always ended in freely admitting he had it coming.

But if a teacher made the mistake of <u>sending</u> a hood out front, instead of <u>taking</u> him, and that hood had the good fortune to draw the principal instead of the assistant principal, his fortune was made, because the principal was most sensitive to neighborhood criticism - especially if the irate parent called him on the phone. At a phone call, he'd go from one fit into another. If a hood of nimble wit, who had the backing of his dam, drew him, his rear end was saved.

And right here, let me say that the most flagrant juvenile hood is fearful for the safety of his back side. None of them will misbehave after a good paddling unless the school official or teacher who gives it to him is punished for it. Of course, if punishment is visited upon the teacher afterward, his paddling will be of no benefit to him. In this school, the punishment of the teacher was left until the end of the yar, and then such derogatory remarks were written into his record, as, "Can't keep order in his class;" "was not respected by the students;" "Weak in discipline," etc., - remarks designed to make it difficult for him to obtain further employment.

Of course, the parents of hoods called in frequently to lodge complaints against the teachers. And the principal rated the teachers according to the number of telephone calls that were made, criticizing him.

At our first meeting, the principal spoke at length of scholarship standards. he held up the report card, and called our attention to the grading scale: 70-74, D; 75 to 84, C; 85 to 100, A. Below 70 was F. And he impressed us with the necessity of conforming to that scale. No matter <u>who</u> the pupil was, or what his father's rank in the air corps, if that boy or girl made a grade below 70, that pupil was to have F.

Well, most of his faculty members were new. it was only later that we found out that he maintained a seventy-five percent annual teacher turn-over. When he issued orders, we believed he wanted them carried out.

He held up the glue card. There was a place for the name of the pupil, and for the time. There was space for a brief description of the offense. he wanted <u>order</u> in those rooms. If anyone persisted in misbehaving, he was to be handed a blue card, and sent, or brought, out front, where he would meet the wrath to come. Those were the positive orders. We believed he meant them.

It was only in private, and towards the end of the year, that he would berate the teachers for using them.

I had a few instances of persistent misbehavior in my classes, during the first thirty weeks of they year, but only a few isolated cases. mainly, my pupils liked and respected me, during those thirty weeks.

One day a colleague of mine caught a big hood cheating on a math test. He made the mistake of <u>sending</u> that hood out front. The hood's luck was running - he drew the principal.

The principal opened his door and smiling affably said,

"Did you want to see me? Come in, son, and be seated."

He seated himself in his swivel chair, leaned back, and folded his hands above his stomach. He said, "Now, Son, I believe you have Mr. Bains for arithmetic. Just what do you think of Mr. Bains?

Is he right smart of a jack leg, at teaching: Now is his classroom manner? Just tell Mr. Gunnarcon all about it!"

The hood had been relaxing visibly under the sunshine of that benigh smile. His confidence rose in this genial atmosphere. He leaned back, crossed his legs, unslung his jaw, and began his broad-minded, man-to-man analysis of his teacher's character, habits, education, and manner.

"Now, Mr. gunnaroon, I wouldn't have you think that Mr. Bains doesn't know his stuff, because he does. I'll bet he used to be a good teacher, back in the old days. (Mr. Bains was just turned fifty).

"Bains wrote on this slip that you cheated on a test. How about that?"

The hood smiled his slow, easy smile.

"That's just the point I'm making. He's old, tired, and embittered. His mind is so set that he's angry at the very appearance of irregularity. He hasn't any flexability - no tolerance. His great trouble is, he's just a back number. He no longer understands young people."

Would you suggest, then, that he be discharged, and a younger person be hired to replace him?"

The hood pursed his lips, and assumed a broad minded, judicious expression:

"Well, I hate to push an old man. But hell! Everybody has to get out of the way of progress. I think it would be to the best interests of the school to have only those people on the faculty who are not older than thirty-five."

The principal was thirty-two. He expaned gratefully under this repression of confidence. Later in the day, he summoned Mr. Bains to his office.

"Bains," he began, fixing the teacher with a narrow-lidded, judicious gaze, "about that boy you sent in for cheating this morning: he says he didn't cheat. You say he did. right now, it's his word against yours. Did anybody else see him cheat? I can't punish him just on the testimony of one person."

Bains blew up, and was slated for dismissal at the end of the term.

The hood swaggered back to class, which had just ended. His claque gathered eagerly around.

"What happened? What did the ol' man say?"

The hood unslung his lantern jaw again.

The ol' man asked me what I thought of Bains, and, By God, I told him. I advised him to fire the old bastard. He won't be around long, blowing his mouth. I decided, some time ago, to have him fired. Now his number is definitely up."

And it was.

It wasn't until the end of the thirtieth week that the idea hit the principal that was the most brilliant that had ever occurred to him in his life: he would have the evaluation of the teacher's professional competence made by their pupils!

He called a delegation of my twelve-year olds, and after receiving them with every indication of courtesy and confidence, told them what he wanted them to do; they were to evaluate their teacher - consider him from every viewpoint, under the guidance of their Big Daddy. In short, they were to sit in judgment on their teacher.

Naturally, they were flattered. And honored. This confidence elated them highly.

They returned to the other children and reported in full. Their teacher no longer enjoyed the respect and confidence of Big Daddy. Buddy, he was on the way out! They no longer needed to carry out Mr. Porter's directions, or follow his leadership!

Those who wanted to, promptly began to conduct themselves like a bunch of apes. The teacher didn't know, at the time, what had happened.

Another circumstance added to the nightmarish character of those last six weeks: workmen came and began the construction of more rooms at the end of the ramp. All day, every day, the deafening rumble, rattle, clatter and roar of concrete-misers, gasoline engines, air drills, trip hammers, and shouts and curses of workmen so filled the air that ordinary tones of voice could not be heard. Those acting like apes had to shriek at each other, to be heard at all.

Every once in a while, a jet plane would hurtle overhead, and out over the Gulf, with a whistle that would wake the dead. Seconds later, there would be an ear busting BOOM that rattled the windows.

Such was the last six weeks period of the year.

It was duging this time that the principal asked me to drop in and see him. He was writing at his desk when I knocked.

"Come in," he bardked. "Ah, Porter! Sit down!"

He finished writing, leaned back in his swivel chair, regarded me with a hostile expression, and spoke:

"You can't teach!"

"Indeed? I replied. "How do you know? You've never heard me. How did you find that out, assuming for the sake of discussion, and for the moment, that your assumption is true."

"Oh, I'm correctly informed, all right. Your own pupils say you can't. Nobody knows about a teacher's ability like his own pupils!"

The ape-like conduct of some pupils stood explained.

One day, in meeting, the principal was in high dudgeon.

He said:

"I've noticed a circumstance, lately, that shames me through and through. I refer to the custom that has broken out, of boys walking with girls - their hand gripping the girls' buttocks. Everytime you see that happening, I want you to send the couple to my office. I won't have it al all!"

In a few days, I saw it happening, and sent the offending couple to his office.

When I reached my classroom, the grape vine had carried the message before me. Five little girls jumped me, verbally. I had "gotten Millie into trouble." They batted me around like a badminton ball. I couldn't stop their chatter at all, short of physical violence. They were going to make that old teacher wish he were someplace else.

Finally, I put the names of the five on a blue slip, and sent them out front.

Just as luck would have it, I remembered a phone call I had to make. I followed them almost immediately. Arriving at the office, I heard my name called, and my attention was, of course, instantly engaged. One of the five was saying, in a tone of sweet reasonableness and transparent innocence,

"We just don't know why Mr. Porter sent us to the office. None of us has done a single solitary thing Wrong. Mr. Porter just stomped in, looking like a thunder-cloud, selected us from the class, and sent us out here, for no reason at all!"

"We'ell," came the placating voice of the principal, "You girls must remember that Mr. Porter is an elderly man - short of patience and easily upset. Old folks often do and say things they don't really mean. You girls must consider the source, and bear with him!"

I stepped into the room.

"Mr. Gunnarson, I am not that old. I am not short of patience, nor am I easily upset. When I sent Millie and roger to you a while ago, these little girls berated me for "getting Millie in trouble" for half an hour. They batted me around like a badminton ball, and what they didn't tell me hasn't been thought of yet. I couldn't stop them at all, short of physical violence. I sent them out, not because I thought you could do anything about it, and not because I want them punished, especially. But I didn want to get their mouths stopped."

Gunnarson turned to the girls:

"So <u>that's</u> it! You know that no teacher would let you get away with that. I'm giving each of you an assignment: write a theme on the subject of the proper way for a little girl to behave in school. Hand them in here tomorrow morning. Now go back to class, and behave yourselves!"

Earlier in the year, we had a young man on the faculty who had been an infantry Colonel, back in the war. He had, on one occasion, parachuted behind the Jap lines with a sub-machine gun in his arms, gunned down a platoon of Tojo's gangsters, and set free fifteen hundred American prisoners of war. While bringing them back to our lines, he chopped up a couple of Jap patrols.

The women of the neighborhood gave the principal a rough time about him. They said it was mighty risky to have a man with so much violence in his past associated with their hoods. A hood might run afout of him most any time, with disastrous results to the hood.

One morning a hood fell off his motor scooter on his way to school, and cracked his arm bone. Though the arm pained him some, he could move it, so didn't think much about it.

Later on, in the Colonel's class, he got mad at another pupil and cussed him out pretty violently. The colonel tried to stop him, but the boy cussed him, too. When told to come along out front, the boy snarled,

"Why don't you take me out, you son of a bitch?"

The Colonel took him by the arm, and the boy howled like a wounded banshee. He loudly proclaimed that the teacher had broken his arm.

Later examination confirmed at least a part of the boy's contention: his arm was indeed cracked.

The bleeding hearts of the community could be appeased in only one say: the teacher must be discharged.

Sometime later, it was disclosed that the police wanted the boy on the charges of breaking and entering, auto stealing, grand larcenty assault and battery, and rape. He is now in Mariana. But the Colonel had long since been dishonorably discharged from the teaching profession.

We had another colonel with us that year. He was the tentlest, finest, most humane man anybody ever had the privilege of knowing. He had retired from the air corps, and was most anxious to succeed as brilliantly in teaching as he had in the Corps.

He worked day and night at his job. He stayed hours after school to help dumb and inattentive pupils, and to counsel with their parents.

There were some, however, who simply couldn't comprehend abstractions and minus quantities. Their dams banded together, organized, and kept up a ceaseless round-robin of phone calls to the principal. Their refrain, "Colonel Anderson just can't teach."

The principal, threatened by a report to the superintendent, whom he greatly feared, agreed. Colonel Anderson was not invited back for the next year.

Moreover, he, along with 75% of the faculty members, was black-listed in that county, which made it next to impossible for any of us to obtain employment elsewhere.

Young men and young women just entering the profession, afire with zeal, altruism, enthusiasm and imbued with the missionary spirit, found themselves stamped with the stigma of failure. But the Great man's hide was saved. In college, he was a "Phys. Ed." major. He is still principal. This year's faculty are not aware that as many of their number as are complained of in anonomous telephone calls will be banished from the profession. The sound of a snarling or whining voice on the phone sets our hero to quivering like an aspen leaf. If the voice demands the degradation of a teacher, the owner of the voice may rest assured; the teacher is a gone sucker.

Just a short time after the cards had gone out for the first six weeks, we had a celebration which we called "open house." The school was full of visiting parents.

I noticed a large, imposing, handsome man standing over toward the side of my room. He looked angry enough to chew spikes. When we drifted together, he introduced himself as the father of one of our lighter-weight girls, he said,

"My daughter received a failing grade. If she doesn't receive a passing grade next time, I'll carry the matter to the school board!"

He proceeded to give me a proper dressing down.

He had sent me a note by his daughter, a few days before. It had read,

"Call my secretary and see if she can set up a conference for you, with me, at my office. I want to see you."

I had replied,

"I will be in room 23, at school, Wednesday evenings from three until four."

He showed my note to the principal - quivering with rage.

"This is what he dared to reply when I summoned him," he bellowed. "I want him discharged immediately!"

But the principal wasn't ready to do that, just yet. He got ready, by the end of the year, and included the Great Man's complaint as part of the Res Gestae, as Perry Mason would say.

I found that there were some pupils who regarded themselves as having an option on grades. If they didn't get them, it was because the teacher just couldn't teach. It was proof positive of his incapacity and unworthiness,

We had three age-echelons in the faculty: myself and two other men of my generation were the "deans." There were about twenty men and women of age 35 to 45: the others were young men who had just finished their hitches in the various armed services, and young women not long out of college.

All these people were of the best. All of us were congenial friends. The young people especially were wonderful folks to know. The boys were so hard and healthy that had a mule kicked one in the stomach, he would only have sprained his own ankle. The girls were just as healthy and hard.

The comeraderie that existed among us was one of the most bright and satisfying experiences of my life. The year was truly a high point of my own career.

God bless you, every one, fellows and girls! You deserved better of the profession you had chosen to serve. Your leaving it is Education's loss.

The ensuling summer was one of anxiety for me. I was within three years of qualifying for retirement. When a man reaches age fifty, it is mighty fine to have even a small pension coming in/ After the unpleasant experience of having been called in and being informed that I couldn't teach, I felt apprehension about getting placed for the next year.

My agent sent me many notices of vacancies. When I received a notice, I called the official by long distance, making preliminary application by phone. I was generally asked to come for an interview in person. If the job was located within two hundred miles of my home, I complied. Description of one such interview will suffice to show prospective teachers what they are up against, after they have served the trade for some years.

I entered the school office, and giving my name, asked for the principal. I was told that, although it was then 2:30 in the afternoon, the principal was in the cafeteria. I was invited to be seated.

After half an hour of waiting, the principal appeared, introduced himself, and asked me into his inner office.

There were two other fellows there - the head of the English department, and the assistant principal.

After introductions and amenities, the Head began the grilling. He cross questioned me carefully and exhaustively concerning my opinion of how the English program ought to be planned for a junior high school. At first, I replied that I wouldn't concern myself with that problem as planning was the prerogative of officials ranging from the state department of education, down to the head of the department in the individual school. The course content is already determined long before the teacher is reached. I said I thought it was the duty of the teacher to move cautiously into the job - find out what the accepted procedure is, follow directions, and give the best performance he can, within the framework of established and agreed-upon procedure.

But that didn't satisfy the Head. I must outline an English course for the school - during that interview.

I wanted that job. I had been cut out of jobs all summer by the testimony of principals I'd had, so I obliged.

He then fell to trying to confuse me on the subject of English grammar. I realized, at that point, that the Great Man had enjoyed a flash of extrasensory perception, and had discerned my "unworthiness" at first glance.

I knew that I would not be given the job.

When the Head had wrung me dry, the Great Man himself took me in hand,

"If a boy in your class shot a spit-wad, what would you do? If a pupil saw a teacher making for a fountain, and shoved in ahead of her, how would you handle the incident?"

I replied,

"No sire! You are postulating imaginary situations, and requiring me to answer questions about them. One never knows what he'd do until the condition arises. cases are altered by circumstances. It is impossible to play the game this way!"

"Excuse me, then, for a few moments, Mr. Porter, We'll give you our final decision presently."

I knew what the verdict would be. Presently they reappeared.

"Mr. Porter, I wouldn't think of offering you the job, while you're unable to get the endorsement of your last two principals."

I replied,

"Very well. But just for the record, haven't I supplied several references that satisfy you? Aren't these enough to prove to you that I am a teacher thoroughly qualified, in good health, and of good moral character?"

"Oh, yes. But they can't be decisive. The last two principals are the important ones; in fact, the others don't bear much weight."

I took a dignified leave as was possible, under the circumstances, came home and busie myself, during the next month, writing this book.

When I had finished all but these last few pages, my agent called me: he had a superintendent in the northern end of the state who desperately needed a teacher for sixth grade. He believed we could swing the deal.

I called the young man, and told him the agent would forward to him the pertinent papers, and made application for the job.

He said he would peruse the papers, and if he liked what he read, the job was mine.

I was ready to work. I had finished my book, and the prospect of earning some money and getting some time in on the years I needed for retirement, was welcome indeed. Like all teachers, I was virtually without funds.

My joy was great, therefore, when I received his telegram:

"Have consulted with principal concerned. He requests you to come immediately. I salary and other conditions are satisfactory, will sign contract."

I packed up, and went - arriving on a Friday evening.

Having checked into a good hotel, I phoned the superintendent, and informed him of my arrival in town.

He said he would come around "sometime Sunday."

I thought the least he could do was come around that same evening. Right then I began to get a vague feeling of apprehension.

I loafed around the hotel that evening, all day Saturday, Saturday night, and most of Sunday. About the middle of the afternoon, Sunday, I noticed two handsome young fellows enter the lobby. They turned out to be the superintendent and the principal of the school I had been engaged to teach in.

We introduced ourselves, and sat down for a preliminary chat. Presently they invited me to drive out to the school.

It was a rambling, one-storied edifice, located at the edge of town - in appearance much like school buildings all over the state.

During our tour of the building, the superintendent began to pry concerning my last two principals. Well, those two fellows had cut me out of half a dozen good jobs already. I felt that surely they had ample recommendations, so I evaded their questions concerning them.

Monday morning I took charge of the job. It was a class of nice kids, for the most part - some outstanding, some fairly good, and a small number below average in ability.

The teacher they'd had, had allowed them to race through their basic tests during the first six weeks. We had to adopt other sets of basis tests; but having done so, we settled to work in earnest.

During the ensuing month, I was happy except for one circumstance: the office staff down town was insistent upon my turning myself inside out, for their information. They had to have detailed listing of my employment. I made it for them.

They then communicated with every principal I'd ever had. The young man at Key East who had gathered up his week, his vicious, his morons, and his homicidal maniacs, dumped them into one class, and given them to me, during the first three months of the year, then accused me of contributing to the delinquency of minors by leaving one of my class-room doors unlocked, reported that my class had been "chaotic."

The young man who had spent the major portion of his time breathing down my collar at Ft. Dune, and building his "case" against me, didn't dare to put this report on paper; he telephoned his in. But he added a new thrust: he said he had advised me to "consult a phychiatrist."

Well, that was a left-handed suggestion that the teacher might possibly be insane. When the boys heard that, they called me into conference, and fires me.

I said,

"You can't do that. I've got the promise of a contract. You can't just fire a teacher, on no valid complaint, as if he were a rascally stable boy. I demand a hearing before the school board!"

"Well, " replied the superintendent: "the board will be in session tomorrow morning. You may meet with us there."

The law requires that written charges must be filed before a teacher is discharged, and a copy furnlshed to the accused teacher, ten days before the hearing.

But I went over the next morning.

the county attorney was there. He stated that, inasmuch as I had no contract, even thogh I had the promise of one, I was not an employee of the board, and the board was, therefore, under no obligation to grant a hearing.

I was outraged, but I spoke civilly and with dignity. I said,

"The superintendent sent me this telegram. He engaged my services in good faith. I served for a month, and was paid for it. How does it come that I am not an employee of the board."

"Ah, but sonny boy, you have no contract. you haven't a leg to stand on!"

I turned to the attorney I had engaged, and who had come with me that morning.

The board president asked him if he had anything to say.

He replied,

"I think not."

Fellow citizens, do not fear the present day struggle to save America from the militia terrorists. Their air is to conquer the world - true. But they don't have to fight to do it. Subversion is their main weapon, in spite of all the rocket-rattling. They can find enough Americans who are Potential Commissars to invade every American institution we have. It is with unbound, and despair, that I behold the terrorizing of American school administration. We have a large scale administrative liquidation of qualified and experienced school teachers.

Recently, The Supreme Court declared the loyalty oath Unconstitutional. The schools have gone, the courts are going. Soon the government will be overtaken by militant terrorists and will be declared the only sensible, authoritative power there is, and anybody who doesn't agree will be anathematized as an enemy of mankind.

As reported by the Washington Post newspaper, even today a Principal with simple assault after a fight with a student at a senior high school in D.C. The school Principal is being sued over the scuffle, but some say it's a flawed system that makes the school dangerous.

It is reported that the Federal Board of Education is on the brink of being disestablished and the entire system be given a through review for improvements to be found and changes made. These facts are based on the program "No child left behind Act" will work. It is not working and will not work unless changes are made. We must look for changing the total school management system THAT IS THE ONLY WAY TO IMPROVE OUR SOCIETY. Maybe the new Administration has seen or will see the light on our school system.